Christ, Church and World

Christ, Church and World

New Studies in Bonhoeffer's Theology and Ethics

Edited by
Michael Mawson and Philip G. Ziegler

LONDON • NEW YORK • OXFORD • NEW DELHI • SYDNEY

T&T CLARK
Bloomsbury Publishing Plc
50 Bedford Square, London, WC1B 3DP, UK
1385 Broadway, New York, NY 10018, USA

BLOOMSBURY, T&T CLARK and the T&T Clark logo are
trademarks of Bloomsbury Publishing Plc

First published in Great Britain 2016
Paperback edition first published 2018

Library of Congress Cataloging-in-Publication Data
Names: Mawson, Michael G., editor.
Title: Christ, church, and world : new studies in Bonhoeffer's theology and
ethics / [edited by] by Michael Mawson and Philip G. Ziegler.
Description: New York : Bloomsbury T&T Clark, 2016. | Includes
bibliographical references and index.
Identifiers: LCCN 2015049304| ISBN 9780567665911 | ISBN 9780567665935 (epdf)
Subjects: LCSH: Bonhoeffer, Dietrich, 1906-1945.
Classification: LCC BX4827.B57 C47 2016 | DDC 230/.044092—dc23 LC record
available at http://lccn.loc.gov/2015049304

ISBN: HB: 978-0-56766-591-1
PB: 978-0-56768-379-3
ePDF: 978-0-56766-593-5
ePub: 978-0-56766-592-8

Typeset by Fakenham Prepress Solutions, Fakenham, Norfolk NR21 8NN

To find out more about our authors and books visit
www.bloomsbury.com and sign up for our newsletters.

Contents

Chapter 6

'COMPLETELY WITHIN GOD'S DOING': SOTERIOLOGY AS
META-ETHICS IN THE THEOLOGY OF DIETRICH BONHOEFFER   101
    Philip G. Ziegler

Chapter 7

CREATURES BEFORE GOD: BONHOEFFER, DISABILITY AND
THEOLOGICAL ANTHROPOLOGY   119
    Michael Mawson

Chapter 8

BONHOEFFER'S TWO-KINGDOMS THINKING IN 'THE CHURCH AND
THE JEWISH QUESTION'   141
    Michael P. DeJonge

Chapter 9

DIETRICH BONHOEFFER AND THE JEWS IN CONTEXT   161
    Andreas Pangritz

List of Abbreviations

The essays in this volume draw extensively upon the newly completed English translation of the critical edition of the *Dietrich Bonhoeffer Werke*, 16 Bände + Registerband (Gütersloher Verlagshaus, 1987–99). Bibliographical details of the volumes of the *Dietrich Bonhoeffer Works*, general editors Wayne Whitson Floyd, Jr., Victoria Barnett, Barbara Wojhoski (Minneapolis: Fortress, 1996–2014) in English (hereafter cited as *DBWE*) are as follows:

DBWE 1   *Sanctorum Communio: A Theological Study of the Sociology of the Church*, ed. Clifford J. Green, trans. Reinhard Krauss and Nancy Lukens.

DBWE 2   *Act and Being: Transcendental Philosophy and Ontology in Systematic Theology*, ed. Wayne Whitson Floyd, trans. H. Martin Rumscheidt.

DBWE 3   *Creation and Fall*, ed. John W. de Gruchy, trans. Douglas Stephen Bax.

DBWE 4   *Discipleship*, ed. Geffrey G. Kelly and John D. Godsey, trans. Barbara Green and Reinhard Krauss.

DBWE 5   *Life Together and Prayerbook of the Bible*, ed. Geffrey B. Kelly, trans. Daniel W. Bloesch and James H. Burtness.

DBWE 6   *Ethics*, ed. Clifford J. Green, trans. Reinhard Krauss, Charles C. West and Douglas W. Stott.

DBWE 7   *Fiction from Tegel Prison*, ed. Clifford J. Green, trans. Nancy Lukens.

DBWE 8 *Letters and Papers from Prison*, ed. John W. de Gruchy, trans. Isabel Best, Lisa E. Dahill, Reinhard Krauss, Nancy Lukens, H. Martin Rumscheidt and Douglas W. Stott.

DBWE 9 *The Young Bonhoeffer: 1918–1927*, ed. Paul Duane Matheny, Clifford J. Green and Marshall D. Johnson, trans. Mary C. Nebelsick and Douglas W. Stott.

DBWE 10 *Barcelona, Berlin, New York: 1928–1931*, ed. Clifford J. Green, trans. Douglas W. Stott.

DBWE 11 *Ecumenical, Academic, and Pastoral Work: 1931–1932*, ed. Victoria J. Barnett, Mark S. Brocker and Michael Lukens, trans. Anne Schmidt-Lange, Isabel Best, Nicolas Humphrey, Marion Pauck and Douglas W. Stott.

DBWE 12 *Berlin: 1932–1933*, ed. Larry L. Rasmussen, trans. Isabel Best, David Higgins and Douglas W. Stott.

DBWE 13 *London: 1933–1935*, ed. Keith Clements, trans. Isabel Best.

DBWE 14 *Theological Education at Finkenwalde, 1935–1937*, ed. H. Gaylon Barker and Mark S. Brocker, trans. Douglas W. Stott.

DBWE 15 *Theological Education Underground: 1937–1940*, ed. Victoria J. Barnett, trans. Victoria J. Barnett, Claudia D. Bergmann, Peter Frick, Scott A. Moore and Douglas W. Stott.

DBWE 16 *Conspiracy and Imprisonment: 1940–1945*, ed. Mark S. Brocker, trans. Lisa E. Dahill and Douglas W. Stott.

DBWE 17 *Indexes and Supplementary Materials*, ed. Victoria J. Barnett and Barbara Wojhoski.

Contributors

Michael P. DeJonge is Associate Professor of Religious Studies at the University of South Florida, where he teaches modern religious thought and the history of Christian thought. He is the author of *Bonhoeffer's Theological Formation* (2012) and co-editor of *The Bonhoeffer Reader* (2013) and *Translating Religion* (2015).

Tom Greggs is Professor in Historical and Doctrinal Theology at the University of Aberdeen, and sits on the Faith and Order Commission of the World Council of Churches. His publications include *The Vocation of Theology Today* (2013), *Theology against Religion* (2011), *New Perspectives for Evangelical Theology* (2010) and *Barth, Origen and Universal Salvation* (2009).

Eva Harasta is the Advisor of Studies for Theology and Interreligious Dialogue at the Evangelische Akademie in Berlin. She is an ordained minister in the Lutheran Church in Austria, and has studied theology in Vienna, Jerusalem, Heidelberg and Erlangen. In 2007, she received the John Templeton Award for Theological Promise. Her books include *Lob und Bitte: Eine systematisch-theologische Untersuchung über das Gebet* (2005) and *Die Bewahrheitung der Kirche Durch Jesus Christus: Eine Christologische Ekklesiologie* (2011).

Christopher R. J. Holmes is Senior Lecturer in Systematic Theology in the Department of Theology and Religion at the University of Otago, and an Anglican Priest. He holds a ThD from Wycliffe College and the University of Toronto and is the author of *Revisiting the Doctrine of the Divine Attributes: In Dialogue with Karl Barth, Eberhard Jüngel, and Wolf Krötke* (2007), *Ethics in the Presence of Christ* (2012), and *The Holy Spirit* (2015). He has also published many articles and book chapters on various Christian doctrines, especially as they relate to the theologies of Karl Barth and Dietrich Bonhoeffer.

Michael Mawson is Lecturer in Theological Ethics at the University of Aberdeen. He is co-editor of *Ontology and Ethics: Bonhoeffer and Contemporary Scholarship* (2013), *The Freedom of a Christian Ethicist: The Future of a Reformation Legacy* (2016) and the forthcoming *Oxford Handbook of Dietrich Bonhoeffer*. He has published articles on Bonhoeffer, political theology and Christian ethics, and is working on a monograph on Bonhoeffer's ecclesiology.

Andreas Pangritz is Professor of Systematic Theology and Director of the Ecumenical Institute at the University of Bonn. He is author of *Vom Kleiner und Unsichtbarwerden der Theologie* (1996), *Polyphonie des Lebens* (2nd edn, 2000), *Karl Barth in the Theology of Dietrich Bonhoeffer* (2000), *Vergegnungen, Umbrüche und Aufbrüche* (forthcoming), and various essays on Dietrich Bonhoeffer, Helmut Gollwitzer, Friedrich-Wilhelm Marquardt and Jewish-Christian relations.

Stephen J. Plant is Dean and Runcie Fellow at Trinity Hall, Cambridge, and an Affiliated Lecturer at the University of Cambridge. He is author of *Bonhoeffer* (2004) and *Taking Stock of Bonhoeffer* (2014), co-editor of *Dietrich Bonhoeffer: Letters to London* (2013) and a commissioning editor of the International Bonhoeffer Interpretations Series for Peter Lang.

Christiane Tietz is Professor of Systematic Theology at the University of Zurich and Head of its Institute of Hermeneutics and Philosophy of Religion. She is the author of *Bonhoeffers Kritik der verkrümmten Vernunft* (1999) and co-editor of *The Bonhoeffer Yearbook* and *Translating Religion* (2015), as well as of various other volumes on Bonhoeffer.

Philip G. Ziegler is Senior Lecturer in Systematic Theology at the University of Aberdeen. He holds a ThD from Victoria University and the University of Toronto. He is the author of *Doing Theology When God is Forgotten: The Theological Achievement of Wolf Krötke* (2007) and the co-editor of several volumes including *The Providence of God* (2009) and *Explorations in Christian Theology and Ethics: Essays in Conversation with Paul L. Lehmann* (2009).

INTRODUCTION

Michael Mawson and Philip G. Ziegler

The theology of Dietrich Bonhoeffer (1906–45) continues to be as contested as it is discussed. His dramatic involvement in the resistance against Hitler and consequent execution have undoubtedly contributed to the widespread and sustained interest in his work, as has the publication of accounts of his life and times written for a non-specialist readership.[1] Today Bonhoeffer remains among the most widely read and taught theologians in Europe and North America, and continues to find an ever-expanding readership around the globe. Most significant debates in contemporary theology have been affected in some way by the influence of widely varied interpretations of his provocative theological legacy.

A generational shift is currently underway in the reception, interpretation and application of Bonhoeffer's theology. The crowning achievement of the senior generation of scholars has been to consolidate Bonhoeffer's varied, diffuse and often fragmentary body of published work and extensive *Nachlaβ* in the seventeen-volume critical edition of the *Dietrich Bonhoeffer Werke*.[2] This massive undertaking, only recently rendered in its entirety into English (with French and other translations underway[3]) establishes a new and invaluable basis for a re-assessment of the *corpus* as a whole. A new generation of scholarship has only just begun to exploit this achievement. Many important tasks still lie ahead.

The present moment is ripe for new research into Bonhoeffer's theology in its own right, and also for projects which endeavour to place it firmly in the context of the tumult of early twentieth-century developments in European intellectual culture generally, and in philosophy and theology in particular. Moreover, recent developments in the historiography of the German Church

Struggle of the 1930s[4] – the formative crucible of much of Bonhoeffer's work – have raised new questions and opened up fresh and highly suggestive perspectives on his central doctrinal and ethical concerns, as well as his vision of the future shape and significance of Christianity in Europe (and beyond).

Alongside such important lines of inquiry stands the equally important need to engage critically with those aspects of Bonhoeffer's theology which have ongoing relevance for contemporary debates in Christian doctrine and theological ethics. If imaginative and fruitful stimulus is to be taken from Bonhoeffer's work in relation to the most pressing challenges in these fields, we must investigate with full critical acumen just what is living and what is dead in Bonhoeffer's legacy, and discern those trajectories which contemporary and creative interpretations must responsibly pursue. Some of these pressing questions are properly internal to theology and its concerns: the church's self-understanding as a community of faith, the nature and interpretation of Christian scriptures, the relation of Christology to the doctrine of God and the normative shape of Christian life. Yet even specifically disciplinary questions like these invariably have important public valences and conse-quences. Moreover, their exploration draws theology into important dialogues with other academic disciplines, many of which are now confronting their own systematic neglect of the theological in light of an increasing '*awareness of what is missing*', as Jürgen Habermas has recently put it. These dialogues are concerned with the nature of human sociality, the ordering and purposes of political life and the role of faith communities, both distinctively Christian and religiously plural, in shaping both.[5] It is one of the signal features of Bonhoeffer's legacy that at one and the same time it drives theological research more deeply into the classical disciplinary questions that constitute its tradi-tional core, even as it demands creative engagement with the most lively and fundamental matters of current public life and cultural debate.

The essays collected in this volume arise out of a series of workshops and colloquia held at the University of Aberdeen during 2014–15 with generous financial support from the Royal Society of Edinburgh. Our contributors – drawn from Europe, the USA and the Antipodes – were invited to investigate current questions relating to Bonhoeffer's theology and to explore possible directions for future research. Given this brief, our common work came to coalesce around the themes of Christology, hamartiology, ecclesiology and Bonhoeffer's engagement with the 'Jewish Question'. As a group, the essays pursue evermore responsible interpretations of Bonhoeffer's work, attending to both its own internal dynamics as well as the formative sources and pressing debates which gave rise to it. They also raise critical questions about the limitations, gaps and *aporia* in Bonhoeffer's theological work, exploring the possibilities for supplementation and reparative critique. Finally, they look to explore the present possibilities for constructive deployment of Bonhoeffer's signal insights in informing, re-shaping and advancing current debates in the field.

In the opening chapter of this volume, 'The Role of Jesus Christ for Christian Theology', Christiane Tietz shows that Bonhoeffer's theology is orientated to and by the living Christ who reveals himself to us *ab extra*. For Bonhoeffer, theology is not possible on the basis of any human idea or experience, but only as and when Christ comes to us and disrupts the human logos. Moreover, Tietz insists that such a Christology can still provide a viable point of departure for theology today. Against those who claim that contemporary theology must be orientated by religious consciousness or the self-representation of faith, she demonstrates that a Christological orientation can authorize rich interreligious dialogue, for example, and guide constructive engagement in current debates about homosexuality.

The second chapter likewise addresses Christological questions. In 'Beyond Bonhoeffer in Loyalty to Bonhoeffer: Reconsidering Bonhoeffer's Christological Aversion to Theological Metaphysics', Christopher Holmes endorses Bonhoeffer's basic Christological orientation, but goes on to ask whether such a Christology can in fact be sustained in and of itself. He suggests that a more robust account of the immanent Trinity is needed to secure both the substance and significance of Bonhoeffer's account of the person and work of Christ. Holmes looks to supplement and expand upon Bonhoeffer by supplying a more adequate doctrine of God, one which draws insights from the first volume of Katherine Sonderegger's recently published *Systematic Theology*.[6]

In the next chapter, Stephen Plant raises questions about Bonhoeffer's Christology lectures from another angle. In '"We Believe in One Lord, Jesus Christ": A Pro-Nicene Revision of Bonhoeffer's 1933 Christology Lectures',

Plant argues that Bonhoeffer sets his Christology over against the early councils and conciliar tradition in a way that is distinctly and problematically modern. He argues that Bonhoeffer's approach affords the individual theologian primacy over the tradition and also displays a typically liberal rejection of so-called 'Hellenistic influences'. These problems are examined by way of a contrast with the more recent work of Lewis Ayres.[7] In Plant's reading, Ayres provides a more thoroughly historical (and less problematically modern) reading of the conciliar tradition, one which allows for greater positive continuity between the early church fathers and contemporary theological work.

While the first three chapters of this volume concentrate on Bonhoeffer's Christology, the next three focus upon a neglected but substantive theme in Bonhoeffer's theology: his doctrine of sin. In 'Adam in Christ? The Place of Sin in Christ-Reality', Eva Harasta considers the question of the ontological status of sin in Bonhoeffer's treatment of it in his *Ethics*. She asks where sin fits with the thoroughly Christological conception of truth and reality with which Bonhoeffer works. If all reality is *Christuswirklichkeit*, then what can sin be? To answer the question, Harasta looks back to the earlier work, *Act and Being*, where ontological questions are to the fore. She demonstrates important continuities, but also material developments in Bonhoeffer's doctrine of sin,

Tom Greggs' chapter, 'Bearing Sin in the Church: The Ecclesial Hamartiology of Bonhoeffer', demonstrates that Bonhoeffer's decision to make ecclesiology the foundational locus or *res* of his theology has ramifications for his treatment of other doctrines. In particular, Greggs shows how this is the case in Bonhoeffer's relational and corporate hamartiology. 'Given Bonhoeffer's ecclesially orientated theological foundation as the ultimate *res* of his theological thought,' Greggs writes, 'the connection between divine-human and human-human relationality cannot be prized apart.'[8] Bonhoeffer makes clear that sin is not only vertical but also horizontal, as it always involves the disruption and overturning of human community and human-human relationality, and simply cannot be understood apart from this.

In the sixth chapter, '"Completely within God's doing": Soteriology as Meta-Ethics in the Theology of Dietrich Bonhoeffer', Philip Ziegler argues that Bonhoeffer's understanding of ethics and the Christian life must be firmly located within his soteriology, that is, his self-consciously Protestant emphasis upon human sin and divine grace. From *Act and Being* he examines the way in which Bonhoeffer rejects any abiding general anthropology prior to the reality of human beings as either 'in Adam' or 'in Christ.' Ziegler goes on to suggest that the full implications of this move for theological ethics become evident in the *Ethics* manuscript, 'God's Love and the Disintegration of the World', where Bonhoeffer contends that moral knowledge is only had by continually looking to Christ who is himself the answer to the question of the good. This means, as Ziegler concludes, that 'a human life "in Christ" is one subjected to the relentless gracious activity of the living God of our salvation.'[9] Bonhoeffer gives priority to divine over human agency in his account of ethics; the moral life is a function of remaining open and attentive to God's action.

In 'Creatures before God: Bonhoeffer, Disability and Theological Anthropology', Michael Mawson draws upon Bonhoeffer to intervene in recent debates about theological anthropology in the field of disability theology. In the first part of his chapter, he traces how disability theologians such as Hans Reinders have sought to develop a relational concept of personhood that can include and affirm the full humanity of those with profound intellectual disabilities. Mawson goes on to question the wisdom and effectiveness of Reinders' appeal to the persons and relations of the Trinity in order to ground this concept theologically: his concern is that this obfuscates the more distinct creaturely and embodied nature of human relationality and personhood. On this basis Mawson argues that Bonhoeffer's theology in *Creation and Fall* may provide a better basis for developing a conception of relational personhood for contemporary disability theology.

The final two essays in this collection explore neuralgic historical and theological questions surrounding Bonhoeffer's theology and the so-called 'Jewish Question' of his day. Michael DeJonge's contribution, 'Bonhoeffer's Two-Kingdoms Thinking in "The Church and the Jewish Question"', makes a strong case for the Lutheran theological background of this important 1933 essay. DeJonge argues that Bonhoeffer's position in this essay must be read in light of Luther's two kingdoms theology and related theological distinction between law and gospel. As DeJonge demonstrates, Bonhoeffer's position on the responsibilities of the church and state closely follow Luther's own understanding of their respective roles. Approaching Bonhoeffer's essay in this way, DeJonge maintains, is essential for making sense of it, since reading with the 'logic of the two kingdoms in mind, some of its apparent contradictions dissolve.'[10]

In the final chapter, 'Dietrich Bonhoeffer and the Jews in Context', Andreas Pangritz also examines Bonhoeffer's theological responses to the so-called 'Jewish question' in the years between 1933 and 1941. Taking a historical approach, Pangritz locates Bonhoeffer's remarks on this theme in their context, comparing them with the statements and positions of a number of his contemporaries, in particular Karl Barth, Elisabeth Schmitz and Wilhelm Vischer. With DeJonge, Pangritz agrees that Bonhoeffer's early approaches are tied to Lutheran theology; but unlike DeJonge, he stresses that this is in fact problematic. Moreover, Pangritz suggests that Bonhoeffer attains a more theologically adequate position in the *Ethics* manuscript, 'Heritage and Decay', a work which displays the influence of that 'network' of Christian thinkers and activists with whom he had interacted. In this way Bonhoeffer's work suggests a constructive trajectory in Christian theological approaches to Judaism beyond his immediate context.

As mentioned earlier, the essays in this volume have been revised from papers that were presented in the series 'The Challenge of Bonhoeffer's Theology for Contemporary Ethics and Public Life' at the University of Aberdeen. We would like to thank all those who assisted with organizing the workshops and lectures in this series, especially our postgraduate assistants Chris Dodson and Claire Hein Blanton. We are grateful to those who contributed to the workshops; those authors included in this volume, as well as Jenny McBride and Ralf Wüstenberg. The series was made possible by an Arts and Humanities Research Workshop grant from the Royal Society of Edinburgh.

We would like to thank Chris Dodson for helping with the final preparation of this manuscript, and several others who read and commented on specific chapters, including Claire Hein Blanton, Brian Brock, David Emerton, Ross Halbach, Caireen Likely, Joe McGarry, Jake Putich, Justin Pritchett, Sam Tranter and Dick Wivell. Finally, we have appreciated the enthusiasm and support for this project from Anna Turton and Miriam Cantwell at T&T Clark / Bloomsbury.

Notes

1   For example, Eric Metaxas, *Bonhoeffer: Pastor, Martyr, Prophet, Spy* (Nashville: Thomas Nelson Publishers, 2010) and Charles Marsh, *Strange Glory: A Life of Dietrich Bonhoeffer* (London: SPCK, 2014).

2   See Clifford Green's 'The Dietrich Bonhoeffer Works, English Edition: A Retrospective', *DBWE* 17: 9–16.

3   *Oeuvres de Dietrich Bonhoeffer*, ed. H. Mottu (Geneve: Labor et Fides, 1996–).

4   For example, see Wolfgang Gerlach, *And The Witnesses Were Silent: The Confessing Church and the Persecution of the Jews*, trans. and ed. Victoria Barnett (Lincoln: University of Nebraska Press, 2000); Victoria Barnett, *For the Soul of the People: Protestant Protest Against Hitler* (Oxford: Oxford University Press, 1992); and Matthew D. Hockenos, *A Church Divided: German Protestants Confront the Nazi Past* (Bloomington: Indiana University Press, 2004).

5   See Jürgen Habermas, *An Awareness of What is Missing: Faith and Reason in a Post-secular Age* (London: Polity Press, 2010).

6   Katherine Sonderegger, *Systematic Theology,* vol.1; *The Doctrine of God* (Minneapolis: Fortress Press, 2015).

7   Lewis Ayres, *Nicaea and its Legacy: An Approach to Fourth-Century Trinitarian Theology* (Oxford: Oxford University Press, 2006).

8   Tom Greggs, 'Bearing Sin in the Church: The Ecclesial Hamartiology of Bonhoeffer', 85.

9   Philip Ziegler, '"Completely within God's doing": Soteriology as Meta-Ethics in the Theology of Dietrich Bonhoeffer', 114.

10 Michael DeJonge, 'Bonhoeffer's Two-Kingdoms Thinking in "The Church and the Jewish Question"', 141.

Chapter 1

THE ROLE OF JESUS CHRIST FOR CHRISTIAN THEOLOGY

Christiane Tietz

If there is one consensus in Bonhoeffer studies it is that Bonhoeffer's theology is essentially Christ-oriented.[1] The question of 'who is Christ actually for us today?',[2] over which Bonhoeffer pondered in prison, can be seen as the *cantus firmus*[3] of all his writings: Bonhoeffer started his academic career in his dissertation *Sanctorum Communio* by defining the essence of the church through the phrase 'Christ existing as church-community';[4] one of his few university lecture series was on *Christology* (in 1933);[5] his 1937 book *Discipleship* is about how to follow Christ;[6] in his *Ethics*, the new ethical perspective of Bonhoeffer is based upon his concept of 'Christ-reality';[7] and Bonhoeffer's ideas of a 'religionless Christianity' and a 'world come of age' can only adequately be understood through his late thoughts about the crucified Christ.[8] Bonhoeffer is a theologian who conceives the task of theology fundamentally as thinking about Christ, not just thinking about religious communities, religious consciousness or the beauty of creation. These topics may well be important too, but theology's first and last thought must be Jesus Christ. The first part of this chapter unfolds in general why Bonhoeffer opted for a Christ-oriented theology. The second part then discusses three particular aspects of Bonhoeffer's theology and demonstrates the relevance of Jesus Christ for each. In all three cases we go on to consider how far these insights can be helpful for theology today.

Some contemporary theologians may think that such an intense orientation towards Christ almost amounts to some kind of fundamentalist theology and so is not open to dialogue. But I am convinced that a strong orientation towards something does not necessarily rule out commitment to dialogue:

indeed, one is an even more interesting dialogue partner if one is able to bring a distinctive standpoint to the conversation. The only requirement, of course, is that such convictions do not lead to violence.

Why Jesus Christ is the orienting point of Bonhoeffer's theology

Bonhoeffer opted for a Christ-oriented theology first of all because of an insight, which he took from Karl Barth's dialectical theology, that there is no path from human beings to God.[9] In a sermon from 1928, Bonhoeffer explains: There are 'two strong lines …, the only possibilities available if one is to conceive of God and the human being together … one line leads from human beings up to God, the other from God down to human beings, and both exclude each other – and yet belong together.'[10] Bonhoeffer parallels these two lines with the distinction of works and grace. The path from humans up to God is the path of works; the path from God to humans is the path of grace. From this, it becomes clear that only the second path from God to humans is acceptable from a Christian perspective with its emphasis on grace. To the path from human beings to God belong history and culture as well as morality and religion. In all this lies a fundamental restlessness, Bonhoeffer observes:

> There is in the soul of human beings, as truly as they are human beings, something that makes them restless, something that points them toward the infinite, eternal …. The soul … wants to transcend itself … it wants to be unchangeable and immortal itself … It wants to take the path itself to the eternal, bring the eternal under its control.[11]

Bonhoeffer appreciates the cultural effects of these attempts at self-transcendence, but at the same time warns: 'The human race might well point proudly to this blossom of its own sirit except for one thing, namely, that God is God, and grace is grace.'[12] Human attempts in religion – and even in the Christian religion – are impressive, but always remain in the human realm and under the dominion of sin: 'Even in their most spiritual spirituality – in religion – human beings remain human beings, and that means sinners; their religion is part of their flesh, and that means part of their desire for happiness, for blessedness, for pleasure, and that means for their own ego.'[13]

Human beings are not able to exit their human, sinful reality and reach and recognize God: 'Human knowledge of God remains precisely that: human, limited, relative, anthropomorphic knowledge.'[14] Bonhoeffer concludes: 'If human beings and God are to come together, there is but one way, namely, the way from God to human beings.'[15] And this way is Jesus Christ. 'Only one thing remains, namely, that God comes to human beings and bestows grace; the path from eternity into time, the path of Jesus Christ ... Not religion, but revelation and grace: this was the word of redemption, revealed to the world.'[16]

Why is Jesus Christ the only path between God and human beings? Bonhoeffer gives several reasons. With Barth (and Søren Kierkegaard) he names as one reason the infinite qualitative distance between God and human beings, but also human beings' sinfulness which lets every human attempt remain within the circle of the *homo incurvatus in se* (the human curved in upon him- or herself).

It is also this: that God is not an idea or principle but a person.[17] You can include an idea or principle in your own intellectual system and thus take possession of it. A person instead is free.[18] A person cannot be extrapolated or calculated by us. A person has to reveal herself to be known, as Bonhoeffer explains in *Sanctorum Communio*.[19] From this it follows that to recognize God, as a person, human beings need a revelation of God.

Furthermore, the *form* of the revelation has to be in accordance with God's character as a person. Because of his or her freedom, a person exists in 'once-ness'.[20] The only place of once-ness is history, because here things happen contingently.[21] Revelation in the once-ness of history has happened in Jesus Christ. In Jesus Christ, God entered into history and spoke his revealing word to the world. For Bonhoeffer, Christ is not a theoretical concept, some principle of humanity or some idea of neighbourly love. The revelation *of the person* of God is the revelation *in a person*, the historical person of Jesus of Nazareth.

But how is the historical person Jesus still relevant for us today? This question is important since, as Bonhoeffer explains in his Barcelona lecture on the essence of Christianity, '[t]he only thing that concerns us is what in history still has the power to speak to us down through the millennia, to make claims on us to which we must respond responsibly and with our entire existence rather than just with our ideology.'[22] This search for Christ's claim on us today leads Bonhoeffer to his abiding question: 'Who is Jesus Christ *for us today*?' It is only if we encounter Jesus Christ today that we cannot include him into our intellectual system. Some content within a system in Bonhoeffer's eyes would always be determined by the past, insofar as the priority of the coherence of reason comes before any present relation to the content.[23] Revelation which is interrupting my existence as *homo incurvatus in se*, and which is really coming from outside, is only possible through a contingent encounter with Jesus Christ *today*.[24]

The relevance of Jesus Christ for Bonhoeffer's theology – and for today

The role of Jesus Christ for ecclesiology

Bonhoeffer's dissertation *Sanctorum Communio* is the first text in which he deals with the question of how we can encounter Christ today, if he has ascended to heaven. Encountering Christ for the Lutheran Bonhoeffer means encountering law and gospel. On the one hand, it means encountering Christ's claim (i.e. the law).[25] This claim of Christ is not abstract but very concrete. Its content is the claim to be there for the other, as we read in Mt. 25.40: 'Just as you did it to one of the least of these who are members of my family, you did it to me'. This means that when we encounter another human being it may be that at the same time Christ encounters us through the other, asking us to fulfil the need of this other. This is not a general rule, an abstract principle, such as: in every other human being Christ encounters us. Such an abstract principle would not lead to deeds on our part. Because we cannot help everybody, we would end up doing nothing. Rather, we have to be open to Christ's claim every time we meet another human being. In Bonhoeffer's view, it may be – and often will be – the case that Christ is asking us to responds to the need of the other. So, where do we encounter Christ's claim? We do so time and again in the concrete other, whenever we understand that through the other Christ is calling us. To understand that Christ is calling us is something which happens through faith.[26] Through the act of faith we continually see Christ standing behind the other and calling us to be there for him or her. Through faith we understand the other as the site where we encounter the claim of Christ.[27] It is this encounter with the claim of Christ through the other that in Bonhoeffer's view makes us a person: 'the person as conscious being is created in the moment of being moved – in the situation of responsibility, passionate ethical struggle, confrontation by an overwhelming claim.'[28]

On the other hand, encountering Christ also means encountering Christ's promise (i.e. the gospel). The content of the promise is that in Christ my own claim upon the other and my own needs are fulfilled.[29] Christ is the one who loves me no matter what. This also is not an abstract idea, but something which happens concretely through other Christians: 'the other member of the church-community is essentially no longer claim but gift, revelation of God's love and heart. Thus the You is to the I no longer law but gospel, and hence an object of love.'[30] This again is recognized only through faith.

The combination of both aspects – in the other human being we encounter Christ's claim, if we have faith, and in the other Christian we encounter Christ's promise if we have faith – leads to the following thesis: we fully encounter Christ only if we have faith. And we encounter Christ only in the other: Christ's law in every human, and Christ's gospel in the Christians.

Bonhoeffer formulates the phrase 'Christ existing as church-community' to explain that today we can encounter him only in the community of Christians. The verb form 'existing' (*existierend*) indicates the fact that the church is a mode of being of Christ. It is not the only mode of being, as Christ is also in heaven.[31] But it is the mode of being in which we can encounter him since he has left the earth.[32]

This 'Christ existing in the church-community' is nothing we can see. I cannot see in a person's face that through him or her Christ is encountering me, or that the other is really a member of the *communio sanctorum* – even if that person should appear to be saved (this could in fact still be faked or an illusion). I can only believe that this person is a Christian. I can only believe that Christ is standing behind that person. Faith is necessary in order to understand the character of the church not only as a religious institution, but as the presence of Christ. Only then does one realize that 'the church ... [and only the church] is simultaneously a historical community and one established by God.'[33] It is only Christ's current presence in the church that constitutes the divine reality of the church. Without Christ presently existing as community, the church would only be a historical community, one constituted by human beings who want to be together and share their religiosity.[34]

So, what is the theological function of this orientation towards Christ for the ecclesiology of *Sanctorum Communio*? It is because and only because of Christ's presence in the church that the church has essential relevance for Christian existence. Bonhoeffer explains: 'Community with God exists only through Christ, but Christ is present only in his church-community, and therefore *community with God exists only in the church*.'[35] From this follows that being a Christian is possible only *in* the church.

In *Life Together*, Bonhoeffer unfolds this aspect in a new historical context. But similarly, he argues that one needs the other to be a Christian:

> Christians live entirely by the truth of God's Word in Jesus Christ … . It can only come from the outside. In themselves they are destitute and dead. Help must come from the outside, and it has come and comes daily and anew in the Word of Jesus Christ, bringing us redemption, righteousness, innocence, and blessedness. But God put this Word into the mouth of human beings so that it may be passed on to others … . Therefore, Christians need other Christians who speak God's Word to them. They need them again and again when they become uncertain and disheartened because, living by their own resources, they cannot help themselves without cheating themselves out of the truth. They need other Christians as bearers and proclaimers of the divine word of salvation. They need them solely for the sake of Jesus Christ. The Christ in their own hearts is weaker than the Christ in the word of other Christians. The Christ in one's own heart is uncertain, the Christ in the word of the other Christian is certain.[36]

In current Protestant debates about the sociological structure of Christian existence, this Christological foundation of the church and of the relevance of the church for Christian existence can and should be of eminent relevance because it makes explicit the special social character of a Christian religious existence. At least in the German speaking Protestant theology of today, a revival of Ernst Troeltsch's concept of Christian existence can be observed. Many German theologians argue that Christian existence does not necessarily take place within the church. It can sufficiently be pursued in an individual, culturally expressed existence outside the institutional church. Martin Laube observes a modern shift and argues for this: in modernity, the 'certainty of faith which is experienced subjectively in being born again, takes the place of the certainty of salvation which is warranted objectively by the word of God.'[37] Laube judges that the ecclesiological concepts of *communio sanctorum* and 'body of Christ' are no longer of any use as they are 'committed to premodern social relations'.[38] The consequence is that now there is also 'Christianity outside the church'.[39]

It is interesting that Bonhoeffer critiques Troeltsch's *The Social Teachings of the Christian Churches*,[40] which stands in the background of this ecclesiological concept, with the following words: Troeltsch 'focuses on the historically contingent social forms, not the essential social structure of Christian community'.[41] Why does Bonhoeffer stress the difference between the historically contingent and the essential? With his historical method, Troeltsch cannot at all discover essential structures. For Bonhoeffer, Christian social structures take place in history, but their essence is defined by the essence of Jesus Christ, existing in those structures. The essential structure is given and defined through the presence of Christ in and only in the church. And because of this presence of Christ the church is necessary for Christian existence. For Bonhoeffer, in contrast to Troeltsch, the church is 'simultaneously a historical community and one established by God'.[42]

Bonhoeffer continues his rejection of Troeltsch in *Sanctorum Communio* by referring to Troeltsch's opinion 'that what matters in the Protestant concept of the church is not the church as community, but solely the word.' Troeltsch 'maintained that where the word is, there is the church, even if there is no one to hear it.' Thus Troeltsch detaches the word from the human community of the speakers and hearers of the word. Bonhoeffer criticizes Troeltsch: 'This is a complete misconception of the Protestant tenet of the importance of the word.'[43] Moreover, Bonhoeffer writes that 'every word of Christ comes out of that community and exists only in it'.[44] For Bonhoeffer, the word happens only between human beings, only in communion. 'Word' is essentially a social category. Thus, if you give up Christian community, you give up Christ who is the word in law and gospel. From this follows, against Troeltsch: No Christianity outside the church is possible.

The role of Jesus Christ for Christology

The title of this part of my chapter sounds unusual. How could the role of Jesus Christ for Christology be discussed? Is it not clear that Jesus Christ stands in the centre of Christology? Yet, if one looks at current Christological debates again in German-speaking protestant theology, this is not so clear at all. There are several approaches in which it is not Jesus Christ who stands in the centre of christological reflection, but religious consciousness.[45]

Bonhoeffer starts his Christology with Jesus Christ. This becomes obvious in his lectures on Christology. Here Bonhoeffer makes clear that Christology has to start with the revelation of God in Jesus Christ: 'The fact that the Logos became flesh, a human being, is the prerequisite, not the proof'[46] of Christology. In other academic disciplines, in the natural sciences and in the humanities, the human mind classifies every new object and sorts it into an already existing system.[47] In Christology, the human mind encounters Christ, who is the 'counter-Logos' and judges over the human logos.[48] Therefore we are not able to categorize Christ, to ask 'How are you possible?', a question answered by combining elements of an existing system. The only adequate question to ask Christ is '"Who" are you?', a question which 'expresses the otherness of the other'[49] as it respects the freedom of the other person and steps away from categorizing the other.

In Bonhoeffer's view, the other is always transcendent. He or she cannot be conceived through the I, but represents a boundary which the I encounters. This insight is important because it helps with conceiving Bonhoeffer's concept of the transcendent. It is not something which you can reach by self-transcending, e.g. by transcending your consciousness, your reason, your will. Whatever you do, you will always remain in your own realm and will not reach the other. In this conception, Bonhoeffer's anthropology is very Lutheran, as one of Luther's own core convictions is that the sinner is curved in upon himself and cannot escape the circle of the I.[50] Only the other, who really comes from the outside, who really is *extra me*, interrupts the circle of the I and lets the I experience its boundaries. Thus, whenever somebody asks Jesus 'Who are you?', he is also asking about the boundaries of his or her own existence.[51] This 'Who are you?' question in Christology, Bonhoeffer adds, is always the question: 'Are you God himself?'[52]

Bonhoeffer adds that even if we ask the Who-question, we will always try to conceptualize the Who-question as a How-question: 'we are always asking the "how" question' ('Tell me *how* you exist, tell me *how* you think, and I'll tell you who you are'), because 'we are chained to our own authority'.[53] We always try to stay the sovereign of our world. Thus the Who-question is only possible when the human logos that asks the question, and which always tries to transform it into a How-question, has already been superseded – namely, superseded by the answer which has already been given in God's revelation.[54] Reflected in the context of the question, 'are you God?', this means that one can only ask the Who-question if one already believes that Jesus Christ is God. Only then is the circle of the I already interrupted. Bonhoeffer summarizes: 'the question of *who* can only be asked on condition that the answer has already been given', that is, when one accepts that the claim of Christ is the Word of God. For Bonhoeffer, the revelation of God is 'a just claim' and 'the christological question can only be asked, as a scholarly (!) question, within the sphere of the church'.[55] Only within the church, when one submits as a believer to the claim that Christ is God, can the Christological question be asked in an academically adequate way. Outside the church no question about Jesus Christ makes sense as Jesus Christ will not be understood.

Bonhoeffer unfolds the life of Jesus Christ as a struggle between Jesus as the Logos of God and the human logos. He stresses that the crucifixion and death of Jesus Christ, the Logos of God, were caused by the human logos, because the human logos was provoked by the existence of the Logos of God, the Counter-Logos, which limited the human logos. The resurrection of Christ showed that the human logos finally is powerless.[56] From then on, the question 'Who are you?' which we pose 'comes back at us: who are you, that you ask this question? Do you live in the truth so you can ask it? Who are you, you who can only ask about me because you have been justified and received grace through me?'[57] Put differently: Christology can only be pursued if one is willing to be asked who oneself is and how one is related to Christ's salvation.

How different does this sound from current conceptions of Christology which understand Christology as 'a reflex of the pious self-consciousness'[58] (Notger Slenczka) or as 'the self-demonstration of faith'[59] (Christian Danz). Notger Slenczka argues that the 'presupposition of Christology is the prefiguration of an expectation', namely the expectation of the Messiah. The historical person is then understood as the 'fulfilment of a projection'.[60] There is no interruption of the human logos, only fulfilment of its projection. Slenczka continues: 'We have the Jesus of scripture only through the interpretation [*Deutung*] of the community'.[61] Christology presupposes a consciousness of one's need of salvation and a consciousness of salvation through Jesus. Traditional Christology, in Slenczka's judgement, is problematic, 'as it object-ifies propositions which originally were the expression of the experience of a salutary influence and which gain sense only in this origin'.[62] The task of theology is to work against the objectification of religious speech.[63] For Slenczka,

> religion does not mean to deal with facts in recognising or acting, but is an understanding which accompanies every dealing with facts and is then explained in objective propositions and transfers itself through the performative appeal of those objective propositions, but always remains prior to this objecti-vation in its knowledge about itself.[64]

As Slenczka continues, 'religious propositions are self-expressions of the religious subject'.[65] Bonhoeffer would agree that you cannot speak about 'religious facts' without faith, but he would deny that making objective claims, speaking of '*Gegenständlichem*', is therefore a mistake.[66] Bonhoeffer speaks without any hesitation of the '*Tatsache, daß der Logos Mensch geworden ist*' – 'the fact that the Logos became flesh' – and makes this the starting point for Christology.[67]

At least Slenczka acknowledges that Christology once started with the encounter with the person of Jesus in whom human beings found their expectations fulfilled. However, such an encounter with Jesus is no longer possible; only words about Christ make the connection.[68] What is the proof for the truth of those words in Slenczka's view? Only that one experiences the understanding of one's existence, which is expressed in these words, as comprehensible and salutary.[69] It is not Christ who is the criterion, but the existential adequateness of the sentences about Christ's function for oneself. Accordingly, Slenczka's Christology does not start with the confession of Jesus Christ as God. Rather, 'God' is a predicate which one awards to Jesus: 'Wherefrom the meaning of reality stems, and wherefrom human life gains the truth of its identity – this is truly God or the Logos'.[70]

Slenczka recognizes that the believer does not understand sentences about Jesus as self-reflection, but as the meaning of that person itself. But this is not evidence for some truth outside the subject. In Slenczka's interpretation, that the believer understands statements about Jesus to be statements about that person directly simply indicates that faith forgets its own productive power in Christology. Accordingly, in Christology a basic element of all religious consciousness becomes visible, namely that religious experience cannot be produced but just *appears*.[71] The *extra nos* is not real, but it is used to explain that religious consciousness is not at one's disposal. How could Bonhoeffer's fear of 'encountering merely my own divine *Doppelgänger*'[72] be addressed by such a concept?

Christian Danz understands Christology as the self-representation of faith.[73] For Danz, faith is 'the event in which human beings are understanding themselves in conscious self-relation. Faith represents itself in its content as a historically embedded event and describes itself.'[74] Faith is not related to external objects but is a self-understanding which expresses itself in a content which is understood to be external. Like Slenczka, Danz stresses: 'The event [of faith] is non-deducible and contingent. This is represented by the religious notion of God. By this notion faith explains itself as event of God in history, so that the notion of God originates at the same time as faith.'[75] And 'the reference to the person Jesus of Nazareth, that is to an extra nos, expresses the embeddedness of all interpretation [*Deutung*] of history in a concrete history with a certain content. The Christ of faith symbolises the event of human self-understanding in its historicity.'[76]

From Bonhoeffer's perspective, such a Christology and theology remains in the realm of human self-understanding and self-interpreting, and thus in the realm of the sinner. A conceptualization of this self-understanding as related to an *extra nos* is very different from the real encounter with an *extra nos* which can only interrupt human self-interpretation. In his habilitation thesis Bonhoeffer judges that for an idealistic approach like that of Danz no communion with God is possible: 'The I remains fixed in itself; its looking into itself, its innermost depths, is religion, but also the revelation of the divine spirit. Revelation is no more than that … . there is no room for faith and word conceived as contrary to reason.'[77] It is obvious that Danz cannot think of a word which is contrary to human self-understanding. But in Bonhoeffer's understanding Jesus Christ is exactly this word. Danz might ask: How can you think of something external if you do not understand it as the thought of the I? Bonhoeffer's answer would be: You cannot think it, you can only believe it. And this believing act is totally receptive, namely a response to the word of God which is really contingent.[78] In Danz' theology, historic contingency is a figure, an abstract category which you represent by the symbol of Jesus Christ. But the concrete historical person has no further relevance, such that the role of Jesus of Nazareth for Christology is arbitrary.

The role of Jesus Christ for the doctrine of creation

For Bonhoeffer, even the doctrine of creation cannot be unfolded without Jesus Christ. Like Karl Barth, Bonhoeffer stresses that the church can only understand the meaning of creation and the meaning of humanity through Jesus Christ.[79] The church cannot speak about this world and of human beings as if the fall had not happened and as if this world is not a sinful world. The church speaks about the sinful world only from the end of this world and from the new, which is Jesus Christ.[80] If one would try to understand creation and humanity without Jesus Christ, then one would ignore the necessity of Jesus Christ and the severity of sin: 'The church … sees the beginning only in dying, from the viewpoint of the end. It views the creation from Christ; or better, in the fallen, old world it believes in the world of the new creation, the new world of the beginning and the end, because it believes in Christ and in nothing else.'[81]

  This leads to Bonhoeffer's critique of the concept of orders of creation, for which he substitutes the concept of orders of preservation (and in his *Ethics* further specifies as 'mandates').[82] Since the fall, there is no relation to the world without pointing 'to the wickedness, the fallen state' of the world and of the laws of the world accordingly.[83] To quote *Creation and Fall*:

> All orders of our fallen world are God's orders of preservation that uphold and preserve us for Christ. They are not orders of creation but orders of preservation. They have no value in themselves, instead they find their end and meaning only through Christ. God's new action with humankind is to uphold and preserve humankind in its fallen world, in its fallen orders, for death – for the resurrection, for the new creation, for Christ.[84]

What is the difference between orders of creation and orders of preservation? Do not the orders of creation also exist for preserving the world? Yes, this is true. But the difference lies in the goal of this preservation. Is it a preservation of creation for itself – because creation is so beautiful that it should be preserved? Or is it a preservation of creation for the gospel and for the new creation through God?[85] In the second case, only an openness to the gospel is a criterion for the adequateness of the orders. In the first case, there is no further criterion for what to preserve, as creation as such seems to be good. Bonhoeffer stresses in his lecture in Čiernohorské Kúpele: 'The danger of this argument [concerning orders of creation] is basically that everything can be justified on its basis. One need only portray something that exists as willed and created by God and then everything that exists is justified for eternity.'[86]

As we know, in Bonhoeffer's time this was an issue of urgency due to the debate with the German Christians.[87] Some theologians of that time, for example Paul Althaus and Werner Elert, argued in the *Ansbacher Ratschlag*, that Adolf Hitler had been given by God:

> [A]s believing Christians we thank God the Lord, that he gave to our people in its need the Führer as 'pious and faithful authority' and will cause in the national socialist order 'good government', a government with 'discipline and honour'. Therefore, we are aware of our responsibility before God, to assist in the work of the Führer in our profession and status.[88]

From the perspective of orders of preservation, this position would have to be tested through the question of whether Hitler is promoting not only discipline and honour, but preserving the world for the gospel of Jesus Christ. For the task of the state, the idea of orders of preservation means that the state should let the church preach the gospel to all citizens of the state. This task of the church questions the order of 'Volk' which is in contradiction to the gospel that is directed towards all people without difference. Any ban of Jewish Christians by the church is in contradiction with this order of preservation.

It may be worth mentioning that Bonhoeffer in his *Ethics* recovers 'the concept of the natural', because he sees it as problematic that within Protestant ethics the concept was for some 'completely lost in the darkness of general sinfulness, whereas for others it took on the brightness of primal creation'.[89] In Protestant ethics, the 'relative differences within … the natural', the 'relative differences within a fallen creation' has been ignored.[90] Bonhoeffer instead wants to recover 'the concept of the natural … from the gospel itself.'[91] And he concludes: 'The natural is that which, after the fall, is directed toward the coming of Jesus Christ. The unnatural is that which, after the fall, closes itself off from the coming of Jesus Christ.'[92] That the natural is directed towards Christ can be understood only from the perspective of Jesus Christ, but the content of the natural can be conceived through reason.[93] This seems to be a shift in Bonhoeffer's theology as compared to *Act and Being*,[94] in that reason now has its own right. But the shift does not take place in how the natural is ascribed value (this is still possible only on Christological grounds). The shift happens only in how to discover good content – in times of chaos and, as Bonhoeffer diagnoses, '"unreasonable" overestimation of the power of the will over against the reality of natural life itself.'[95] Bonhoeffer deduces natural rights and natural duties through reason. Yet in the priority of natural rights over natural duty, the truth of the gospel is reflected.[96]

Could this difference between orders of creation and orders of preservation still be relevant today, in times when we – thank God – don't have to deal with the German Christian ideology anymore? Is Bonhoeffer's critique of natural theology still of any importance? I would suggest that it is in two respects. Nowadays, it has become common to assume – following Friedrich Schleiermacher – that most human beings have a religious feeling of something greater, that they are somehow religious. This religious feeling very often is linked to some experience of creation. We experience 'mother earth', the 'power of being', the 'connectedness of all'. And theology often interprets this as already Christian, at least as already inclined towards Christian faith. Within this interpretation, the idea of sin has almost disappeared. As in Schleiermacher's theology, which speaks of the sin of human beings in a very weak way as 'inhibition of God-consciousness',[97] current appreciations of general human religiosity have no strong concept of sin either. That people are religious already seems to be something. Only a small distinction is made between a selfish religiosity and a healthy religiosity, for example. As Bonhoeffer argues in his *Ethics*, it is not wise to understand everything after the fall in the same sense as sinful because this makes you blind to elements in this world which can be understood as being in conformity with Christ.[98] But it is also not wise – and even not Christian – to understand every religious impulse of human beings as already leaning towards Christianity. Creation as such is no longer good, it is fallen. If we go with Bonhoeffer's concept of unconscious Christianity, it might be possible that people somehow relate to Jesus Christ without explicit Christian faith. Even so, this relation still has criteria: the conformity with Christ or at least the openness for Christ. Only from here does something become Christian.

The second way in which I think Bonhoeffer's distinction between orders of creation and orders of preservation can be helpful is in the debate about homosexuality and the often heard argument in Christian circles that homosexual relationships are 'not natural'. Heterosexual relationships are seen as natural orders, set up already in paradise by God and therefore the only way in which Christians may live partnership. From the perspective of orders of preservation, this argument would be too weak. It would ignore the fall, after which Christian marriage also is now located. From the perspective of orders of preservation, the criterion for a 'Christian partnership' would not be the sexual orientation of the two partners, but the question of whether this order helps to preserve the world for Christ. This is also possible in a same-sex relationship. Here as well the partnership can help the partners to live a life of Christian discipleship. And they can help children, e.g. through God-parenthood, to become Christians. They can have 'children' in a metaphorical sense, e.g. in taking responsibility in a parish or in accompanying friends, whom they help to live a life oriented towards Christ. The only thing a homosexual couple is not capable of is having naturally born children. But giving birth to one's own children is – seen from the criterion of Christ-orientedness – not in itself a defining value. So this should not be an argument for continuing to ban homosexual couples from Christian blessings.

In both cases we see that through an orientation towards Christ we can find criteria for dealing with our world. Of course, we still have to consider how we know about this Jesus Christ and who Jesus Christ is. The history of Christian theology has been shaped by this debate. But this debate is what makes Christian theology Christian.

Notes

1   For example, see Ernst Feil, *Die Theologie Dietrich Bonhoeffers. Hermeneutik – Christologie – Weltverständnis* (Münster: LIT, 2014), 137–40.

2   *DBWE* 8, 362.

3   For example, see Andreas Pangritz, 'Who is Jesus Christ, for us, today?' In *The Cambridge Companion to Dietrich Bonhoeffer*, ed. John W. de Gruchy (Cambridge: Cambridge University Press, 1999), 134.

4   See *DBWE* 1, 189.

5   *DBWE* 12, 299–360.

6   See *DBWE* 4, 59.

7   See *DBWE* 6, 58–75.

8   *DBWE* 8, 478–82.

9   On this issue see my book *Bonhoeffers Kritik der verkrümmten Vernunft. Eine erkenntnistheoretische Untersuchung* (Tübingen: Mohr Siebeck, 1999), 122–9.

10   *DBWE* 10, 481.

11   Ibid., 481–2.

12   Ibid., 482.

13   Ibid., 484.

14   Ibid., 353.

15   Ibid.

16   Ibid., 484.

17   Ibid., 455. Like Barth, Bonhoeffer speaks of 'personality' instead of person, but the meaning here is person or personhood. In *Act and Being*, he writes, 'Gott offenbart sich in der Kirche als Person'. Bonhoeffer, *Act und Sein: Transzendentalphilosophie und Ontologie in der Systematischen Theologie. Dietrich Bonhoeffer Werke* 2, ed. Hans-Richard Reuter (München: Chr. Kaiser Verlag, 1988), 108.

18   See *DBWE* 10, 455.

19   *DBWE* 1, 56.

20   See *DBWE* 10, 456.

21   Ibid.

22   *DBWE* 10, 346.

23   See *DBWE* 2, 111.

24   Ibid.

25   See *DBWE* 1, 51–4. That it finally is Christ's claim can also be seen in *DBWE* 2, 126–8. See also my book *Bonhoeffers Kritik*, 119.

26   *DBWE* 2, 89.

27   Ibid., 126–8. It is interesting and quite untypical for a Lutheran theologian that Bonhoeffer judges faith to be necessary for recognizing Christ's claim or the law. Without faith, without acknowledging Christ as boundary, human beings would still not be able to recognise any 'outside': 'the exteriority … of the person of Christ … is known as genuine *outside* only where human beings are *in* Christ.' Ibid., 127. This is because the law is not a general law, but *Christ's* law.

28   *DBWE* 1, 49.

29   Ibid., 166.

30   Ibid.

31   See *DBWE* 2, 112, fn. 39: 'The tension between "Christ existing as community"
and the heavenly Christ, whom we await, persists.'

32   See *DBWE* 1, 140.

33   Ibid., 126.

34   On Bonhoeffer's critique of Schleiermacher, see Tietz, 'Friedrich Schleiermacher
and Dietrich Bonhoeffer.' In *Bonhoeffer's Intellectual Formation. Theology and
Philosophy in His Thought*, ed. Peter Frick (Tübingen: Mohr Siebeck, 2008),
129–32.

35   *DBWE* 1, 158.

36   *DBWE* 5, 32. Translation altered.

37   Martin Laube, 'Die Kirche als "Institution der Freiheit."' In *Kirche,* ed. Christian
Albrecht (Tübingen: Mohr Siebeck, 2011), 151.

38   Laube, 'Die Kirche', 152.

39   Ibid.

40   Ernst Troeltsch, *Die Soziallehren der christlichen Kirchen und Gruppen*
(Tübingen: Mohr, 1912).

41   *DBWE* 1, 32, fn. 4.

42   Ibid., 126.

43   Ibid., 144–5.

44   Ibid., 158.

45   Tietz Christiane. 'Jesus von Nazareth in der christlichen Theologie heute.'
Zeitschrift für Dialektische Theologie, 31, Heft 62 (2015), 90–108.

46   *DBWE* 12, 301.

47   Ibid.

48   Ibid., 302.

49   Ibid., 303.

50   Ibid. Bonhoeffer refers to Luther's *cor curvum in se.*

51   Ibid.

52   Ibid., 302. Translation altered. The German reads: 'bist Du Gott selbst?'
Bonhoeffer, *Berlin 1932–1933. Dietrich Bonhoeffer Werke* 12, ed. Carsten
Nicolaisen and Ernst-Albert Scharffenorth (München: Chr. Kaiser Verlag,
1997), 282.

53   *DBWE* 12, 303.

54   Ibid.

55   Ibid.

56   See ibid., 305.

57   Ibid.

58   Notger Slenczka, 'Die Christologie als Reflex des frommen Selbstbewusstseins',
     Jesus Christus, ed. Jens Schröter (Tübingen: Mohr Siebeck, 2014), 181–241.

59   Christian Danz, *Grundprobleme der Christologie* (Tübingen: Mohr Siebeck,
     2013), 193–240.

60   Ibid., 182.

61   Ibid., 183.

62   Notger Slenczka, 'Problemgeschichte der Christologie', *Marburger Jahrbuch
     Theologie XIII: Christologie*, ed. Elisabeth Gräb-Schmidt and Reiner Preul
     (Leipzig: Evangelische Verlagsanstalt, 2011), 81.

63   See Slenczka, 'Christologie als Reflex', 232. Religious self-consciousness
     and theology differ at this point: 'Die Rede von Gott, die der theologischen
     Reflexion nichts anderes als Reflex des frommen Bewusstseins ist, [wird] als
     solcher Reflex vom frommen Bewusstsein nicht wahrgenommen.' Ibid.

64   Ibid., 222.

65   Ibid., 232.

66   Ibid., 223.

67   *DBW 12*, 281. The English translation is from *DBWE* 12, 301.

68   Slenczka, 'Christologie als Reflex', 222.

69   Ibid., 223.

70   Ibid., 231.

71   Ibid., 233. In German: 'Diese Selbstvergessenheit verweist auf die
     Unableitbarkeit der religiösen Erfahrung, die nicht von einem Subjekt oder eine
     Gruppe von Subjekten generiert wird, die sich vielmehr einstellt.'

72   *DBWE* 14, 169.

73   Also compare this with Tietz, 'Jesus von Nazareth.'

74   Danz, *Grundprobleme*, 203.

75   Ibid., 212.

76   Ibid., 204–5.

77   *DBWE* 2, 52–3. Translation altered.

78   Ibid., 58.

79   See *DBWE* 3, 21, 62.

80   Ibid., 21.

81   Ibid., 22.

82   See ibid., 139–40. In his *Ethics*, Bonhoeffer prefers to call these structures
     'mandates' because the term 'order' 'contain[s] the inherent danger of focusing
     more strongly on the static element of order rather than on the divine
     authorizing.' *DBWE* 6, 389. He continues: 'If these misinterpretations could be
     purged from the concept of order, then it would be very capable of expressing

the intended meaning in a strong and convincing way.' Ibid., 389–90. See also
Ibid., 68–9: 'We speak of divine mandates rather than divine orders, because
thereby their character as divinely imposed tasks, as opposed to determinate
forms of being, becomes clearer.'

83 *DBWE* 3, 139.

84 Ibid., 140.

85 See *DBWE* 11, 268.

86 Ibid., 363.

87 See ibid., 267, fn.1 by the English editors.

88 Quoted from *Die Ambivalenz der Zweireichelehre in lutherischen Kirchen des 20.
Jahrhunderts*, ed. Ulrich Duchrow and Wolfgang Huber (Gütersloh: Gütersloher
Verlagshaus, 1976), 55–7, 56.

89 *DBWE* 6, 171.

90 Ibid., 172.

91 Ibid., 173.

92 Ibid.

93 See ibid., 174. Compare this with the German. 'Während von Jesus Christus her
die Selbstzwecklichkeit des Lebens als Geschöpflichkeit und das Leben als Mittel
zum Zweck als Teilnahme am Gottesreich verstanden wird, findet im Rahmen
des natürlichen Lebens die Selbstzwecklichkeit ihren Ausdruck in den Rechten
und das Leben als Mittel zum Zweck seinen Ausdruck in den Pflichten, die dem
Leben gegeben sind.' Bonhoeffer, *Ethik. Dietrich Bonhoeffer Werke* 6, ed. Ilse
Tödt, Heinz Eduard Tödt, Ernst Feil, and Clifford Green (München: Chr. Kaiser
Verlag, 1992), 173.

94 See my book *Bonhoeffers Kritik der verkrümmten Vernunft*.

95 *DBWE* 6, 184.

96 Ibid., 174.

97 *DBWE* 1, 114 fn.11. See Friedrich Schleiermacher, *The Christian Faith*, 2
volumes, 2nd edn, ed. H. R. MacKintosh and J. S. Stewart (Edinburgh: T&T
Clark, 1968). Here, vol. 1, 271–3.

98 *DBWE* 6, 172.

Chapter 2

BEYOND BONHOEFFER IN LOYALTY TO BONHOEFFER: RECONSIDERING BONHOEFFER'S CHRISTOLOGICAL AVERSION TO THEOLOGICAL METAPHYSICS

Christopher R. J. Holmes

Introduction

I have for several years wrestled with Bonhoeffer's Christology lectures of 1933. What first attracted me to them was Bonhoeffer's dogged insistence on Jesus Christ as the 'counter Word' who teaches us to speak truthfully of himself.[1] Responsible and truthful talk about Christ begins with silence before him. While immersed in a church environment that thought (and still thinks) it could talk about Jesus Christ by talking about human aspirations for justice, inclusivity, etc., Bonhoeffer's talk was music to my ears. Such talk recognizes that were it not for Christ's ongoing agency in giving rise to words of witness, the human would have nothing (truthful) to say about him. Indeed, the human would be forever concerned with the wrong question, the 'how' question.[2] The counter Logos crucifies the human logos, raising it anew, teaching it to talk in a way that conforms to the Logos' own self-revelation. The human logos learns from the Logos himself to ask the right question, the 'who' question.[3]

What also attracted me to the lectures, as I first began formation for holy orders, was Bonhoeffer's insistence that the 'who' of Christ cannot be uncoupled from his form as Word, sacrament and church.[4] The risen and ascended Christ's presence is a concrete one that takes up space in that form. Such thinking has significant resources, I thought and still think, for an account of the church grounded in Christ's presence as a person in history, especially in a church environment that detaches Christ from where he wills to be found.

What attracts me to Bonhoeffer's lectures these days is his treatment of the conciliar tradition of Christology and, more broadly, the classical doctrine of God and of the Trinity. There is much that I find myself questioning in Bonhoeffer's treatment of the tradition, indeed in his understanding and assessment of theology proper, of classical Christological and Trinitarian metaphysics. In this chapter I discuss what Bonhoeffer calls 'the first premise of all theology'.[5] I take up Bonhoeffer's account of 'Critical or Negative Christology' in Section II of his Christology lectures so as to not only present what Bonhoeffer thinks is the first premise of all theology but also to offer some evaluation of it in conversation with the Episcopalian theologian Kathryn Sonderegger. I think this is worthwhile because I am more and more convinced that Bonhoeffer's Christological concentration obscures at times important dimensions of the Christian doctrine of God and of the Trinity.

Bonhoeffer on critical (conciliar) Christology

Bonhoeffer says many interesting things about the conciliar tradition. His reading of the various heresies is informed and, while at times a bit rough, instructive. What one recognizes nearly right away in his treatment of heterodox teaching is the need to avoid thinking '*in abstracto* the divine and human natures'.[6] An abstract or speculative doctrine of God – 'abstract' and 'speculative' are synonymous terms for Bonhoeffer – is problematic by virtue of 'the opposition between idea and appearance'.[7] Jesus is not the idea behind whom exists an invisible substance, that is the divine nature. For example, the problem with enhypostatic teaching, as Bonhoeffer sees it, is that it assumes the existence of a divine nature in which the man Jesus exists. Enhypostatic thinking is prisoner to 'above and beyond thinking' that isolates the man Jesus from the substance that is God.[8] What Christology must avoid, Bonhoeffer argues, is any account of the Christ event that would make the becoming human of the Son incidental to God. 'Liberal' Christology does just that insofar as it shares in the docetic tendency to make the humanity of Christ into a 'symbol'.[9] Liberal theology shares in the prejudices of what Bonhoeffer calls 'Greek idealistic thinking' by distinguishing 'idea and appearance'.[10]

It is at this point in the lectures that Bonhoeffer's thinking on theology's first premise emerges. Theology's first premise is 'that God, out of mercy freely given, truly became a human being'.[11] Neither Docetism, and its offspring 'Greek idealistic thinking', nor Ebionitism can acknowledge that.[12] There is not any identity of being between God and the man Jesus, the man Jesus and God. Both heresies stumble precisely because of their preoccupation with the 'how' question. Each heresy in its own way threatens 'the identity of God with the human'.[13]

Chalcedon is helpful in affirming 'the identity of God with the human' but in a way that ends up subverting itself.[14] How so? Bonhoeffer thinks that Chalcedon encourages us to leave behind talk of the 'substance' of Jesus Christ, indeed of 'the thinking about relationships between natures', in favour of thinking about 'states'.[15] This is a subtle move. Bonhoeffer does not write off Chalcedon as being hopelessly imprisoned by Hellenistic paradigms, substance metaphysics, etc.; rather, for Bonhoeffer, the genius of Chalcedon is that it 'reveals the limitations of its own concepts'.[16] Not only that, Chalcedon's own concepts are fruitful for asserting Christ in a way that is 'objective' and 'living'.[17]

Bonhoeffer's cautious approval of Chalcedon has to do with the way Chalcedon directs us to move beyond 'beyond all conceptual forms', which is something that the doctrine of the hypostatic union does not encourage us to do.[18] In short, what is wrong with the doctrine of the hypostatic union is that it overturns Chalcedon. The doctrine wants to preserve 'the integrity of both natures' by keeping Jesus' humanity separate from his divinity.[19] There is a high level of abstraction here, so Bonhoeffer argues. The doctrine of the hypostatic union takes attention away from the one God-human by talking about him in terms of natures rather than as an event. Hence Bonhoeffer's preference for the language of 'states' over 'natures'. The former points to one person who is both humiliated and exalted.

Doctrinal teaching on the person of Jesus Christ is only salutary if it promotes attention to 'one of the first statements in theology – that wherever God is, God is wholly there'.[20] Herein we see another emphasis that is programmatic for Bonhoeffer's thinking. 'To say that Christ became a human being compels us to say that Christ is identical with God in substance'.[21] Talk of the *homoousios* of the Father and the Son is derivative of the confession that Christ became human. That God is wholly in Christ assumes an 'identity of substance between the Son and the Father'.[22] Such an affirmation is not a product of 'Greek thinking'.[23] *Ousia* language is able to help us to better understand the essential identity of the first and second persons of the Trinity. However, *ousia* language is problematically deployed when it 'speaks of the nature [Wesen] of God and human nature in the theoretical manner of an onlooker, as if these were two material things, normally distinguished from each other, which only come together in Jesus Christ'.[24] Over and against Harnack's hasty dismissal of *ousia* language, Bonhoeffer argues that it is serviceable to the Gospel insofar as it is freed from thought forms that set apart God and humanity. *Ousia* language can point to the sheer facticity of the God-human, Jesus Christ.

To rehearse Bonhoeffer's thought on the conciliar tradition, the problem is not with terms like 'ousia' but rather with 'materiality' and the many forms of thinking in agreement with it. Material ways of thinking do not receive encouragement from Chalcedon as Chalcedon is quite content to let the 'fact of the God-human stand as the presupposition'.[25] Where the doctrine of the hypostatic union errs is that it thinks of Christ's person in terms of natures, natures as material things that can stand independently of one another; whereas the God/human relation is, for Bonhoeffer, between 'two persons'.[26] God is a triune mystery in which there is identity of substance between the three. Nature talk does not yield (much) insight into this mystery. However, dynamic talk, talk of 'states' does. That God and humanity are united in Jesus Christ is a mysterious *event* that must be left to stand. The 'ultimate mystery of the Trinity', says Bonhoeffer, is that 'God glorifies himself in the human'.[27] God does so freely, precisely because God is not a nature but a person who is 'wholly there' in Jesus Christ.[28] Thus Christology's task is to let 'the fact of the God-human stand'.[29]

Assessment

Possible gains

There is much that is laudable in Bonhoeffer's handling of the critical or negative tradition. Most helpful, I think, is his sense that Chalcedon does not take away from the mystery of God the Trinity and of Jesus Christ but rather, when rightly deployed, heightens them. Chalcedon does not get bogged down in talk of 'how' two natures can co-exist in one person. Instead, as Bonhoeffer points out, it surmounts such a concern, thereby drawing attention to 'the fact that Jesus Christ is God'.[30] That fact is Christology's ultimate concern.

Bonhoeffer acknowledges the Church Fathers' concern with the consubstantiality of the Father and the Son, with the unity of being between the three. However, Bonhoeffer does not think that Christology ought to be slavishly devoted to conciliar (i.e. critical) formulations of the mystery of Christ's person in relation to the Father (and the Spirit). Only talk that enables us to say that 'God is wholly there' is necessary.[31] To the extent that the conciliar tradition encourages that, is it useful. Laudable then is Bonhoeffer's sense that the language of *ousia* is edifying to the extent that it remains permeable to the actuality of God's becoming human.

Salutary, furthermore, is Bonhoeffer's refusal to succumb to Harnack's and Ritschl's anti-Hellenism. To be sure, Bonhoeffer criticizes 'Greek idealistic thinking'.[32] But what he means by this is thinking that remains 'above and beyond history'.[33] This liberal theology does insofar as Jesus Christ simply becomes something of a symbol. By way of contrast, Bonhoeffer does not dismiss the classical tradition as entirely beholden to paradigms antithetical to the Gospel as does, for example, his first dissertation supervisor R. Seeberg.

Seeberg's *Zum dogmatischen Verständnis der Trinitätslehre* argues that Trinitarian doctrine is 'an observation of religious experience'.[34] While Bonhoeffer develops Seeberg's sense that 'the personal element' of the doctrine of God warrants explication, Bonhoeffer does not think that Trinitarian doctrine expresses the 'experience of the religious life of the Christian community in God'.[35] Such a formulation is too anthropocentric. Similarly, Bonhoeffer does not adjudge that 'the triadic idea is a product of platonising reflection', or worse, reflective of a 'naïve platonic doctrine of knowledge'.[36]

That said, Bonhoeffer does share some of Seeberg's aversions to metaphysical teaching about the processions of the persons in God's life. For example, nowhere in his Christology lectures does Bonhoeffer discuss the function of the language of begotteness to describe the Son's originating relation with respect to the Father in God's life. Seeberg deems talk of the processions 'speculations' that do not reiterate the 'truths of revelation'.[37] Although Bonhoeffer would not be so crude as to suggest such, that this important tract of Trinitarian teaching does no work for Bonhoeffer's Christological project is worth noting. I suspect Bonhoeffer's silence regarding the procession of the Son from the Father is because such teaching, as Bonhoeffer understands it, does not support the kind of *material* thinking he is trying to encourage.

Material thinking is thinking that yields at every point to what God actually does, to events as it were.[38] A doctrine of God that describes the immanent processions of Son and Spirit in an expansive way would, in Bonhoeffer's mind, detract from the main thing, the 'who'. That is why Bonhoeffer does not say anything about them. I think that Bonhoeffer's reservation must be taken seriously, limitations notwithstanding. Put again, talk of the originating relations of the Son (and Spirit) in relation to the Father in God's life *may* just be another way of asking the wrong question, that is, the 'how' question. Instead, what Christological and Trinitarian doctrine must say at every turn is that Jesus 'in his being humiliated and in being exalted, … remains wholly human and wholly God'.[39]

If we were to follow Bonhoeffer's lead in remaining (relatively) silent about the processions, are we not freed from 'the backward reference'?[40] Bonhoeffer argues that we are not. In his ruminations on the mystery of the eternal unity of word and Spirit in DBWE 14, he states that their unity is not 'to be understood temporally'; for theirs is an eternal unity intrinsic to the immanent Trinity.[41] Likewise, in a fascinating sermon outline on Exodus 20.2–3 in *DBWE* 14, Bonhoeffer recognizes that preaching on the economic Trinity 'always risks turning into an outline of the entire doctrine of soteriology, and [the sermon] becomes more a report' if the immanent Trinity is ignored.[42] To speak of 'weakness and manger' as Bonhoeffer insists, does not mean that we speak of them without God, for they are *God's* weakness and *God's* manger. The doctrine of the immanent Trinity reminds us of just this. Accordingly, Christology is much more than a matter of reporting on what God has done:

such is the domain of soteriology. Christology, as derivative of the doctrine of God, needs always be alert to its foundational premise, God's life as Father, Son and Spirit.

In his outline for a Sermon for Trinity Sunday Bonhoeffer writes, 'What good does a God do us who is in eternity and is stronger than the majesty of the world, stronger than sin and death? This God does not concern us.'[43] The God that does not concern us is the God that does not come to us and help us in Jesus Christ – that God is an idol. That is the God we are to disbelieve: a God locked up in and by his own eternity that does not 'inquire after me'.[44] The God in whom the church is summoned to believe is a God who does inquire after me, and that God is the Father, 'Christ the Son, God the Holy Spirit'.[45] The God in whom we are commanded to trust is the Trinity. The function of the doctrine of the immanent Trinity, for Bonhoeffer, is to remind us that it is *God* who acts savingly for us.

God, for Bonhoeffer, *is* an event, 'the God who became human'.[46] Trinitarian doctrine's task is to speak of this God who glorifies himself in the human. What is gained in all of this is a kind of discipline, I think, the discipline of remembering that it is *God* who acts for us and for our salvation. God is the acting subject. With Bonhoeffer, I do not want to speak of an 'idea of God' but of the one who delivered his people from bondage in Egypt and raised Jesus from the dead.[47] But moving beyond Bonhoeffer, I also want to speak of God as one whose perfect life is revealed in these acts, not conflated with them. In the next section I develop this point.

Possible losses

What *may* be lost via Bonhoeffer's intense Christological concentration? Katherine Sonderegger helps us to discern what may be lost, namely, the earlier appreciation of metaphysics. In the recently published first volume of her *Systematic Theology*, she writes that 'the impulse of much modern theology is to assimilate the question of Deity into the question of Identity … . [whereas] always the reality of God presses us to set forth and praise both God's Deity, His Nature, and His Identity. Almighty God, we say, is both Object and Subject; both What and Who.'[48] God is Deity (Object) and Person (Subject). Now, I am not suggesting Bonhoeffer is immediately vulnerable to the critique of neglecting God's deity. What I am signalling, however, is that the overwhelming orientation of Bonhoeffer's Christology to the economy may generate some doctrinal problems.

Martin Rumscheidt, in his assessment of Seeberg's influence on Bonhoeffer's thought, argues that Bonhoeffer's preoccupation with 'the social aspect of existence' informs his 'antispeculative inclinations'.[49] Indeed, Bonhoeffer's efforts in his first dissertation to recognize 'the social intention of all fundamental Christian concepts'[50] leaves him with a diminished capacity to appreciate dimensions of the traditional doctrine of God that would seem – at first glance, anyhow – to reflect an unedifying interest with the 'how'. Here again I am thinking of talk of the processions of Son and Spirit from the Father in God's life as the ground of their missions and the principle of their intelligibility.

Commenting on Irenaeus's use of the problematic imagery of 'two hands of God', Sonderegger states that 'not all relations of God to the world are the Acts of the Persons! God relates to the world through His Nature as well'.[51] God is both 'Nature and Person', and God relates to his creature *via* both.[52] That is Sonderegger's basic point. How does this match up with Bonhoeffer's powerful insistence that 'there is no "divine nature" as all-powerful and ever-present'?[53] Well, Bonhoeffer's concern, most strongly attested in his aversion to the doctrine of *enhypostasia*, is to negate the idea that something lies behind Jesus – a divine nature – that makes him who he is. Again, Bonhoeffer: 'This person's being God is not something added onto the being human of Jesus Christ'.[54] Sonderegger would undoubtedly agree. She, as with Bonhoeffer, wants to build the doctrine of God and of Jesus Christ on Scripture. But she undoubtedly reads Scripture *differently* than Bonhoeffer. For Bonhoeffer, the primal theological question for Christology – indeed, all of theology – is whether it is possible to speak of Jesus Christ in a way that does not render him incidental to the divine substance. Bonhoeffer wants to know whether Jesus can be loved, served and confessed as he is, wholly God. Speculative thought – which Bonhoeffer associates with Hegel – says that the Creator's relationship to the creature in Jesus is a necessity. The world is necessary to God's being God. Sonderegger and Bonhoeffer obviously want to uphold what speculative and Greek idealist thought cannot: 'the Word became flesh and dwelt among us'.[55] But the way in which Bonhoeffer and Sonderegger advance that truth by describing the God/world relationship as rooted in God's freedom differs in some significant ways. In the rest of this section of the chapter, I will explore some of these ways, arguing that losses accrue to Bonhoeffer as result of his Christology.

Bonhoeffer's aversion to the language of natures and relationships between them in favour of 'states' language in order to describe Christ's person provides a reflective point of contrast with respect to Sonderegger's thought. So Bonhoeffer: Jesus is God in his humiliation and exaltation. The doctrine of the hypostatic union errs because (unlike Chalcedon) it thinks of the natures of Christ (divine and human) as 'things' that relate to one another. The more dynamic language of states is preferable, for Bonhoeffer, as it obviates the notion that there is a 'substance' in which the natures subsist. Jesus is a person who is identical with God in his humiliation and exaltation. Accordingly, we cannot think God apart from the God-world relation, which is not to make God dependent on that relation. In making this move, however, Bonhoeffer does take Christology into the very doctrine of God. The result is that with Bonhoeffer we do not really get a doctrine of *God*. To be sure, we get a rich Christology, but do we really get a sense of what Sonderegger calls 'the Lord's own Unique Metaphysics'?[56]

In Sonderegger's and Bonhoeffer's treatments, we see different accounts of theology's 'first premise' at work.[57] For Bonhoeffer, it is 'that God, out of mercy freely given, truly became a human being, rather than becoming, out of necessity, the realization of some human principle'.[58] Quite the opposite, for Sonderegger: theology's first premise is 'the Unicity of the God of Israel', a unity at one with 'Divine Subjectivity – His Utterly Concrete Reality as I AM'.[59] With Bonhoeffer, the emphasis is entirely on what Sonderegger calls 'Divine Subjectivity'.[60] This is (again) evidence of Bonhoeffer's 'antispeculative inclinations'.[61] God's objectivity, important to acknowledge in order that the doctrine of God is not reduced to soteriology, does little *material* work for Bonhoeffer. This is not to suggest that Bonhoeffer is indifferent to the truth of God's aseity, God ontological self-sufficiency in relation to all that is not God. Recall Bonhoeffer's polemic against Hegel.[62] There is not any necessity driving the incarnation other than the love and freedom of God. But – and here is the fault line – Bonhoeffer, the Lutheran theologian, does not conceive of the God/world relation outside of the act of God's becoming human, whereas for

Sonderegger, the Reformed Catholic theologian, God's nature – and herein lies her appreciation for the transcendentals – is germane for expounding God's relationship to the world. Expressed differently, for Sonderegger, Christology presupposes a sophisticated theology in the form of a doctrine of God that unfolds, as does Augustine in *On the Trinity*, the processions of the persons in God's life as the ground for understanding and receiving the missions of Son and Spirit in the world. Of course Sonderegger would affirm what Bonhoeffer says about the freedom of God to act as God does; but more than that, she would disagree with what Bonhoeffer says is theology's 'first premise'.[63] Sonderegger's sense is that incarnation is derivative of the life of God, full and complete as it is, and that we need to expound God's Life (objectivity) in all its fullness so as to receive the incarnate one in all his truthfulness.

I think that the doctrine of the processions and missions of Son and Spirit – understood along Augustinian and Thomistic lines – deepens what is salutary in Bonhoeffer's account. The eternal procession of the Son from the being of the Father is revealed among us in 'the fullness of time'.[64] Everything that Jesus does and says attests his origin from the Father: as true God and true man, he reveals his origin from the Father. The basic fault line in our Lord's ministry has to do with disputes about his origin. Is he from the Father, or does he cast our demons by Beelzebub's power? Jesus' mission not only reveals his origin; his mission reveals the glory he had with the Father 'before the world existed'.[65] If we take John's lead here, theology ought not to be concerned with an abstract something that lies behind Jesus. The Lord Jesus, true God and true man, can only be described with reference to the Father who begets and sends him. To know the one who sends and the one sent is 'eternal life'.[66] To use a different idiom, Christology makes sense only within a doctrine of God's life and of the Trinity. Jesus himself can only be known in relation to the one to whom he is obedient, with whom he is one in being from eternity.

With Bonhoeffer, we do not want to think of Christ as a kind of puzzle to solve in terms of how natures may or may not relate to a substance behind them.

With Sonderegger we do want to talk about God's nature, the perfections of the one God, common to the three, and we do want to talk about God's reality, his substance, not as what lies behind the three, but as one with God's subjectivity – but not in such a way as to collapse substance and subjectivity! The 'Abstract Divine Nature is Subject, Pure and True Personal Subject'.[67] Yes: 'Not all is Christology! … and not every Doctrine of God begins with Trinity' or Christology.[68]

If Jesus is true God, he is unchangeable, immutable. But his divinity can only be expounded in relation to God the Father. Jesus *is* truth and life eternally and therefore in time; he just *is* truth and life; and it is his nature to be such. And he is truth and life as the Father's truth and life. He has this truth and life as the Son of the Father, and the Father has truth and life as the Father of the Son. As true man, Jesus is truth and life in time, and he is truth and life unchangeably and infinitely, for he is true God. *Contra* Bonhoeffer, human nature need not be changeable to be human. The Son exists fully humanly, even unto death; he dies as the Father's Son. Even the manner of his death is revelatory of his origin. Expressed in a Bonhoefferian idiom, he is wholly there as the one he has always been, the Father's Son. The humanity of Jesus is thus understandable only as the humanity of the Father's Son. God exists humanly, so to speak, in the Son.

What remains then of what Bonhoeffer says 'is one of the first statements in theology – that wherever God is, God is wholly there'?[69] Well, if we follow Sonderegger's lead, we can say 'yes' insofar as God's *nature* is 'Invisibly Present, Hidden in the world, as its Truth, its Light'.[70] God's divine nature is one that is 'wholly there' to us insofar as it is that by which we see and know – 'in your light we see light'.[71] But more, the Light by which we see light is the light of the world, our Lord Jesus Christ. Our sight, our knowledge *is* Jesus Christ. Who is wholly there? Just as God is 'Invisibly Present, Hidden in the world, as its Truth, its Light', so is our Lord Jesus Christ present through the powerful operation of the Spirit.[72] It is this God who is wholly there, Father, Son and Spirit.

What, then, of an eschatological reserve? Of longing for the day when we shall see him as he is? The ascended Jesus, the Father's beloved Son upon and in whom the Spirit rests from and to eternity, is wholly here, yes, and here as the Son who sits at the right hand of the Father. He is among us as the transfigured one. More broadly, he is wholly here as 'Limitless Truth, and the Truth of all our earthly truths; yet is not One with them, not reduced to nor identified with nor limited to any one of these human truths'.[73] Sonderegger reminds us that in the admixture with the creature, God remains sovereign. The 'Utterly Unique communicates His Being to creatures'.[74]

In sum, what I think is somewhat lost or obscured in Bonhoeffer's treatment of the 'first premise' of theology is *God*. As William Hoye writes, 'Jesus himself presupposes an elaborate theology'.[75] That theology is God. Knowledge of God is an effect of this most glorious truth. Theology studies the being of God. That is its premise, and its goal is love of God. Christology is derivative of *theology*. In this life we can know that God is; we can know that in the events of manger and cross the great 'I am' is present. But if we follow Bonhoeffer too closely, I think that we lose a sense of the splendour of God's absolute being, and the knowing of God through his essence and not just his acts.

With Bonhoeffer I want to awaken to reality. I want to be conformed to reality, to see reality become real in our sin soaked and death obsessed world. That is my prayer. With Bonhoeffer I want to follow the one who is wholly God, the Word who became flesh. And I would like to do so in a way that recognizes and takes the time to describe his truth and life as the truth and life of theology's first premise, God.

Conclusion

In this chapter I have presented Bonhoeffer's account of negative Christology. Bonhoeffer argues that Chalcedon is helpful because it discourages us from attempting to talk about Christ in terms of natures, thereby letting the facticity of his person as wholly God and human stand. There is much that is to be commended in his treatment. It encourages us to be disciplined in our talk of who he is by what he actually does. That said, the kind of Christological concentration Bonhoeffer champions discourages, as Sonderegger suggests, recognition of Christology's foundation and first premise: God; for from God do we understand the manger, the life, cross, resurrection, ascension and heavenly session of Jesus Christ in all their fullness.

Notes

1   *DBWE* 12, 302.

2   For example, Ibid., 303.

3   Ibid.

4   Ibid., 315–22.

5   Ibid., 338.

6   Ibid., 349. This is said of the doctrine of enhypostasia.

7   Ibid., 335.

8   Ibid., 336.

9   Ibid., 337.

10 Ibid., 338.

11 Ibid.

12 Ibid.

13 Ibid., 341.

14 Ibid.

15 Ibid., 343, 355–60.

16 Ibid., 343.

17 Ibid.

18 Ibid.

19 Ibid.

20 Ibid., 349.

21 Ibid., 350.

22 Ibid., 351.

23 Ibid., 352.

24 Ibid.

25 Ibid.

26 Ibid.

27 Ibid., 355.

28 Ibid., 349.

29 Ibid., 352.

30 Ibid., 350.

31 Ibid., 349.

32 Ibid., 338.

33 Ibid., 336.

34 Reinhold Seeberg, *Zum dogmatischen Verständnis der Trinitätslehre* (Leipzig: Deichert, 1908), 12. All translations of Seeberg's text are my own.

35 Ibid., 13.

36   Ibid., 8, 4.

37   Ibid., 6.

38   In this regard, Bonhoeffer writes: 'The early church stood against this, because it knew what the docetists of every age have forgotten, namely, that Christ was not an idea but rather an event.' *DBWE* 12, 336.

39   Ibid., 355.

40   John Webster, 'Principles of Systematic Theology', in *The Domain of the Word: Scripture and Theological Reason* (London: T&T Clark, 2012), 143.

41   'On the Doctrine of the Holy Spirit', *DBWE* 15, 486.

42   'Outline of Exodus 20:2–3 (Student Notes) as a Sermon for Trinity Sunday', Ibid., 635, fn.10.

43   Ibid., 636.

44   Ibid.

45   Ibid., 637.

46   *DBWE* 9, 354.

47   This is not to suggest that I want to conflate God with these events. The point is that *God* does these things in fulfilment of the promise made to Abraham.

48   Kathryn Sonderegger, *Systematic Theology: Volume 1: The Doctrine of God* (Minneapolis: Fortress Press, 2015), xii.

49   Martin Rumscheidt, 'The Significance of Adolf von Harnack and Reinhold Seeberg for Dietrich Bonhoeffer', in *Bonhoeffer's Intellectual Formation*, ed. Peter Frick (Tübingen: J. C. B. Mohr, 2008), 204; Eberhard Bethge, *Bonhoeffer: A Biography*, rev. edn (Minneapolis: Fortress Press, 2000), 70.

50   *DBWE* 1, 21.

51   *DBWE* 12, 391.

52   Ibid., 414.

53   Ibid., 354.

54   Ibid., 353.

55   Jn 1.14.

56   Sonderegger, *Attributes*, 199.

57   *DBWE* 12, 338.

58   Ibid.

59   Sonderegger, *Attributes*, 444, 443.

60   Ibid., 445.

61   Bethge, *Bonhoeffer*, 70.

62   See *DBWE* 13, 355: 'It is wrong to derive the God's becoming from an idea, such as the idea of the Trinity.'

63   Ibid., 338.

64   Gal. 4.4.

65   Jn 17.5.

66   Jn 17.3.

67   Sonderegger, *Attributes*, 441.

68   Ibid., 394.

69   *DBWE* 12, 349.

70   Sonderegger, *Attributes*, 441.

71   Ps. 36.9.

72   Sonderegger, *Attributes*, 441.

73   Ibid., 452.

74   Ibid., 491.

75   William J. Hoye, *The Emergence of Eternal Life* (Cambridge: Cambridge University Press, 2013), 26.

Chapter 3

'WE BELIEVE IN ONE LORD, JESUS CHRIST': A PRO-NICENE REVISION OF BONHOEFFER'S 1933 CHRISTOLOGY LECTURES

Stephen J. Plant

Introduction

In an appendix to the second edition of his book *Arius*, Rowan Williams notes some pained reactions by reviewers to allusions in his first edition to parallels between the doctrinal crises of the fourth century and the German Church struggle of the 1930s.[1] Williams wryly acknowledges the aptness of Maurice Wiles' comment that he appears to give the impression that 'Arius' problem was that he had not read Barth'.[2] The exchange relates to Williams' observation in the theological postscript to the first edition that:

> If we seek to understand Nicaea … I suggest that we might think of certain aspects of the 'German Church Struggle' in our own century. Here we have a church faced, in the aftermath of the First World War, with the challenges of 'modernity' … offered an integral place – on certain conditions – in the new Reich, it is pitiably eager to abandon theological self-questioning and to allow the political *deus ex machina* to brush aside the uncomfortable residue of inner conflict or self-doubt.[3]

Williams acknowledges that the analogy can be pressed too far – 'with Arius as Emmanuel Hirsch and Eusebius of Nicomedia as Reichsbischof Müller' and, irresistibly, with Athanasius as Karl Barth, 'difficult and ambivalent figures, both of them', but both witnesses to the question of the distinctiveness of the gospel in their insistence that there is 'no gap conceivable between God as he acts towards us – as the Father of Jesus Christ – and the activity in and by which God is eternally what he is'.[4]

Williams is right to handle such an analogy with a light touch. But that doesn't mean that considering the relation between fourth- and fifth-century Trinitarian disputes and modern theology need be frivolous. In this chapter I want to suggest, to the contrary, that a reconsideration of fourth-century Trinitarian theology is not only potentially useful, but affords an essential corrective for modern theology in at least two ways. First, recent scholarship of the early Church aims to correct a number of misreadings of the development of Christological and Trinitarian theology. Second, and on the evidential basis of its re-reading of early doctrinal disputes, revisionary scholarship offers to correct several methodological errors characteristic of much modern theology. To develop this suggestion I plan to make use of Lewis Ayres' book *Nicaea and its Legacy: An Approach to Fourth-Century Trinitarian Theology* that entails proposals for a revisionary approach to what he calls 'pro-Nicene theology' and, in its final chapter, makes several constructive suggestions about how a pro-Nicene legacy should function within modern theology.[5] In part then, I simply want to see how Bonhoeffer's proposal that the task for contemporary theologians is 'to construct a positive Christology on the foundation of this critical [i.e. negative] Christology' stacks up against recent revisionary approaches to the fourth- and fifth-century doctrinal disputes.[6] But if my instincts are right, then what this enquiry will reveal is that Bonhoeffer's approach is typical in at least some respects of theological strategies for appropriating early theology in ways that improperly privilege the modern over the classical or traditional. It is precisely such strategies that are called into question by recent revisionary scholarship of the early Church. The order in which I want to develop my argument is, first, to put some questions to Bonhoeffer's Christology lectures. Next, I will sum up quite briefly the thrust of revisionary scholarship on the fourth- and fifth-century doctrinal disputes in the early Church, before turning in more detail to Lewis Ayres' particular contribution. This will lead in conclusion to several suggestions about how modern theology might better appropriate the culture of pro-Nicene theology.

Bonhoeffer's 1933 Christology lectures

The Christology lectures mark the high-tide mark of Bonhoeffer's career as a *Privatdozent* at the *Friedrich-Wilhelms-Universität* in Berlin. Bonhoeffer began the course on 1 May 1933 and the course ended on 22 July. The lectures coincided, therefore, with months in which the new Third Reich moved efficiently to build on Adolf Hitler's appointment as Chancellor at the end of January. The lectures as they appear in volume 12 of the *Dietrich Bonhoeffer Werke* were transcribed in 1960 by Gerhard Riemer from his lecture notes, at which point Riemer destroyed the originals. This distinguishes the DBW version from that of 1966, which reconstructed Bonhoeffer's lectures in a composite text from notes taken by several students. Bonhoeffer's surviving correspondence in the second half of 1932 and the first half of 1933 gives no indication of what was in his mind in nominating Christology as the topic of his lectures,[7] but it cannot be fanciful to speculate that a desire to make clear the distinction between the Christ and the Führer lay somewhere in the background.

The lecture course was intended to be in four parts: an introduction, followed by sections on 'The Present Christ', 'The Historical Christ' and 'The Eternal Christ'. The course ended before the third part could be given and no notes towards it in Bonhoeffer's hand survive. In this context, where some knowledge of the lectures can be assumed – and also for pragmatic reasons – I don't plan to undertake an extensive description or exegesis of the lectures as a whole but rather to engage the lectures by means of three diagnostic questions. The diagnostic questions are:

1. What narrative strategy does Bonhoeffer employ in presenting the development of Christology in the early Church?
2. What roles does Bonhoeffer ascribe respectively to God, individuals and Church Councils in the development of Christology?
3. What function does Bonhoeffer believe the theology of the early Church has for modern Christology?

Bonhoeffer defines Christology early in his introduction as 'doctrine, speaking, the word about the Word of God'.[8] Like all forms of doctrine Christology is therefore a form of human speaking, but it is a human speaking that has as its object Jesus Christ as the Logos of God. In the opening paragraphs Bonhoeffer distinguishes this kind of speaking, on the basis of its unique object, from other forms of scholarship: Christology is uniquely concerned with a personal encounter that asks the question 'who are you?' and whose subject is herself asked the question 'who are you?' by the Logos of God encountered in Christology. Bonhoeffer tells us that, understood this way, two further questions are prohibited by any genuine Christology:

1. Whether the answer that is given is the right answer …
2. … how the 'that' of the revelation can be *conceived*.[9]

Bonhoeffer's reason for excluding both these questions is that 'there can be no authority for our own human logos to cast doubt on the truth' of the Logos of God,[10] since all that our human logos can know is what is given it to know in God's self-revelation. An alternative approach that made the human logos the arbiter of truth about the Logos of God would be an act of idolatry, in which the human logos made itself like a god. In his opening remarks, Bonhoeffer has already given us partial answers to two of our three diagnostic questions.

In answer to the second question concerning the roles of God, individuals and Church councils in the development of Christology, Bonhoeffer answers that the roles were the same in the early centuries of the Church as they are now and as they always are: God's role is to give himself as a Word of address and the role of human individuals is to be addressed by God's revelation. Christology is concerned with an event of personal encounter; Christology is, as Clifford Green puts it, sociality.[11]

In answer to the third question, concerning the function of the theology of the early Church for modern Christology, Bonhoeffer's clear view is that in genuine Christology 'Jesus's own witness to himself, then and now, stands on its own and substantiates itself'.[12] Consequently, the early Church has as its role the same role that modern theologians have, which is to hear and joyfully receive the Word's witness to himself. Christ for Bonhoeffer is God's Word of personal address and Christology may not, therefore, be an outcome or product of reification, deduction or speculation either by the early Church or by contemporary theologians.

This sense of Christology occurring in personal encounter is taken up in section one on 'The Present Christ', which spells out the ways in which the encounter between Christ and human beings takes place concretely. It is clear in this section that Bonhoeffer means to preserve God's freedom in the encounter of Christ and the human person. Focusing on revelation as a personal address – as an 'event' or 'happening', as Bonhoeffer does and as Barth also does – means that the truth of God is not conceived as something preserved in formaldehyde and bottled so that later theologians can simply take it from the shelf. Christology is not about an idea of God embodied in Christ which a 'person needs only take possession of'.[13] This insight conditions Bonhoeffer's understanding not only of the form taken by Christ in the world as Word, but also as sacrament and as Church community. With respect to the sacrament (by which, somewhat oddly, he refers only to the Lord's Supper) he spells out the distinction between Christology as address and Christology as idea by maintaining that Christ is in the sacrament – in his essence – Christ is 'not *doctrina*', that is, he is not a generalized truth which is at the Church's disposal.[14]

If Christ is not at the Church's disposal, then where is he? Bonhoeffer makes use of Luther's understanding of Christ's presence in the Eucharistic elements as a *repletive* presence, a way of being in a place such that 'something is everywhere and yet not measurable in any place'.[15] Christ is present in the bread in a theological or spiritual way; one may not, as Bonhoeffer colourfully puts it, 'grope for him in the rustling leaves'.[16] In the second section of the first part of his lectures, he goes on to give a positive account of Christ's presence in the centre of life in being there for humankind, being there for history and being there for nature. In this 'being there' of Christ the Church has, literally, a central place. While he does not mention the Church in relation to human existence, he places it at the centre of the state and – in her sacraments and in her preaching – makes the Church instrumental for the liberation of the 'old creation' for the 'new'. Returning to our three diagnostic questions, we can now make a comment on the first question, which concerns the narrative *strategy* Bonhoeffer employs in the lecture with respect to the early Church. He hides in full view a significant methodological decision, which is to place the Christology of the early Church second in the order of his presentation after the Christ *pro me*. It is just possible that the order of the sections is purely practical, after the fashion of Calvin's *Institutes of the Christian Religion* which, Calvin tells us, he might have begun just as well with the study of 'ourselves' or of God.[17] But to my mind it is clear that this order is an enactment of a methodological decision that Christology begins with the direct address of God. The present Christ is thus primary to the historical Christ in two distinct senses: He is primary in a temporal sense and primary in a methodological sense. The address of Christ to the contemporary theologian as it were trumps the address he made in the early centuries of the Church's history. Such a method comports, of course, with that of Barth, who was also clear that God needs only himself as the basis of His claim upon humanity, with the consequence that history, even the history of Jesus or the history of the Church, may not be understood as in any way another independent authority for contemporary theology.

With this in mind we turn now to the second part of the lectures in which Bonhoeffer considers the historical Christ. It is here that he begins to discuss Christology in ways that are connected to the development of doctrine in the early Church. As a prelude, he rejects a distinction he believes central to liberal theology between the Jesus of the Synoptic Gospels and the Christ of Paul, between the historical Jesus and the Christ of faith. Bonhoeffer believes such a distinction to be illusory. It is an illusion historically because the Synoptic Gospels too are theologically constructed; but it is also an illusion theologically since 'dogmatics does need the certainty of Jesus Christ's historical existence.'[18] According to Bonhoeffer – following here in Johannes Weiss and Albert Schweitzer's boot prints – historical research can neither affirm nor deny historical facts and, because of this, absolute certainty about historical facts is made impossible. It is for this reason that theology must begin not in historical data but with Christ *pro me*.

With this clarification in mind Bonhoeffer turns to the history of dogma in the early Church. His presentation of the development of Christological doctrine continues with the sharp distinction between, on the one hand, a critical or negative Christology (he thinks the terms interchangeable), and, on the other, positive Christology. Bonhoeffer's initial description of critical Christology comes straight to a very sharp point: critical Christology 'seeks to make the incomprehensibility of the person of Jesus Christ comprehensible.'[19] 'It is critical', he continues, 'because it tests every assertion about Christ against this limitation', that is, the question of intelligibility. It is for this reason that one may accurately describe critical Christology as 'negative'.

Bonhoeffer gives further clarification to his meaning in proposing that while 'approaches to a positive theology have always been launched by individual theologians … [t]he decisions of the councils … expressed only the conclusions of critical Christology'. Between councils individuals proceeded with a positive Christology; the official Church, however, made 'critical Christology its business – setting limits [and] issuing negative statements'.[20]

A number of remarkable things are going on here. Note, first, the sharp distinction being asserted to exist between the positive Christological work undertaken by individuals in the early Church and the negative work of the institutional Church in the decision of its councils. Note too that the negative theology of the councils is described as being motivated by the effort to comprehend that which is properly incomprehensible in Christology and Trinitarian theology. The suggestion is that individual theologians innovate while councils restrain innovation. Here we have Bonhoeffer's clear answer to the second of our diagnostic questions. One may still allow that he ascribes a useful function to the early Church in its councils. He indicates three things gained from negative theology – an opening up of Christological talk to the two natures, the overcoming in the immanent of 'material thinking in Christology' and stepping beyond 'how' questions in Christology, again within the immanent. Nonetheless the more heroic role goes to the individuals who pioneered Christology against the tide of the negative power of the Church. In answer to our third diagnostic question – concerning the function of early Church Christology, it turns out that there are two functions, not one. The Church functions to establish negative limits to Christology while individuals function to provide us with positive Christology. While the suggestion is not, I think, that positive Christology should aim to *overcome* negative Christology, it is clear that positive Christology should aim to move beyond the limits of critical Christology in the form of the limits of the council's creeds. In changing tack towards the end of his lectures from reflecting on the historical Christ to a positive Christology, Bonhoeffer sets out this task with the question: 'How can we now construct a positive Christology on the foundation of this critical Christology?'[21]

Bonhoeffer makes one further brief comment on the early Church that may be illuminating in the context of the questions I am asking of him. Acknowledging that 'doctrine must always be set over against false doctrine' he states all the same that '[f]or us the concept of heresy no longer exists'.[22] The reason he gives is that there are no longer Church councils of a truly ecumenical nature. This may be a straightforwardly factual remark following unresolved divisions of the Church in 1054 and 1517, but it may also imply that ecumenical councils belonged to the first phase of the history of the Church and that is an era that has now permanently passed.[23]

In the description I have given I have already made mention of a correspondence between Bonhoeffer's views and those of Karl Barth with respect to conceptualizing God's revelation as a word of *address*. Before moving on I want to take note of another figure with whose views Bonhoeffer's appear to overlap: those of Adolf von Harnack. If it were to prove the case that Harnack's approach to the development of doctrine in the early Church had rubbed off on Bonhoeffer it would hardly be surprising: in 1925 Bonhoeffer wrote to his parents that he had seriously considered Harnack as a possible doctoral supervisor, but had ruled out the septuagenarian because of his age. On Harnack's retirement Bonhoeffer collected essays from students in Harnack's seminar on the topic of 'joy' in early Christianity; when he finally died in 1930, Bonhoeffer was the student deputed to offer a eulogy.[24] The key to Bonhoeffer's obvious personal affection for Harnack was, as Bonhoeffer says on his *Curriculum Vitae* in 1927, he had attended Harnack's Church history seminar for three semesters, for one of which he wrote an extant essay on 1 Clement. As an important figure in the study of the early Church Harnack's views played a key role in shaping the consensus against which recent revisionary accounts have reacted. In light of what we have read it may be worth singling out two aspects of Bonhoeffer's theology that correspond with his teacher's views. First, like Harnack, Bonhoeffer was keen to promote the idea of a tension between institutional ecclesial intransigence on the one hand, and the positivity of religious genius on the other. This is an idea with a long history in Lutheran theology, stretching back at least to Philip Melanchthon, whose classical humanism led him to see God's providential work in the 'great men of history'.[25] Second, Harnack's historical theology was influenced significantly by Hegelian assumptions about the progress of the human spirit in ways that gave priority to the modern over the classical.

'New perspectives' on the early Church

As far as I am aware none of the scholars who are leading revisionary treatments of Nicaea and its legacy use the term 'new perspectives', which I am, of course, borrowing, somewhat wryly, from trends in Pauline scholarship. The term is not, however, inappropriate. There are at least two major fault lines, which are not unconnected, that divide older Patristic scholarship and an emerging new scholarly consensus. The first fault line lies along questions of historical interpretation. Earlier scholarship tended to narrate the development of Christian doctrine in terms of clearly distinguishable party lines in which, typically, key figures played the leading role. The *locus classicus* of this approach was the so-called Arian controversy, which was narrated as a clash between, on the one hand, one or perhaps two Arian or neo-Arian parties with Arius himself as a heresiarch, and on the other of Athanasius and, following in his footsteps, the Cappadocians as a sort of theological collective. Revisionary scholarship has argued, in contrast, that fourth-century disputes were much more complex. Individuals such as Athanasius certainly played significant roles – Arius himself much less so – but it makes better sense to characterize these disputes as debates between competing theological cultures, some of which overlapped with others in shifting alliances. Earlier historians, such as Harnack, tended to present this history in terms of a pure original Christian truth that was periodically interrupted and corrupted by heresy. Revisionary scholarship is re-narrating the historical evidence in terms of a series of fraught family disputes in which the early Church tried to make the best sense of what the Scriptures gave them to believe about God and about Jesus Christ in ways that expressed an essential continuity with the teaching of the Apostles. There remain some, for example Thomas Weinandy, who continue to place greater emphasis on the role of individuals such as Athansius in the development of Nicene Trinitarian orthodoxy; but revisionary scholarship seems to be winning the day.[26] In addition to the interpretive issues, a second methodological fault line has also emerged from what I am calling 'new perspectives' on Nicaea. This second fault line concerns the question of what role the theology of the early church ought to play in contemporary theology. Earlier scholarship has tended to draw quite sharp lines between historical study and doctrinal theology. Those associated with the new perspectives tend to be less willing to distinguish the historical and the theological, with the result that fresh examination of the work of the Fathers leads directly to new theological proposals. Returning to Bonhoeffer's key terms, proponents of the new perspective are treating the theology of Nicaea and Chalcedon not only as a negative theology that asserts a creedal limit, but as a living partner in contemporary theology.

A simple way to flesh out this contrast is to turn to Lewis Ayres' 2004 book *Nicaea and its Legacy*. Ayres sets out to demonstrate that pro-Nicene theology is best considered as a theological culture comprising a number of diverse theologies. Such historical study is, for Ayres, not merely propaedeutic for contemporary theologians; rather, the practice of disciplined, patient and rigorous historical theology is continually demanded of theologians if they are to have any chance of doing their work in ways that acknowledge any continuity that might or ought to exist between contemporary theology and historical theology.[27]

It takes a while for Ayres to reach a point when he has gathered enough descriptive evidence to warrant pinning down a definition of a fully pro-Nicene theology. Along the way there are several surprises. One in particular is relevant to our earlier diagnostic question concerning the function of the councils of the early Church. According to Ayres, there is little evidence that creeds in general, and Nicaea's creed in particular, were either intended to function or functioned in practice as regulative statements of belief. Both before and after the council of Nicaea in 325, creeds were primarily intended for use in baptismal liturgies and in catechetical preparation for baptism. Many if not most episcopal sees had such creeds, and after Nicaea there was no sudden disappearance of local baptismal creeds. Moreover, wherever there were meetings of bishops in the third, fourth and fifth centuries, even where such meetings were quite local and relatively small, creeds were frequently issued. Sometimes individuals too published credos stating their beliefs, either for polemical reasons or occasionally to defend themselves against charges of heterodoxy. It took several decades before the creed of the Nicene council began to function as something that was especially regulative for orthodox doctrine.

For Ayres, a fully pro-Nicene theology is, of course, in part a matter of one's doctrinal convictions. But in order to qualify for the accolade 'fully pro-Nicene' in Ayres' book it is inadequate simply to list a set of doctrinal statements to be ticked off one by one. The significance of defining pro-Nicene theology as a culture becomes apparent when, more than half way into his argument, Ayres states its three central principles:

1. a clear vision of the person and nature distinction, entailing the principle that whatever is predicated of the divine nature is predicated of the three persons equally and understood to be one (this distinction may or may not be articulated via a consistent technical vocabulary);
2. clear expression that the eternal generation of the Son occurs within the unitary and incomprehensible being [note the importance of *not* transgressing the incomprehensibility of the union of natures];
3. clear expression of the doctrine that the persons work inseparably.[28]

Following the achievement of this working definition of a pro-Nicene theology, Ayres moves on to identify three theological strategies characteristic of pro-Nicene theologians. By a theological strategy Ayres means 'a pattern of argumentation, a way of relating together particular themes or topics for discussion: a strategy is thus a matter of both form and content'.[29] Each of these three pro-Nicene strategies is treated at chapter length, but it is enough for our purposes to illustrate what Ayres means with a brief mention of each of them. The first and most basic strategy identified by Ayres 'is a style of reflecting on the paradox of the irreducible unity of the three irreducible divine persons'.[30] There is no suggestion in this strategy of making the incomprehensible comprehensible, and indeed the reverse is true, as pro-Nicene theologians attempted to articulate the divide between God and creation and express analogical relations between them. A second strategy characteristic of pro-Nicene theological culture identified by Ayres is more narrowly Christological in focus and subdivided into two sets of issues: the 'Christological determination of spiritual purification' on the one hand, and, 'the interweaving of Christology and ontological speculation' on the other.[31] In relation to the first of these twinned themes, pro-Nicene theologians were deeply interested in the transformation of the life of the Christian by Christ. Christ shapes Christian life in a variety of intellectual and contemplative ways, some of which, if we are to judge from Bonhoeffer's opening dismissal of silence in patristic thought as 'mystagogical … prattle',[32] he is not especially sensitive to. Finally, pro-Nicene theologians operated with recognizably common elements in the approaches taken to reflections on the purification of the soul and on appropriate ways of reading Scripture. In relation to the former theme, purification, Ayres pays attention to the theologies of baptism and Eucharist. In relation to Scripture, Ayres suggests that 'the distinctive character of pro-Nicene exegesis is to be found in subtle twists given to common reading practices, and in the links drawn between these reading practices and the principles of pro-Nicene Trinitarianism.'[33]

Towards a conclusion

I want now – still in dialogue with both Bonhoeffer and Ayres – to begin drawing some conclusions from their juxtaposition. The first point to make quite clear will I hope be obvious: in no sense do I intend to imply by this discussion of his attitude to the creeds of the early Church that Bonhoeffer is anything other than wholly doctrinally orthodox, by the standard of Nicaea entailed by the three central principles Ayres identifies. Any concerns I have relate, in the first instance, to the distinction made in the lectures between negative and positive Christology that seems to me overly polemical and perhaps somewhat casual. However, as I hinted in my opening remarks, I think this minor exegetical issue may be the tip of an issue that is of some importance concerning Bonhoeffer's theological methodology. My suspicion is that Bonhoeffer's views of the function of the creeds and of the relation between historical theology and systematic or dogmatic theology may be typical of his time in certain ways that we should not wish now to pass unchallenged.

In the final chapter of *Nicaea and its Legacy*, Ayres moves beyond his re-narration of fourth-century Trinitarian disputes to spell out his concerns about the ways that the legacy of Nicaea has been appropriated in modern theology. One difficulty comes, Ayres thinks, from the way that the discipline of theology has been subdivided into distinct scholarly guilds within the modern academy, with biblical studies, historical theology and systematic theology each operating in isolation from one another. One consequence of this has been that systematic theologians have conceived part of their job as *appropriating* classical theology and the work of historical theologians, their lack of expertise often meaning that such appropriation is shallow. It is certainly the case, for Ayres, that the theology of early theologians needs appropriation – what he questions is the separation of expert disciplined attention to classic texts from that of drawing out systematic theological conclusions from them. In Bonhoeffer's terms Ayres calls into question the habitual modern distinction between negative and positive theology in which Bonhoeffer colludes – at least with respect to the early Church (his reading of Luther may well be a case we should treat differently). On the other side of the same intra-disciplinary divide historical theologians have tended to think of their job as purely historical – that is, exegetical and interpretive. In modern systematics, narratives of the development of Trinitarian theology in the early Church

> frequently serve as quasi-confessional statements, indicating existing options, setting out a narrative that results in a range of possibilities for current use, as they narrate a story of error such that certain modern assumptions seem necessary.[34]

Narratives of the pre-modern in systematics, Ayres thinks, are frequently interwoven with assumptions about how theology should be practised and how theology has developed, ones which hold at arm's length the real challenge that pro-Nicene theologies present. He suggests three narrative strategies – modern alternatives to the strategies of pro-Nicene theologians in the pre-modern period – that serve to justify systematic theology in marginalizing, misinterpreting and misappropriating the pre-modern.

The first of these strategies is manifested in the assumption that 'modern theological method must differ from the methods of pre-modernity because of supposedly necessary features of post-Enlightenment rationality'.[35] Just such an assumption is made in a distinction between negative and positive Christology. A second strategy in modern theology for keeping the theology of the early Church at arm's length is to present 'classical Christian theology as unsustainable because of its debt to "Greek metaphysics", or because of its "Platonizing" of Christianity'.[36] This stratagem was widespread until quite recent times at least in English-speaking theology. It is evident too in attempts in liberal theology to scrape Hellenistic accretions away from the genuine teachings of Jesus. However, Ayres, writing in 2004, precedes the recent revival of interest in

Augustine and Thomas Aquinas that is doing much to immunize contemporary English-speaking theology against an allergic reaction to metaphysics. How does Bonhoeffer fare on this count? In a passing remark in the lectures he tells us that there is no implication of 'Greek thinking' in the Chalcedonian definition. Yet, strongly influenced by Luther in a suspicion of forms of theology in which metaphysical speculation plays an important role, Bonhoeffer's modern assumptions do sometimes get the better of him. A privileging of modernity may also be evident in his apparent lack of sensitivity to the ways that the Fathers related prayer and theology, ascetic and intellectual practices, perhaps particularly in the apophatic tradition – 'mystagogical silence is prattle'. Finally, modern theology, according to Ayres, makes assumptions 'about the nature and function of philosophy and about the appropriate use of the text of scripture'.[37] In several important ways Bonhoeffer's theology resists this particular temptation in modern theology. For example, Bonhoeffer's commitment to reading the Bible with the primary intention of hearing God speak in it has more in common with Gregory Nyssa and Augustine than with many of his contemporaries, though he stops short of some ways of reading scripture common to pro-Nicene theologians, such as allegorical readings of biblical texts.

Rowan Williams' loose analogy between the Christological debates leading up to and beyond the Council of Nicaea and the German Church Struggle of the 1930s does not make much of Dietrich Bonhoeffer. If we allow in this playful parallel that Barth is a kind of modern Athanasius and Hirsch a kind of modern Arius, then might we also speculate which Nicene and post-Nicene theologian prefigures Bonhoeffer? If such mind games are permitted then my money is on Basil of Caesarea.

Notes

1   Rowan Williams, *Arius*, 2nd edn (London: SCM Press, 2001), 266.

2   Ibid., 266.

3   Ibid., 237.

4   Ibid., 237–8.

5   Lewis Ayres, *Nicaea and its Legacy: An Approach to Fourth-Century Trinitarian Theology*, (Oxford: Oxford University Press, 2004).

6   *DBWE* 12, 353.

7   In a letter to Helmut Rössler on the 25 December 1932, Bonhoeffer discusses *Christus praesens*, a theme that appears in the lectures, but without making an explicit reference to the lectures: *DBWE* 12, 83.

8   Ibid., 301.

9   Ibid., 304.

10 Ibid., 304.

11 Clifford J. Green, *Bonhoeffer: A Theology of Sociality*, rev. edn (Grand Rapids: Eerdmans, 1999).

12 *DBWE* 12, 304.

13 Ibid., 316.

14 Ibid., 319.

15 Ibid., 320–1.

16 Ibid., 321.

17 John Calvin, *Institutes of the Christian Religion*, trans. Henry Beveridge, (Peabody: Hendrickson, 2008), 4.

18 *DBWE* 12, 329.

19 Ibid., 331.

20 Ibid., 332.

21 Ibid., 353.

22 Ibid., 332.

23 I may mention in passing here that Bonhoeffer's characterization of the Ebionite heresy as heresy with roots in 'Israelite thinking' exhibits a casual, derogatory use of the term 'Israelite' in a way that ought to trouble his readers more than it has done so far. Ibid., 338.

24 See *DBWE* 9, 148.

25 As Timothy Wengert writes: 'He [Melanchthon] never missed an opportunity to connect the study of time and history to the providence of God.' Wengert, 'Philip Melanchthon on Time and History in the Reformation'. *Consensus* 30:2 (2005): 18.

26 Thomas Weinandy, *inter alia*, argues that Ayres has underplayed the significance of individuals such as Athanasius in the development of a 'pro-Nicene culture' and also under-emphasized the role of pro-Nicene faith as foundational for pro-Nicene theology. Weinandy, *Athanasius: A Theological Introduction* (Aldershot: Ashgate Press, 2007), 60, 78.

27 The same point of view is expressed by Khaled Anatolios in *Retrieving Nicaea: The Development and Meaning of Trinitarian Doctrine* (Grand Rapids, MN: Baker Academic, 2011). Anatolios aims to 'destabilize the division of tasks of

historical and systematic theology' in the conclusion to his study, which, while distinct from Ayres', makes a number of similar points. Anatolios reiterates the point by arguing that 'the task of retrieval involves both a receptive and an active constructive posture'. Ibid., 281.

28   Ayres, *Nicaea*, 236.

29   Ibid., 273.

30   Ibid., 278.

31   Ibid., 302.

32   *DBWE 12*, 300.

33   Ayres, *Nicaea*, 335.

34   Ibid., 385.

35   Ibid., 387.

36   Ibid., 388.

37   Ibid., 390.

Chapter 4

ADAM IN CHRIST?
THE PLACE OF SIN IN CHRIST-REALITY
Eva Harasta

Bonhoeffer and the question of sin

It seems natural to turn to Dietrich Bonhoeffer when dealing with hamarti-ology. Bonhoeffer is famous both for his clear perception of political injustice and for his clear theological analysis of sin and its confession. Yet a closer look at Bonhoeffer's writings reveals some reluctance on his part to discuss 'sin' and 'evil' as themes on their own. Throughout his writings, Bonhoeffer emphasizes the Lutheran principle that sin can only be perceived clearly from the perspective of faith, that is, from the perspective of those that are freed from sin. Sin becomes recognizable only retrospectively, from the perspective of reconciliation. This strong emphasis on reconciliation culminates in the concept of Christ-reality – *Christuswirklichkeit* – in Bonhoeffer's last work, the *Ethics*, where he aims to establish reconciliation as *the* guiding principle of theological ontology. In his own words:

> There is no part of the world, no matter how lost, no matter how godless, that has not been accepted by God in Jesus Christ and reconciled to God. Whoever perceives the body of Jesus Christ in faith can no longer speak of the world as if it were lost, as if it were separated from God; they can no longer separate themselves in clerical pride from the world.[1]

But does Bonhoeffer refuse to acknowledge sin and evil in a systematic and conceptual way even as he is surrounded by injustice in his daily experience? Does he succumb to the temptation to becalm himself with hopes for reconciliation in a thoroughly unreconciled world? He is clearly very much aware of this temptation, invoking a literary figure in order to express the underlying problematic ambiguity. Since his time in Barcelona as a young vicar, Bonhoeffer was fascinated by the figure of Don Quixote, who even as he bravely faces evil refuses to acknowledge it. In 'Ethics as Formation', Bonhoeffer writes with gentle appreciation of Don Quixote:

> The perennial figure of Don Quixote has become contemporary, the 'knight of the doleful countenance' who, with a shaving basin for a helmet and a miserable nag for a charger, rides into endless battle for the chosen lady of his heart, who doesn't even exist. This is the picture of the adventurous enterprise of an old world against a new one, of a past reality against a contemporary one, of a noble dreamer against the overpowering force of the commonplace.[2]

In spite of his literary appreciation for Don Quixote, in the end Bonhoeffer appeals to Don Quixote as a metaphor for ethical concepts that have failed in establishing clear criteria against National Socialism. However well-regarded and well-grounded these ethical concepts were in the past, their failure in the face of Nazism disqualifies them for future use. And still, the quixotic method of simultaneously evading and opposing evil evokes a sympathetic reaction on Bonhoeffer's part. As he remarks, 'Only the mean-spirited can read the fate of Don Quixote without sharing in and being moved by it.'[3] Even failed models of ethics continue to exercise a certain tragic appeal that goes beyond pity. For although they fail to grasp injustice and evil, their cause remains noble. Indeed, exactly by their failure these ethical models illustrate the profound complexity of the ethical endeavour. For Bonhoeffer, this deep complexity can only be resolved theologically. This testifies to the thoroughly Lutheran quality of Bonhoeffer's approach. For the Lutheran perspective typically stresses that 'sin' affects the whole human being, thus corrupting the very ability of perception itself. Even theologians are in no position to disrespect Don Quixote.

Yet Bonhoeffer does not intend to write an ethics for dreamers of doleful countenance. The deep complexity of evil and sin at the root of ethics does not discourage him at all. Rather, he aims to find firm ethical ground, and wants to establish solid criteria by which to differentiate justice from injustice, and to provide guidelines for practical resistance against injustice. Bonhoeffer chooses a typically Lutheran way of approaching the problem of sin: his guiding principle remains that sin has no real power, and that justification is the only true reality – even as his surroundings seem to testify ever more strongly to the very opposite, i.e. to the abiding reality of injustice, of sin, of guilt, of evil, even as '[t]he gray on gray of a sultry, rainy day has turned into the black cloud and bright lightening flash of a thunderstorm'.[4] Bonhoeffer remains reluctant to discuss sin on its own in a more systematic manner because of the quixotic ambiguity described above. However, in this essay I want to focus precisely upon the hamartiological presuppositions that underlie his position. For though Bonhoeffer does not discuss the reality of sin extensively in the *Ethics*, his earlier works are replete with discussion of this topic, and his earlier insights continue to influence his thinking right up and into the argument of his *Ethics*.

Sin in the *Ethics* (1): Guilt

Why exactly is Bonhoeffer reluctant to discuss sin in the *Ethics*? Once we begin to look at that text with a specifically hamartiological interest, we start to find one clue after the other. Even the quotation above which established Bonhoeffer's reluctance and ambiguity on the hamartiological front may be read differently. For the universality of Christ's salvific claim on all parts of reality – 'no matter how lost, no matter how godless'[5] – could be interpreted on the basis of Christ's vicarious suffering (2 Cor. 5.21): reconciliation implies Christ's radical acceptance of human sin. Bonhoeffer re-interprets this traditional Lutheran tenet in an ontological way such that Christ's acceptance of sin does not only apply to individual justification before God, but rather constitutes the principle of the world's justification, the principle of reality itself, of Christ-reality. In terms of theological anthropology, Bonhoeffer here identifies Christ with Adam. This needs further substantiation and explanation.

The starting point for examining Bonhoeffer's hamartiology in the *Ethics* is the text 'Guilt, Justification, Renewal'. In this passage, Bonhoeffer focuses on the active form of sin, on sin-as-deed. Such a focus on the act-dimension of sin follows naturally in and from the ethical perspective. Characteristically, Bonhoeffer is interested in the social dimension of sin-as-deed; his emphasis as ever lies on the relational quality of reality.

The place where this acknowledgment of guilt becomes real is the church. This does not mean that the church, alongside other things it is and does, is also the place where guilt is genuinely acknowledged. Instead, the church is that community of people that has been led by the grace of Christ to acknowledge its guilt toward Christ. It is tautological to say that the church is the place where guilt is acknowledged. If it were otherwise, the church would no longer be church.[6]

This passage includes two ideas that are supremely relevant to the present investigation: first, that the church is defined as a discrete social entity by Christ's soteriological work, and second, that Bonhoeffer transforms the contemporary notion of 'Confessing Church' in a way that might have astonished some of his colleagues in the German church struggle. Let me briefly touch on both aspects.

First, we consider the definition of the church as a real community by Christ's soteriological work. Defining the church by Christ's salvific work is of course one of the most basic of ecclesiological thoughts, but Bonhoeffer re-interprets it in a specific way. He balances between the *high* ecclesiology of his earlier work *Discipleship* on the one hand – where the (confessing) church becomes almost identical with Christ, even participating in his salvific work – and the more *humble* ecclesiology of his later prison writings on the other hand, where we find the famous dictum: 'The church is church only when it is there for others.'[7] In the brief passage from the *Ethics* cited above, Bonhoeffer describes the social implications of the acknowledgment of guilt by the church. The church is *the* confessing community. Moreover, it is the group that is formed as a community by acknowledging and confessing guilt. It is not sin itself that is assumed by the church, but guilt. The church, in short, does not remedy or carry the reality of evil. This would surpass its ability as a community of human beings. Rather, the church's field of expertise concerns the actual consequences of sin. The church's business is the acknowledgement of sinful deeds; the church's special gift, so to speak, lies in discerning guilt while being aware of the fact that such discernment is made possible only by divine justification. In this act, the church begins to realize its nature as Christ's community. It does not take the place of Christ himself (contrary to what might be signalled in *Discipleship*). In the *Ethics*, the concept of acknowledging guilt seems rather retrospective, but Bonhoeffer already stresses that the confession of guilt paves the way towards renewal, towards 'personal and corporate rebirth'.[8] It is a very small step from there towards the active 'church for others' in the *Letters and Papers from Prison*.

The second issue is Bonhoeffer's hamartiological transformation of the notion 'Confessing Church'. The acknowledgment of guilt is only the first step; the second step is giving voice to this acknowledged guilt *coram Deo*. By articulating the consequences of sin before Christ, the church realizes its nature as Christ's community. That is its defining characteristic, the unique prerogative of the church among all institutions and communities. Bonhoeffer is careful to distinguish between the actions of the church and the actions of Christ in this respect as well as in the first respect. He writes: 'The church is today the community of people who, grasped by the power of Christ's grace, acknowledge, confess, and take upon themselves not only their personal sins, but also the Western world's falling away from Jesus Christ as guilt toward Christ.'[9]

Behind the English expression 'grasped by the power of Christ's grace' lies the German expression '*erfasst von der Gewalt der Gnade Christi*'. The crucial word here is '*Gewalt*'. 'Power' is an apt, but also cautious translation of this word. The German expression '*Gewalt*' refers to a more forceful and concrete form of action than the general term 'power' (which is more precisely equivalent to the German '*Macht*'). When Bonhoeffer writes that the church is being grasped by the '*Gewalt*' of Christ's grace, he hints at the possibility of resistance within the church. Does Christ need to take matters quite forcefully in his hands in order to establish a clear acknowledgment and confession of guilt in his church? In any case, by using the expression '*Gewalt*' in this context, Bonhoeffer gives a strong signal: there is an external player who initiates the confession of guilt within the church; the church needs Christ's intervention in order to become the confessing church, in order to 'realize' its own being. If we were to take this thought a step further, the '*Gewalt*' of Christ's own intervention would have to be interpreted by the cross, i.e. by a situation where force is used upon Christ, and where this force is transformed through its very application to Christ into a new and completely different kind of power.

In his approach to guilt as the 'act-quality' of sin, Bonhoeffer stresses its social reality. He speaks about the political and historical dimensions of guilt, and describes how guilt may accumulate, forming a specific guilt-laden 'heritage'.[10] However, this is not meant in the sense of an ontological 'original sin' (*peccatum originale*) that is passed down through the generations. In his historical assessment of guilt, Bonhoeffer continues to focus on the act-quality of sin. And this means not only that he does not need to wrestle with the old ontological baggage of the *peccatum originale*, but also that he is free to imagine the 'scarring over' of historical guilt. The concept of 'scarring over' is central for Bonhoeffer's interpretation of guilt *coram mundo*. It helps him avoid an abstract dialectical opposition between 'guilty reality' and 'reconciled reality', or between 'sinful reality' and 'the reality of acknowledged and forgiven guilt'. In this way it helps illustrate his claim that world-reality is identical with Christ-reality. Bonhoeffer is interested in a realistic interpretation of guilt as an experience of actual communities. In this regard, he observes that historical guilt may remain unforgiven even though over time its hurtfulness may lessen, and justice may grow from unjust ground. 'To be sure, the guilt is not justified, not removed, not forgiven' in this manner.[11] The reality of sin behind the concrete historical guilt is not removed, neither is it forgiven. Such forgiveness of sin and removal of guilt can only be accomplished *coram Deo*, by God's own reconciling work. But *coram mundo*, the act that caused the guilt may recede more and more into the past and its consequences grow more remote and less pressing.

So far, I have emphasized Bonhoeffer's interpretation of the act-quality of sin, that is, guilt. But Bonhoeffer always takes into account that the removal of guilt demands a thorough change in reality itself. That is, underneath the actual guilt, there lies a deeper stratum of 'sin', which retains a doubtful and blurry ontological status even as it asserts its effective presence in the concept of 'scarred over' guilt. For the wound that led to the scar cannot be completely undone by scarring, but remains inscribed into the reality of the body. A deeper healing process is needed if the deepest reality of guilt is to be transformed.

A short section in the *Ethics* hints at the underlying *ontological* problem. It is a somewhat irritating passage at the beginning of 'Ethics as Formation', one which has an almost Aristotelean flavour. Nevertheless, it proves Bonhoeffer's continuing awareness of the ontological complexities connected with the concept of sin. He writes: 'It is worse to be evil than to do evil. It is worse when a liar tells the truth than when a lover of truth lies, worse when a person who hates humanity practices neighborly love [*Bruderliebe*] than when a loving person once falls victim to hatred.'[12]

Here Bonhoeffer almost sounds like a proponent of virtue ethics! It certainly expresses a surprising thought within the context of Bonhoeffer's theological consequentialism. The passage hints at the ontological dimension of sin, an aspect that lies beneath actual sinful deeds, beneath guilt. Bonhoeffer does not intend to offer a systematic reflection on the ontology of sin with these short remarks; after all, he worked out just such a systematic ontology in his second book. Here Bonhoeffer merely wants to criticize deontological ethics as he views them suggesting that practitioners of that kind of ethics cannot recognize 'the evil in the form of light',[13] because they focus solely on the ethical *principles* of an action, and tune out the underlying 'reality' behind the action. In order to clarify the notion of sin's being, I turn to Bonhoeffer's treatment of this theme in *Act and Being*.

Being in Adam

'If sin were no more than a free act of the particular moment …, a retreat to sinless being would in principle be possible.'[14] But such an assumption of 'sinless being' *remoto Christo* cannot be tolerated within a Lutheran perspective! Bonhoeffer's *Habilitation* dissertation *Act and Being* is his ontological manifesto. Published in 1931, Bonhoeffer wrote this second book in the course of a single year between his pastoral appointment in Barcelona and his return to Berlin, completing it when he was twenty-four years of age and a newly ordained minister of the old Prussian Union of Churches. Though Bonhoeffer later distanced himself from his *Habilitation*, its thoughts and concepts remained influential for his thought all the way to the *Ethics*.

With regard to the present topic, namely the ontological status of sin, we need to discuss the concept of 'being in Adam' which is developed in that early work. The sentence just quoted is found in the section of that work which bears this subtitle. Here, Bonhoeffer approaches sin from the exact opposite direction than he does in his *Ethics*, concentrating upon the specifically ontological dimension of sin. Bonhoeffer criticizes traditional approaches to the being of sin that employ the notion of human nature as the seat of sin within the human. For the young philosophical theologian influenced by Heidegger and Barth, such theories of original sin confuse 'beings' (*'Seiendes'*) and 'being' (*'Sein'*). Such theories naturalize and historicize human being, that is, they 'freeze' the flow of being, which conceptually must always be connected to becoming. Instead of the general term 'nature', Bonhoeffer uses the term 'being in Adam', which aligns with his overall relational and soteriological framework. In contrast to the term 'nature', 'being in Adam' allows for integrating the specifically personal and social manner of human being;[15] in short, 'being in Adam' expresses Bonhoeffer's relational ontology. Bonhoeffer had already begun to use the concept of 'being in Adam' for this purpose in his dissertation *Santorum Communio*.

I contend that Bonhoeffer's idea of 'being in Adam' underlies his interpretation of sin in the *Ethics*. Some brief consideration of the concept as he develops it in *Act and Being* will help us interpret the corresponding hamartiological blank space in the later work. The *Ethics* is almost solely concerned with 'being in Christ', i.e. with Christ's conforming work on the world. Yet Bonhoeffer continues to be aware of the underlying anthropological problem posed by evil, as can be seen clearly in remarks like the one cited above. Sin belongs to the realm of personal being. The names of Christ and of Adam stand for the two opposite ways of personal being, of that being-in-relation in which a person finds himself or herself. These ways of being-in-relation precede and qualify all individual actions and interactions; they are not the product of individual actions. Rather, by 'being in Adam', Bonhoeffer means a general social reality that manifests itself individually. 'Adam' here stands for a fundamental way of living out one's personhood; this way of personhood becomes real only when 'lived out' actively, when it becomes guilt. In this manner, Bonhoeffer can say that 'I' am Adam, just as 'Adam' is humanity as such.[16] The name of Adam signifies the way of being human under the conditions of sin.

In *Act and Being*, Bonhoeffer further delineates 'being in Adam' by three terms: 'Everydayness' (*'Alltäglichkeit'*), 'Knowledge of Conscience' (*'Gewissen'*) and 'Temptation' (*'Anfechtung'*).[17] The clear centrepiece of this sinful triptych is *conscience*. Even for specialist readers it might be a helpful reminder that Bonhoeffer places conscience in a hamartiological context as early as *Act and Being*. His later thoughts on conscience in the *Ethics* build on this earlier material. In his *Habilitation*, the concept of conscience lies at the centre of 'being in Adam': it is the very expression of being in sin. And what Bonhoeffer says about conscience here is especially relevant for understandings the particular ontological status of sin in the *Ethics*, for Bonhoeffer further developed his theory of conscience in the latter work, even though he neglected to mention its ontological background in his earlier writing. Apart from explicit reference to Bonhoeffer's remarks on conscience in *Act and Being*, the ontological background of Bonhoeffer's late conception of conscience can scarcely be discerned. Bonhoeffer's interpretation of conscience in the *Ethics* actually further develops his thoughts on the 'reality' of sin, on its 'being-dimension' even as he also modifies his earlier thinking on this theme.

In his *Habilitation*, Bonhoeffer identifies conscience as *the* main characteristic of 'being in Adam' within the individual and he describes conscience in stark existentialist terms: a person in the grip of conscience experiences a chilling awareness of immortality and complete solitude.[18] This particular combination of immortality and solitude might sound slightly vampiric when heard within the context of today's popular culture. One wonders what Bonhoeffer would think of today's fascination with the figure of the vampire. From the point of view of *Act and Being*, the figure of the vampire certainly seems like a strong metaphor for 'being in Adam', with its thirst for life and inability to change, that is, its inability to really *live*. Be that as it may, immortality and solitude are the defining characteristics of Adam's conscience. In a sense, the term 'immortality' is misleading in this context. Bonhoeffer does not speak of true immortal life under the conditions of sin, but rather he points at the incapability of the sinner to imagine the world without himself or herself. Within the context of sin, immortality means an imagined endlessness of one's own existence, an inability to view the limits of one's existence. This feeling of immortality runs along the lines of Kierkegaardian despair. Conscience 'in Adam' signifies the human being's last stand in the face of insecurity and fear, in the face of one's own powerlessness. Later, in the *Ethics*, Bonhoeffer will express a certain respect for this 'last effort' of the 'I' in the face of the unknown external power, even if it is a worse than quixotic stance. In his *Habilitation*, however, Bonhoeffer stresses the sinful character of conscience: following one's own conscience here amounts to trying to define good and evil. Or in biblical terms, following one's own conscience is equivalent to attempting to be *sicut deus*, to assume as a human privilege something which belongs to God. This attitude may take the form of an everyday indifference towards revelation or the form of special obstinacy in individual situations.

By describing sin as 'being in Adam', Bonhoeffer interprets sin within his framework of relational ontology. He criticizes substantialist interpretations of sin, and counts Augustine's notion of original sin (*peccatum originale*) prominent among such interpretations. Within Bonhoeffer's position, the being of sin stands for a certain type of personal relationality, namely self-chosen solitude, or a pursuit of autonomy to the point of isolation. It does not refer to some portion of an essential human nature, or a fixed quality of such human nature. Rather, 'being in Adam' corresponds to a narrowing down of the horizon, until only the single moment of one's consciousness seems real. Fear and a general feeling of insufficiency accompany this way of living.

Five years after publishing *Act and Being* Bonhoeffer described the feverish year of his life during which he wrote his *Habilitation* in very self-critical terms. Did he unwittingly portray himself in Adam? His self-critical portrayal of his own state of mind during the work on his *Habilitation* almost seems to point that way:

> I threw myself into my work in an extremely unchristian and not at all humble fashion. A rather crazy element of ambition, which some people noticed in me, made my life difficult and withdrew from me the love and trust of those around me. At that time, I was terribly alone and left to myself. It was quite bad … . Despite this isolation, I was quite happy with myself.[19]

But then, as he noted in *Act and Being*, human beings for the most part remain psychologically opaque to themselves.[20]

Yet two questions remain open regarding Bonhoeffer's ontological interpretation of sin: first, his conception of 'being in Adam' does not integrate the *structural* aspect of sin, to use a term that is more familiar in liberation theology circles. And second, the correlation of sin and guilt remains very much in the background, although this might also be due to the non-ethical character of *Act and Being*. How serendipitous, then, that the *Ethics* should pick up exactly these two loose ends!

Sin in the *Ethics* (2): Adam in Christ?

Having clarified Bonhoeffer's ontological approach towards sin in his earlier second dissertation, we now return to the *Ethics* in order to address the two open questions: that is, the correlation of sin and guilt and the structural aspect of sin as 'being'. Bonhoeffer's further development of his theory of *conscience* helps tackle the correlation of sin and guilt. And his concept of *conformation* points towards the relational structures that may underlie 'sin in being'.

'Conscience is the call of human existence for unity with itself.'[21] Bonhoeffer's well-known definition of conscience in the *Ethics* may sound self-evident in its clarity and brevity, but it is the product of quite some preparation. This definition applies both to natural (sinful) conscience and to the reconciled conscience 'in Christ'. It testifies to the underlying relational structure of being human; said theologically, it expresses the creatureliness of Adam. Even in his wildest dreams of splendid isolation, Adam remains a creature, i.e. a deeply relational being; this is why it is against his very being to live in isolation, solely in relation to oneself. By defining conscience as the call of human existence into unity with itself, Bonhoeffer adapts his earlier notion of conscience from *Act and Being*. Now, in the *Ethics*, he proposes this definition as the common ground for two different forms of conscience: natural conscience and conscience in Christ. In the earlier work he focused almost entirely on *natural* conscience and did not pause to ask what became of conscience in the reality of revelation. Neither did he pause to consider how exactly conscience relates to moral action: does conscience become active only retrospectively or may it propose a course of action in an ambiguous situation? With this fully developed concept of conscience in the *Ethics*, however, he offers answers on both accounts.

In natural conscience, a human person calls himself or herself into existence, so to speak. Natural conscience focuses on the authenticity and inner coherence of 'my' deeds with my convictions. Thus, natural conscience is a self-affirming authority, however critical it may seem at first glance. If 'I' argue with myself about values, it is obvious who will win this argument. Conscience in Christ, on the other hand, leads into freedom and responsibility, Bonhoeffer's key words for identifying and characterizing reconciled human relationality. In this liberated conscience, the 'call to unity with oneself' is no longer self-serving but is received from the outside, from Christ.[22] By stressing that liberated conscience implies receiving the call to unity with oneself from the outside (*extra nos*), Bonhoeffer re-interprets the Lutheran separation between doer and deed, between sinner and sin. Reconciliation means that the determining power of 'being in Adam' is broken, and a new manner of relationality is established. Bonhoeffer explains that 'responsibility is bound by conscience, but conscience is set free by responsibility. It has now become evident that these two statements are saying the same thing: those who act responsibly become guilty without sin; and only those whose conscience is free [in Christ] can bear responsibility.'[23]

From a hamartiological perspective, the idea of becoming guilty without sin represents a most remarkable development. Reconciliation in Christ liberates from the very reality of sin, or rather, Christ's work of reconciliation overcomes all claims of sin to be real, to have its own power of being. Becoming guilty without sin seems a strange concept, especially within the context of theological ethics. But Bonhoeffer had already prepared the way for this concept in the text about 'Guilt, Justification, Renewal' discussed above. For the central way of becoming guilty without sin seems to be the acknowledgment and confession of guilt, be it one's own guilt, the guilt within society or the guilt of the world. Thus Bonhoeffer gives a clear interpretation of the relation between sin and guilt: he acknowledges the 'reality' of sin behind individual acts, but at the same time, he emphasizes that within the reality of reconciliation sin retains only a very tenuous hold on being.

By referring to Bonhoeffer's concept of conscience in the *Ethics*, I have interpreted the correlation of sin and guilt within Christ-reality. Now I want to investigate the relational *structures* that may underlie 'sin in being' by turning to Bonhoeffer's concept of conformation.

Without a doubt, the concept of Christ-reality is Bonhoeffer's fundamental ontological model within the *Ethics*. With the notion of *Christuswirklichkeit* he develops his earlier thoughts about revelation and reality further, putting an ever stronger Christological spin on his approach. While 'revelation reality' in *Act and Being* is mostly characterized by the Word of God, in the *Ethics* it becomes a thoroughly Christological concept. Bonhoeffer's relational ontology, with his re-interpretation of being human in terms of personal relationships, comes to its conclusion and summit at this point. The concept of *conformation* is the heart of his mature ethical ontology. However, Bonhoeffer does not really expand on the hamartiological connotations of Christ-reality, other than to emphasize that all of reality, without exception, is under the rule of Christ. In the final stages of this chapter, we will reflect further on the hamartiological implications of Christ-reality by investigating Bonhoeffer's model of conformation to Christ.

In 'Ethics as Formation', Bonhoeffer describes the inner structure of Christ-reality in terms of Christ's conforming work.[24] The three forms of Christ represent the structure of reconciled relationality; they are Christ incarnate, Christ crucified, and Christ resurrected. By conforming reality to these forms of himself, Christ counteracts the reality of Adam with its corruption of genuine creaturely relationality. Christ thereby establishes a new way of being-in-relation. The liberated conscience is one central expression of this all-encompassing work of conformation, i.e. it concerns the re-orientation of individual human action. But the reality of justification runs deeper. It touches upon the basic structure of reality, as it takes away the very necessity of scarring over. Yet the very concept of conformation also implies judgement and rejection, for whatever does not conform does not belong to Christ-reality.

The form of Christ incarnate, of 'God become human',[25] reveals God's love of human beings as they are, even as it also reveals God's rejection of contempt for or idolization of humanity.[26] The form of Christ crucified reveals God's love for the human being as a being that falls under God's judgement, that has become guilty before God. The form of the crucified Christ refers to the judgement of grace, the separation between sinner and deed; it refers to the destruction of sin's power over human life.[27] It reveals God's rejection of both contempt for and idolization of success.[28] Bonhoeffer emphasizes that judging humanity is the sole privilege of God; ascribing success or failure to the lives of others implies the usurpation of this privilege on the part of the human being. Being conformed to the form of the crucified Christ leads to the acknowlededgment and confession of guilt. Last, the form of the resurrected Christ reveals the new human being, the establishment of a new way of relating to each other.[29] With the resurrection of Christ, God rejects the contempt and idolization of death.[30]

With these two key words – *contempt* and *idolization* – Bonhoeffer hints at relational structures that are opposed to Christ's conforming work. Opposition to Christ's conforming work in the form of contempt and idolization sums up the structure of sinful relationality still active in Christ-reality. In this way, Bonhoeffer further develops the position of *Act and Being*, where he described 'being in Adam' generally as attempting to live in splendid isolation, independent of others, governed solely by one's own autonomy. In the *Ethics*, Bonhoeffer hints at a more nuanced understanding of sin's structures in terms of its relational reality. The development within his concept of relationality mirrors the development within his concept of conscience: Bonhoeffer moves away from his former dialectical opposition between Adam and Christ because he radicalizes his understanding of Christ's vicarious representative work (*Stellvertretung*). Bonhoeffer stresses Christ's universal claim and irresistible power over all reality ever more strongly. But this does not follow from a turn towards a *theologia gloriae*, but rather from a growing emphasis upon the cross. For the cross is where Adam and Christ become one. The cross is Adam's place in Christ-reality, because it is the place of judgement and renewal, of justification. The cross is Christ's place in Christ-reality, because it is the place where Christ identifies himself with Adam, conforms himself to Adam, and thereby transforms Adam's reality and brings about the reality of reconciliation.

Notes

1   *DBWE* 6, 67.
2   Ibid., 80.
3   Ibid., 81.
4   Ibid., 76.
5   Ibid., 67.
6   Ibid., 135.
7   'Outline for a Book.' *DBWE* 8, 503.
8   *DBWE* 6, 135.
9   Ibid., 135.
10 Ibid., 143.
11 Ibid.

12 Ibid., 77.

13 Ibid.

14 *DBWE* 2, 145.

15 Bonhoeffer, *Act und Sein: Transzendentalphilosophie und Ontologie in der Systematischen Theologie. Dietrich Bonhoeffer Werke 2*, ed. Hans-Richard Reuter. (München: Chr. Kaiser Verlag, 1988), 144: 'Adam als Ich und als Menschheitsperson-Sein.'

16 Ibid., 145.

17 Ibid., 146; *DBWE* 2, 147.

18 Bonhoeffer, *Act und Sein*, 147. The German: 'Der Mensch weiß sich unsterblich und bleibt allein.'

19 'Letter to Elisabeth Zinn, January 27, 1936.' *DBWE* 14, 134.

20 Bonhoeffer, *Act und Sein*, 141. The German: 'Wir bleiben uns psychologisch undurchsichtig.'

21 *DBWE* 6, 276.

22 Yet 'the conscience freed in Jesus Christ still essentially remains the call to unity with myself.' Ibid., 281. From the perspective of contemporary theology, Bonhoeffer's nonchalance in speaking about the 'call of Christ' is remarkable, even provocative.

23 Ibid., 282.

24 Ibid., 76–102.

25 Ibid., 84.

26 Ibid., 85.

27 Ibid., 88.

28 Ibid., 89.

29 Ibid., 91.

30 Ibid., 91–2.

Chapter 5

BEARING SIN IN THE CHURCH:
THE ECCLESIAL HAMARTIOLOGY OF BONHOEFFER
Tom Greggs

Systematic theology is a theological discipline which involves not only the rational explication of the Christian gospel through description, reflection and critique of the church's teaching, but also the selective placement, arrangement and locating of doctrinal loci within the theological description offered. The arrangement of doctrines in the description is significant in the enterprise not only in terms of the presentational form of the doctrine offered, but also in terms of the material dogmatic content. Within systematic theology it is possible always to have ultimate and immediate foundational *res* for different loci. Beginning with, let us say, the inner life of God as a foundation will determine that all other loci exist underneath or stem from this doctrine: one could imagine a doctrine of God's immanent life leading to an account of God's economy and from there to an account of creation, Christology, reconciliation and so forth – each locus stemming from a previous intermediate *res* or directly from the ultimate foundational *res*.[1] Key here is this ordering and differentiation – the point that there are immediate foundational *res* and there is an ultimate foundational *res*. Here, in this example, the ultimate foundational *res* is the inner divine life, and we might consider that the other dogmatic loci have their foundation in this doctrine; but other doctrines which have their foundation in the ultimate foundational *res* might also become immediate foundational *res* for successive dogmatic loci. For example, the inner divine life is the ultimate foundational *res* for the external works of God, of which we might list creation, but creation itself might become the immediate foundational *res* for, let us say, theological anthropology, which in turn might become the immediate foundational *res* for accounts of sin, and so forth: all of these doctrines have their ultimate foundational *res* in this scheme in the account of the inner life of God, but each may also have successive immediate foundational *res* in other dependent loci.[2] The derivative doctrines will take a particular form materially by virtue of the structural dogmatic foundation on which they rest: having a particular dogmatic foundation will give a particular shape to the doctrine which exists underneath it. For example, a theological anthropology which has Christology as its immediate foundational *res* will have a distinctive account of what it means to be human in comparison to an account of theological anthropology which has its immediate foundational *res* in the doctrine of creation. Similarly, an account of the person and work of Jesus Christ as a human will take a particular form and shape dependent on whether its immediate foundational *res* is theological anthropology, or the external operations of the divine life, or the doctrine of reconciliation and so forth; or dependent on whether it is itself the ultimate foundational *res* for the given system. All of this is to say that dogmatic topography matters: where a particular doctrine becomes the focus or foundation of theological thinking, it may well become a foundational *res* for other areas of dogmatic enquiry. By doing so, it will invariably shape the material form of the locus which has its foundational *res* in the more primordial doctrine. This account of the systematic task in theology clearly concerns primarily the order of derivation rather than the order of presentation, though we might think that in a mature account of theology these two become one or can be seen as one (even if certain material derivations of doctrines receive only more explicit presentational statements in later work).

What has this abstracted engagement with the scientific task of theology to do with Dietrich Bonhoeffer? Within Dietrich Bonhoeffer's account of the Christian gospel and the Christian life, one might identify the ultimate foundational *res* of his theology as ecclesiology;[3] this may be a contentious claim, but I think it can be made. While Bonhoeffer's theology does not form a regular dogmatics offering a systematic account of the whole breadth and schema of Christian doctrine, as an irregular dogmatics it nevertheless follows from a foundational basis,[4] or else is at least a theology which is centred upon the theological account of the church. From a first doctoral dissertation on the theological study of the sociology of the church to final searching questions on the meaning of the church in a post-Christian era, Bonhoeffer's theology is resolutely and continuously ecclesiologically orientated, or better still ecclesiologically founded. Such an orientation and foundation determines that the loci which flow from and derive from Bonhoeffer's account of the church will take a particular form and have particular dogmatic content by virtue of the ecclesiological centredness of the theological account offered. This shapes in interesting ways the doctrines which have their immediate derivative *res* in this ecclesiological account. This has material as well as presentational effects (effects on content as well as form), and determines that creative and new ways of thinking about derivative loci occur: thinking loci from the doctrine of the church has a material effect on dependent loci which are formed in different ways because of the dogmatic ultimate *res* and the subsequent intermediate immediate *res*.

In this chapter, I wish to examine the effect of this ultimate foundational *res* of ecclesiology on one (under studied) area of Bonhoeffer's thought in which he offers distinctive and creative accounts of Christian doctrine – his hamartiology. Given Bonhoeffer's ecclesio-centrism, the account offered of the doctrine of sin has a significantly corporate dimension, compared to accounts of sin which find their *res* (immediately or ultimately) in the doctrine of creation or human freedom, and so forth. Exploring this ecclesial effect on the materially derived doctrine of sin, the first section of this chapter will consider the individual and corporate nature of sin for Bonhoeffer, and his account of the way in which these inter-relate. The nature of the fall as being separated from the community and choosing the life of an individual will be explored in the second section of this chapter; here, I consider what it means to speak of sin as 'horizontal' as well as 'vertical'. The third section seeks to understand the act of God, for Bonhoeffer, in putting right this horizontal disorder both internal to the church and in relation to the church's role in the world. A brief conclusion will seek to discuss what contemporary theology might take from Bonhoeffer on this topic and how the theme might further be explored.

The individual and corporate nature of sin

Bonhoeffer's account of original sin is one which recognizes both the individual and the corporate nature of sin. Rather than focusing primarily on the nature of the original sin and its effects, Bonhoeffer recognizes the relationship between the culpability of the individual and the culpability of the entire race. In the classical Augustinian account, through Adam's turning away from God in the fall, the soul of the human is made chaotic and subject to perturbation. It is, for Augustine, the pride of the first human which is wholly the basis for his fall.[5] It is the character of the first sin which is the reason for its heinousness: it is worse than any other sin because Adam was nobler than any other subsequent (fallen) human. Indeed, such was the gravity of the first sin that it resulted in the ruin of the entire race (the *massa damnata*): sinful itself, the first sin propagates sinners. Through this first sin, humans have no freedom over their sinfulness. Augustine uses the analogy of the inherited disease to illustrate this: the disease has weakened humanity and cannot be cured by human agency. In Adam's fall, humans lost the power to do good because a permanent twist had occurred; and Adam lost the freedom of choice for the good because he could choose only one thing (for ill) and this had a universal effect which required God to put it right. Sinning, in a sense, becomes a natural thing for humankind, as Augustine sees in Adam a sin which flaws the very nature of the human; humans can no longer turn God-wards unaided by God and require God to enable them to do good, as a permanent change in human nature has occurred through corruption in sin. Thus, in Augustine it is possible to see a system of *inherited* sin as a result of Adam's fall.

For Bonhoeffer, the incapacity of humans to escape sinfulness (the universal quality of sin) is affirmed in classical Augustinian manner (as one would expect from a Lutheran).[6] But Bonhoeffer draws out or focuses particularly on individual humans' *co-operation* with and *participation* in the first sin (rather than primarily the inheritance of its effects): original sin is, for Bonhoeffer, corporate and something for which we are co-responsible. He writes:

> The culpability of the individual and the universality of sin should be under-
> stood together; that is the individual culpable act and the culpability of the

human race must be connected conceptually ... . Everything obviously depends upon *finding the act of the whole in the sinful act*, without making the one the reason for the other.[7]

For Bonhoeffer the individual human participates fully in the act of Adam. This is a drawing out of a particular emphasis of Augustine's account of original sin, which points to the co-responsibility of every human being for human fallenness: we too are culpable in the sharing of our wills in Adam's willing. Augustine writes: 'all sinned in Adam on that occasion, for all were already identical with him in that nature of his which was endowed with the capacity to generate them.'[8] Although Augustine has a system of inherited sin passing like a disease from Adam through to all his descendants in humanity,[9] Augustine nevertheless also points to the reality that all human beings are identical with Adam,[10] though he leaves space for this to be further developed or explored. Bonhoeffer expands on and develops this tradition away from straightforward notions of inheritance. He writes:

> In *my* fall from God, humanity fell ... . [B]efore the cross, the debt of the I grows to monstrous size; it is itself Adam, itself the first to have done, and to do again and again, that incomprehensible deed – sin as act.[11]

One's own individual sin is the first sin, is original sin, for Bonhoeffer. The reason for this is that for Bonhoeffer each individual is connected to humanity as a whole.[12] There is not simply inheritance on display in this concept; instead, there is a *reciprocity* here. He continues:

> in this act, for which I hold myself utterly responsible on every occasion, I find myself already in the humanity of Adam. I see humanity in me necessarily committing this, my own free deed. As human being, the I is banished into this old humanity, which fell on my account. The I 'is' not as an individual, but always in humanity. And just because the deed of the individual is at the same time that of humanity, human beings must hold themselves individually responsible for the whole guilt of humankind ... . I myself am Adam – am I and humanity in one. In me humanity falls. As I am Adam, so is every individual; but in all individuals the one person of humanity, Adam, is active.[13]

Bonhoeffer's account of original sin is a *corporate* account in Adam – an account of human co-responsibility which develops the Augustinian account and moves away from notions of sin as inherited towards the participation in and culpability of all individual humans in the first sin, and the first sin's presence in and responsibility for any individual sin. The hamartiology here is concerned with the corporate and the individual in relation to the corporate: there is no capacity to separate Adam from other individuals or other individuals from Adam; the human being is understood in her fallenness in Adam as identical with Adam and fully responsible not only for her own sin but for the sin of all human beings. This corporate effect is a result of the immediate theological *res* of Bonhoeffer's account of the doctrine of sin finding its locus within an account of the church. The topography of the doctrine shapes its form, and determines its content.

Let me explain what I mean. The metaphysical underpinning for this manoeuver lies in Bonhoeffer's theological ontology of 'being in'. For Bonhoeffer, the essence of humanity is found not in an independent metaphysics of humanity, but in a genuine *theological* account of human ontology.[14] For him:

> There is no ontological specification of that which is created that is independent of God being reconciler and redeemer, and human beings being sinners and forgiven. In the Christian doctrine of being, all metaphysical ideas of eternity and time, being and becoming, living and dying, essence and appearance must be measured against the concepts of the being of sin and the being of grace or else must be developed anew in light of them.[15]

The prior knowledge that there is no humanity independent of being in Adam or being in Christ establishes the theological anthropological ontology necessary for the individual and corporate understandings of sin that Bonhoeffer gives. For Bonhoeffer, this point about ontology is a fundamental distinctive of Protestant theology compared to Roman Catholic theology. Any account of metaphysics based upon an account of being in creation, rather than being in Adam and sin, leads, according to Bonhoeffer, directly to the *analogia entis* and a pure metaphysics of 'being'. Instead, for Bonhoeffer, the human is either in Adam (in sin) or in Christ (in the church): 'The human being only "is" in Adam or in Christ, in unfaith or in faith, in Adamic humanity and in Christ's community'.[16] There is no humanity apart from these two communities – the community of Adam (of sin), and the community of Christ (which is concretely the church).[17] Clearly, the church continues to sin and fall (and exists within the *communio peccatorum*),[18] but humans do not exist independent from the community of which they are a part; and the ontology of both individual humans and all humanity must be thought of in relation to the *community* of Adam or of Christ. Adam and Christ are both in one sense corporate persons [*Gesamtperson*].[19] Again, this account flows from the ecclesial (community) *res* of the account of humanity and sin offered.

There is, furthermore, an epistemic consequence of this claimed ontology: the order of being (as being in) affects the order of knowing, as this knowledge of human ontology as 'being in' is known only in the context of being in Christ, that is being in the 'corporate person of the Christian community of faith'.[20] It is only within the corporate context of the church that humanity can know itself as sinful and the individual know herself as a sinner. Since for Bonhoeffer, there is no independent metaphysics beyond the ontology of 'being in', and that reality is one that is only known theologically, true knowledge of who one is is only possible in relation to one's being in the life of the church. There is no knowledge of who one is outside of Christ, and outside of the church there is no knowledge of Christ:

> For only through the person of Christ can the existence of human beings be encountered, placed into truth, and transposed into a new manner of existence. But as the person of Christ has been revealed in the community of faith, the existence of human beings can be encountered only through the community of faith.[21]

Or, as Luther puts it: '*sola fide credendum est nos esse peccatores*'.[22] The possibility of knowing one's own sin outside of the community of faith is itself (we might say) semi-Pelagian: it would mean that outside of the Gospel and faith one could know the truth of oneself by oneself. This consequence is not simply intellectual: the epistemic component of sin is as a result of the ontology of 'being in Adam'. For humans in Adam, knowledge begins and ends in themselves: pulling themselves away from God and the community of faith, they stand alone. That standing alone is in itself an untruth about human existence: it is a making of oneself lord and creator, a standing alone in a false belief in one's own individual identity.[23] Standing alone is the desire to be creator and creature all at once: 'Only in Christ,' writes Bonhoeffer, 'do human beings know themselves as God's creatures; in Adam they were creator and creature all at once.'[24] This theme is developed in *Discipleship* where Bonhoeffer is able to state arrestingly:

Only those who are bound to Jesus in discipleship stand in complete truth-fulness. They have nothing to conceal from their Lord. They live unveiled before him. Jesus knows them and places them into the truth. They are revealed as sinners before Jesus. They did not reveal themselves to Jesus, but as soon as Jesus revealed himself to them in his call, they knew themselves revealed in their sinfulness. Complete truthfulness emerges only from sin that is unveiled and forgiven by Jesus.[25]

Yet, this relationship to Jesus is not possible without living in community with other people: the two cannot be prized apart. It is an untruth that one tells to oneself outside of Christ not to recognize and confess oneself a sinner. This untruth is itself an aspect of the heart turned towards itself, and only turned outside of itself (in salvation, we may say) can it live in the community of Christ with other people: 'There is no truth toward Jesus without truth toward other people.'[26] In denying one's sinfulness and standing outside of community with Christ (known only in the community of the church), the human does not know herself and corrupts her own being from one of relationality towards others to one of self-preservation over and against others. This standing alone aside from the community is in itself a horizontal component (and not merely consequence) of the fall. It is to this we now turn.

Horizontal sin: The individual separated from the community

For Bonhoeffer, the sinful act is not simply a disruption of the divine-human relationship, but a fundamental altering of the human in Adam such that the person ceases to be a person in relation and instead believes that personhood is an individual standing alone. Thus, the vertical fallenness (humanity in relation to God) and the horizontal fallenness (humans in relation to one another) are two sides of the same coin: in the fall humans cease to be persons in relation and become those whose hearts are turned in on themselves. Bonhoeffer is able to write, therefore,

Community with God by definition establishes social community as well. It is not that community with God subsequently leads to social community; rather, neither exists without the other ... . With their act of disobedience against God ... [a] rupture has come into the unbroken community. Losing direct community with God, they also lose – by definition – unmediated human community. A third power, sin, has stepped between human beings and God, as between human beings themselves.[27]

Given Bonhoeffer's ecclesially orientated theological foundation as the ultimate *res* of his theological thought, the connection between divine-human and human-human relationality cannot be prized apart, as both belong within an account of theology which stems from an account of the life of the church. Sin is not about a single individual's relationship with God which has consequences for her relationship with other humans: sin is about the alteration of human beings such that we cease to be orientated eccentrically and relationally and become orientated interiorly and individually.

For Bonhoeffer, the *cor curvum in se* determines that humans are pulled away from community – both from God and other humans – and 'stand alone' in solitude.[28] Humans have rent themselves away from God and each other, and continue to seek to defend themselves and decide for themselves. This is a theme which Bonhoeffer develops in *Creation and Fall*. In seeking to remove his limits by disobeying God and seeking to be like God, Adam finds himself alone in his desire to be his own god, his own creator; in this Adam seeks to lose his creaturely identity.[29] But this rejection of creatureliness is not only a rejection of God, but also a rejection of the relationality which comes from God: it is a binding of oneself to oneself and one's own limits, having rejected the limits placed upon one by God; it is a stepping out of relationship and a stepping into individualism. The fall, therefore, is horizontal as much as it is vertical since Adam and Eve exist not only in relation to God, but in relation to one another. Having been created from the rib of Adam,[30] the violation that takes place towards God at the tree and the subsequent discussion of blame is at the same time a violation of the other person.[31] What was a gift of God in the alterity and unity of the other becomes a perceived curse of God in division and seeking to place responsibility for the fall at the feet of the other. As the human is turned in on herself, the other exists not as gift but as a burdensome limit. Bonhoeffer writes:

> [Adam] no longer sees the limit that the other person constitutes as grace but as God's wrath, God's hatred, God's begrudging. This means that the human being no longer regards the other person with love. Instead one person sees the other in terms of their being over against each other; each sees the other

as divided from himself or herself. The limit is no longer grace that holds the human being in the unity of creaturely, free love; instead the limit is now the mark of dividedness.[32]

This dividedness is symbolized in the act of the human in covering herself up: in the perceived shame of nakedness, the human recognizes her limited nature over and against the other.[33] The heart turned in on itself is not only a standing apart as an individual in relation to God; it is also a standing alone in relation to other humans beings. This is an idea which Bonhoeffer rehearses in *Sanctorum Communio*: 'With their act of disobedience against God, human beings realize their sexual difference and are ashamed before one another. A rupture has come into the unbroken community,'[34] writes Bonhoeffer. It is by losing their direct relationship with God that they lose their direct relationship with each other and the community is broken.

If sin is a life turned in on itself, then sin arises from altered human relationality, a relationality which now fails not only to be orientated towards God but also towards one another. We see this in Bonhoeffer's unpacking of the effect of the fall. Humans find themselves in solitude, and in this solitude, they cling to themselves and their own self-knowledge. This self-knowledge is untruthful and self-justifying or despairing in its form; Bonhoeffer names this 'conscience'.[35] This post-lapsarian situation is a desperate one in which in their solitude humans find themselves hopeless in light of their limits and guilty in light of their conscience.[36] The turning in on the self produces an existence in which one cannot know one's reality in light of God and of others and in which we hide in our solitude from one another.

The intermediate dogmatic *res* for Bonhoeffer between his ecclesial-centric doctrinal foundations and his hamartiology is his concept of the person.[37] Altered personhood determines that humans no longer share in the divine form of personhood as that which exists in relation. Bonhoeffer is clear that 'community with God by definition establishes social community as well'.[38] It is clear in his thought that the '*concepts of person, community, and God* are inseparably and essentially interrelated'.[39] For him, it is not that one is the subsequent creation of the other (presumably, we would wish to add doctrinally, within the created order). He asserts: 'It is not that community with God *subsequently* leads to social community; rather, neither exists without the other'.[40] The basis for this claim is the personhood and relationality of

God. For Bonhoeffer, 'God only "is" as the creator, reconciler, and redeemer, and that being as such is personal being'.[41] There is no independent divine metaphysics for Bonhoeffer without the relationship of God to humanity: or else, we might say, there is (at least for humanity) no immanent trinity independent of God's divine economy.[42] As Bonhoeffer famously states in the second doctoral dissertation: 'There is no God who "is there" [*Einen Gott, den "es gibt", gibt es nicht*]; God "is" in the relation of persons, and the being of God is God's being person [*das Sein ist sein Personsein*].'[43] This is something which accompanies Bonhoeffer throughout his theological career,[44] and to which he points later in his life in his suggestive *Letters and Papers from Prison* in his questioning and critique of metaphysical approaches to speaking of God.[45] For Bonhoeffer, personhood and sociality are concepts which are bound together. Human personhood arises from the gracious external operations of divine personhood; and each is known only in relationship to the other. Since the only God there is is the God who is for creation, and who is known only in relation to creation, it is necessary to think of creation only in relation to the creator, reconciler and redeemer God.

To unpack what this means, it is useful to turn to Bonhoeffer's account of the likeness of God in humanity in relation to his account of the *analogia relationis*.[46] Bonhoeffer yet again firmly rejects the *analogia entis*, and affirms that the image of God in humanity is one based on an analogy of relationship. Although Bonhoeffer affirms divine aseity in the order of being (and by virtue of this differentiates God's being from human being), Bonhoeffer nevertheless points to God's relationship which he freely establishes with that which is not God in creation. Divine aseity protects the graciousness of God's relationality, but there can be no concept of God independent of God's free self-offering to humanity. Bonhoeffer writes:

> God – who alone has self-sufficient being in aseity, yet at the same time is there for God's creature, binding God's freedom to humankind and so giving God's self to humankind – must be thought of as one who is not alone, inasmuch as God is the one who in Christ attests to God's 'being for humankind'. The likeness, the analogia, of humankind to God is not analogia entis but *analogia relationis*. What this means, however, is, firstly, that the relatio too is not a human potential or possibility or structure of human existence; instead it is a given relation, a relation in which human beings are set, a justiti passiva![47]

For Bonhoeffer, moreover, this likeness is not something which humans have in possession in and of themselves, but which they have only strictly in likeness from the prototype and which always points back to the prototype: 'Analogia relationis is therefore the relation which God has established, and it is analogia only in this relation which God has established. The relation of creature with creature is a relation established by God.'[48] This establishment finds its analogy in God's own freedom to be for another in creation based in the form of personhood the divine life has: a form of personhood which lives in relationality not only internally in the eternal trinity but also externally in the economy of grace – in creation, reconciliation and redemption. What we can see here is that the intermediate *res* of Bonhoeffer's doctrine of sin, based upon the foundational *res* of ecclesiology, is an account of divine personhood in external relationality. This forms itself as an immediate foundational *res* of Bonhoeffer's theological anthropology through the *analogia relationis* in his description of the divine likeness in humanity. The fall, therefore, relates to human relationality which is both vertical (centred upon God) and horizontal (centred upon other humans): one is not a consequence of the other, but both are a consequence of the altered fallen human ontology of being 'in Adam'. Being in Adam, and seeking to be one's own creator and god, the human is tempted to a life *in se* – a sinful replication of the divine aseity which fails to understand that the freedom of the divine life *a se* is not something which God has grasped and claimed for Godself, but something which only establishes the full graciousness of the God who, although He is free from creation, chooses in creation to be free for creation in the divine economy of salvation. It is only in re-learning what it means to be a creature in light of Christ that the human can once again become human in the community of Christ, and be saved from the individualistic solitude that seeking to be *sicut deus* produces in its perverted attempt at the false replication of divine aseity. As Bonhoeffer puts it: 'To be in the center and to be alone means to be sicut deus. Humankind is now sicut deus. It now lives out of its own resources, creates its own life, is its own creator; it no longer needs the Creator.'[49] It is only an act of God which can rescue humanity from this desire to be as it considers wrongly and falsely God to be.

Horizontal salvation: Turning out towards the other

Existence in Christ is the only way in which the human is able to know herself as creature, and the only way in which she can be saved from the desire to be her own creator and a creature all at once. Existence in Christ is a salvific act of God's economy as the human moves from being 'in Adam' to, in the life of the church, being 'in Christ': 'the person *in se conversus* is delivered from the attempt to remain alone – to understand itself out of itself – and is turned outwards towards Christ.'[50] This turning out towards Christ involves gaining a new humanity found in Christ as the one 'for others'. Humanity being 'in Christ' regains its original created human form, regains the likeness of God in the *analogia relationis*, through the work of Christ. For Bonhoeffer, the being and work of Christ is such that in Christ's human form, humanity finds its restored and renewed human form. Reversing the classical account of divine salvation which acclaims that God became human in order that humans might become like God,[51] for Bonhoeffer Christ takes human form in order that humans can become like Jesus in His humanity: God became human, we might say, so that humans might become genuine human creatures. For Bonhoeffer, salvation is by *anthroposis* not *theosis*. Bonhoeffer writes: 'In Christ's incarnation all of humanity regains the dignity of bearing the image of God … . In community with the incarnate one, we are once again given our true humanity.'[52] Through community with the incarnate one, humanity is saved from the individualized isolation of its uncreaturely inhumanity. This *anthroposis*, therefore, is one which allows the fulfilment of the *analogia reationalis* in mirroring the personhood of God as a personhood which exists in relationship and sociality – not in isolation, even though God's divine aseity determines that God is the only One who can live in and of Godself. Bonhoeffer continues in relation to human solitude: 'With [our true humanity given by Christ], we are delivered from the isolation caused by sin, and at the same time restored to the whole of humanity.'[53] Salvation is, for Bonhoeffer, in part a sharing in the corporate life of the whole of humanity. For him, '[t]he destruction of humanness is sin.'[54] In the reception of salvation, the Christian takes on the form of Christ, and the form of Christ takes form in human beings.[55] Christians live in the world like anyone else, and differ seemingly only little from those others who are 'in Adam'. The difference is that they are not individualized and isolated from others, concerned to promote themselves and their own individual ego; instead, writes Bonhoeffer, they are 'not concerned to promote themselves, but to lift up Christ for the sake of their brothers and sisters'.[56] Their life is not ordered to themselves but is ordered to Christ and through Him to others. As Bonhoeffer writes in *Act and Being*:

> Only through the person of Christ can the existence of human beings be encountered, placed into truth, and transposed into a new manner of existence. But as the person of Christ has been revealed in the community of faith, the existence of other human beings can be encountered only through the community of faith. It is from the person of Christ that every other person first acquires for other human beings the character of personhood.[57]

Christ, known in the community of faith, enables humans to be open in relationality to the personhood of other humans, and by this creates a new existence for the believer who now has an ontology 'in Christ'.[58]

This life in Christ is experienced and known concretely in the church, and it is in the church that the forgiveness of God is found. The mechanism for forgiveness is confession, but even confession, for Bonhoeffer, has an immediate *res* in ecclesiology. Confession is not an individual's engagement with God apart from the community, since sin is itself corporate. Confession involves the community, and is a break-through of community. As Bonhoeffer writes in *Life Together*:

> In confession there takes place a *breakthrough to community*. Sin wants to be alone with people. It takes them away from the community. The more lonely people become, the more destructive the power of sin over them.[59]

Sin in its individualism wants to hide, to be alone to be in darkness. It, therefore, needs to be exposed and to have light shone on it. This exposure is by necessity ecclesial: it involves there being others in front of whom this exposure can take place, individuals who can be present as a gift to overcome the solitude and hiddenness of sin. In public confessing, sin is taken away from the individual and is exposed to the community; as such its individual-izing power, which tears the individual away from community, is undermined. In Bonhoeffer's words:

> Sin that has been spoken and confessed has lost all of its power ... . It can no longer tear apart the community. Now the community bears the sin of the

individual believer, who is no longer alone with this evil but has 'cast off' this sin by confessing it and handing it over to God. The sinner has been relieved of sin's burden. Now the sinner stands in the community of sinners who live by the grace of God in the cross of Jesus Christ. Now one is allowed to be a sinner and still enjoy the grace of God. We can admit our sins and in this very act find community for the first time. The hidden sins separated the sinner from the community and made the sinner's apparent community all a sham. The sins that were acknowledged helped the sinner to find true community with other believers in Jesus Christ.[60]

To confess sin means that the individual joins a community of confession, in which individuals confess sins *to one another*. It is in this community that one finds forgiveness because by acknowledging and confessing our sin before one another, the human is enabled to participate in a community and by that is freed from her individualized solitude in which by her conscience she attempts to adjudicate her sinful standing herself and yet in that finds her guilt. In the act of confessing publically, Christians are joined in solidarity to one another in the church.

There is a subjective and objective component to this act of confession and the forgiveness which flows from it. First, subjectively, so long as Christians confess their sins to each other, there is no way in which the Christian can feel alone anywhere.[61] Bonhoeffer unpacks this idea from *Life Together* in his Finkenwalde material, which formed the basis of his later book. In this, confession before others means that for us subjectively God is not a phantom who makes us *feel* as though we are forgiving our own sins by ourselves. Public confession means that our sins are brought into the open and that the pride which is the root of sin is in public confession before others uncovered such that we are made to feel small. From this smallness we are enabled to surrender entirely to the mercy of God, and in this surrender and joint confession, there emerges the creation of fellowship. For Bonhoeffer, we are not alone in our confession.[62] It is not that the church *qua* church releases people from their personal confession of guilt: the church does not give absolution; only Christ judges and restores humanity. But in confessing guilt together, the church draws people into a community of confession.[63] This, in itself, overcomes the fall – taking away the human's covering over of sin, sense of blame, individual conscience and solitude.

Second, objectively, forgiveness is not only given existentially to the believer through the words 'I am forgiven', but also objectively in the life of the community. The believer may know forgiveness only in the life of the community through the practices of the community in word and sacrament:

> The community of faith really does have the word of forgiveness at its disposal. In the community faith the words 'I am forgiven' can be spoken not merely existentially; as the Christian church, the congregation may declare in sermon and sacrament that 'you are forgiven'. Through such proclamation of the gospel, every member of the church may and should 'become a Christ' to other.[64]

Furthermore, it is not simply that *my* hearing and reception of forgiveness is grounded in the individual self even in the context of the community. It is the church *qua* church which hears and receives forgiveness *and* the individual within the life of the church, that is the individual whose being is 'in Christ'. This is what preserves the *being* of forgiveness vis-à-vis the *act* of forgiveness in time and space. The words of forgiveness are proclaimed and heard *in the community of faith,* that is in the community of Christ. Continuity of human reception of forgiveness does not stem, therefore, from any individual state of faith or existential individualism or subjective identity, but from the word of the gospel addressed to, heard in and proclaimed by the church. In Bonhoeffer's words: 'The continuity does not lie in human beings, but rather it is guaranteed suprapersonally [*überpersönlich*] through a community of persons.'[65] The reception of forgiveness by the community in Christ, one could say, is in part an overcoming of the solitariness of the guilt and conscience of the human in Adam.

This corporate sin and confession is itself expanded to a confession and acceptance of guilt by the church on behalf of the whole world. The internal ordering of individuals towards the other in the church is replicated in its community orientation corporately in an external ordering towards the world. Just as the individual confesses sin in the context of the church, and through the church is ordered towards another (becomes, we might say, a true person), so the church as the individual corporate community of Christ is ordered towards the world and its sin. This outwards, relational orientation is not simply something which the individual has in relation to the corporate identity of the church, but something which the church has corporately in relation to the whole world. The church has a vicarious role in accepting the sin of those outside of the church. This idea clearly relates to the sharing of the individual's sin in original sin: we are all co-responsible for the sin in the world and in the church's confession of its members' own sins, it must also confess the sin of the world to which it has contributed. In his provocative *Ethics,* Bonhoeffer writes:

> With this confession [*mea culpa, mea culpa, mea maxima culpa*] the whole guilt of the world falls on the church, on Christians, and because here it is confessed and not denied, the possibility of forgiveness is opened … for there are people here who take all – really all – guilt upon themselves, not in some heroic self-sacrificing decision, but simply overwhelmed by their very own guilt toward Christ. In that moment they can no longer think about retributive justice for the 'chief sinners' but only about the forgiveness of their own great guilt.[66]

Even in the church there is a contribution to the sin of the world in the church's continued sinfulness as the sins of those who previously had been in Adam and now find themselves in Christ. In recognition that to calculate or weigh sin is in and of itself fallen, part of the individual's activity of conscience and self-justification (a result of eating from the tree of the knowledge of good and evil), genuine admission of guilt simply confesses itself: genuine admission of guilt is that which 'no longer calculates and argues, but … acknowledges my sin as the origin of all sin, as, in the words of the Bible, the sin of Adam'.[67] We require the other to be forgiven, indeed, as we have the power to excuse every other sin but our own, and concomitantly we too require the other to be excused. Furthermore, the church as Christ existing as community shares in the work and power of Christ in accepting vicariously the sins of those outside of the community which exists in Christ.[68] Brought together in Christ's forgiveness in the collective I [*Gesamtich*] of the church, the church confesses and acknowledges its guilt in and through the rest of the world. The nexus of sin 'in Adam', in the individual, community and world determines that there is an ecclesial and relational component to forgiveness as well. Sin and forgiveness are not simply about the individual in relation to God, but also simultaneously and resultantly about the individual in relation to others in the church, and the church in relation to the rest of the world.

Conclusion

For Bonhoeffer, theological thought finds its ultimate foundational *res* in the doctrine of the church. This provides that his thought in other areas of theology has its locatedness in relation to this ultimate *res* of ecclesiology. This approach to the system of systematic theology shapes subsequent and dependent loci which emerge from this ultimate and the intermediate immediate dogmatic *res*. Bonhoeffer's hamartiology takes a distinctly corporate and ecclesial focus as a result. The doctrine of sin that Bonhoeffer produces is one which explores more fully than most the horizontal nature of sin, but distinctively from social gospel accounts of corporate sin, Bonhoeffer offers a determinedly biblical and classical account of original sin:[69] the key distinctive for Bonhoeffer is the nature of the church and the effect of thinking about the church on the dogmatic locus of hamartiology.

But what does this mean for theology today? On a meta-level in terms of the nature of doctrinal thought, Bonhoeffer offers us an important lesson. Clearly, there are different ways of accounting for each locus depending on the differing foundational and immediate *res* that one offers for dogmatics. Or else, we might suggest different irreducible narratives of the Christian faith and life,[70] and the theologian is wise to explore how dogmatic locatedness and topography in relation to immediate and foundational *res* affects individual loci. Bonhoeffer may help us to learn that thinking of doctrines from different loci as immediate or foundational *res* may create a plurality of accounts of doctrines and may help us both recognize the descriptive and critical task of systematic theology as well as the possibility for new and creative ways of thinking rationally about the gospel, which can never be reducible to a single system.

On a micro (or locus-specific) level, thinking with Bonhoeffer on the corporate nature of sin, we might be prepared to say that Bonhoeffer makes plain for Magisterial Protestant believers what it means in a deeply Protestant setting to speak of the church as salvific: or, in more classical theological terms, to claim that *extra muros ecclesiam nulla salus est*.[71] To be in the church is to be in Christ, and to have a distinctive ontology. Realizing the horizontal as well as the vertical nature of sin makes the church a genuine act of the salvation of God as in the church we are given forgiveness and restored to true humanity as a humanity not ordered to the self but to others.

Should we, then, simply repeat Bonhoeffer's findings uncritically? Here, I am not so sure as a theologian, and especially as one interested in ecclesiology. Bonhoeffer opens interesting and exciting avenues, but mere repetition does not do justice to his thought: to be a true student of Bonhoeffer is surely to learn from him and respond to him, to take his promise and think along with and beyond it.[72] Thinking beyond Bonhoeffer, there are questions to be asked about the role of the Spirit in his account. Recognizing that (despite caricatures to the contrary) Bonhoeffer does talk about the Spirit (especially in terms of actualization), does locating the church so closely with the person of Christ risk the danger of reducing the particularity of the historical person, Jesus, and the once-for-allness of the cross and resurrection? Might contemporary theology, drawing from Bonhoeffer, wish to deepen an account of the Spirit to unpack the way in which the church is Christ existing as community – a church which is such as the Spirit enables it to participate in, encounter and be transformed by the Living Lord Jesus. Perhaps for Bonhoeffer, the foundational *res* of ecclesiology requires being founded upon the divine person who creates and sustains the church, and either a more foundational *res* of pneumatology is needed or an intermediate *res* of pneumatology should be offered in relation to how the church is 'in Christ'. Either way, there is much to be learned and developed from Bonhoeffer's understanding of the corporate and ecclesial nature of the way in which we should think of sin and the way in which God in His grace offers humans salvation, especially within the Protestant and more particularly Pietistic communities.

Notes

1   We might think of Thomas Aquinas' *Summa Theologica* in this way; Karl Barth's *Church Dogmatics* might be thought to take a foundation of Christology; Friedrich Schleiermacher's *Christian Faith* might be considered to have its foundation in a theology of human experience; and so forth.

2   Anna Williams sees this aspect of the task of theology as being related to the desire for coherence. On the interconnection of doctrines in relation to the issue of rational coherence, see A. N. Williams, *The Architecture of Theology: Structure, System, and Ratio* (Oxford: OUP, 2011), 4–6.

3   See Bonhoeffer *DWBE* 1, 141: one should 'start with the doctrine of the church'. Others have suggested different hermeneutical keys. For example, sociality has been offered in Clifford J. Green, *Bonhoeffer: A Theology of Sociality* (Rev. edn) (Grand Rapids: Eerdmans, 1999); a theology of life has been offered by Ralf K. Wüstenberg, *A Theology of Life: Dietrich Bonhoeffer's Religionless Christianity* (Grand Rapids: Eerdmans, 1998); reality as a key by André Dumas, *Dietrich Bonhoeffer: Theologian of Reality* (London: SCM, 1971) and Hienrich Ott, *Reality and Faith: The Theological Legacy of Dietrich Bonhoeffer* (London: Lutterworth, 1971); or freedom in Ann Nickson, *Bonhoeffer on Freedom: Courageously Grasping Reality* (Aldershot: Ashgate, 2002). Even those such as Nielsen who claim that Christology forms the centre of Bonhoeffer's theology nevertheless see Christology as existing surrounded by an 'ellipse' of anthropology and ecclesiology; see Kirsten Busch Nielsen, 'Community Turned Inside Out: Dietrich Bonhoeffer's Concept of the Church and of Humanity Reconsidered', in *Being Human, Becoming Human: Dietrich Bonhoeffer and Social Thought*, ed. Jens Zimmerman and Brian Gregor (Eugene: Wipf and Stock, 2010), 91–2.

4   On regular and irregular dogmatics, see Karl Barth, *Church Dogmatics* I/1, trans. G. T. Thomson (London: T&T Clark, 2003), 275–87. Williams helpfully differentiates between two approaches to systematicity: one a 'reasonably comprehensive account of Christian doctrine, ordered locus by locus'; the other 'theological writing in which the treatment of any one locus indicates, at least in some measure, how it is informed by other loci or how it will itself determine the shape of others'. See Williams, *The Architecture of Theology*, 1–2.

5   Augustine, *De Civitate Dei, Patrologia Latina*, vol. 41, ed. J. P. Minge (Paris: 1864), 13–14; and *De Libero Arbitrio, Patrologia Latina*, vol. 32, ed. J. P. Minge (Paris: 1841), 2–3.

6   On the relation of Luther to Augustine (and for very helpful accounts of the hamartiology of both Luther and Augustine), see Matt Jenson, *The Gravity of Sin* (London: T&T Clark, 2006), Chapters 1 and 2. On the relation of Bonhoeffer to Lutheran accounts of sin, see Michael P. DeJonge, *Bonhoeffer's Theological Formation: Berlin, Barth, and Protestant Theology* (Oxford: OUP, 2012), 121–8.

7   *DBWE* 1, 110–11, 115. Emphasis original.

8   Augustine, *De Peccatorum Meritis et Remissione et de Baptismo Parvulorum, Patrologia Latina*, vol. 44, ed. J. P. Minge (Paris: 1865), 3.14.

9   See Karl Barth's critique of inheritance, *Church Dogmatics* IV/2, ed. T. F. Torrance and G. W. Bromiley, trans. G. W. Bromiley (Edinburgh: T&T Clark, 2004), 501–2.

10 Bonhoeffer relates this to Luther (see *DBWE* 2, 147–8), but Luther himself, a former Augustinian monk, draws upon the tradition of Augustine for this.

11 *DBWE* 2, 146.

12 See Nielsen, 'Community Turned Inside Out', 96–7.

13 *DBWE* 2, 146.

14 Ibid., 109.

15 Ibid., 151.

16 Ibid., 153.

17 Bonhoeffer: 'Being in Christ means being in the church.' *DBWE* 1, 199.

18 Ibid., 213.

19 *DBWE* 2, 111.

20 Ibid., 111.

21 Ibid., 114.

22 Martin Luther, *Lectures on Romans*, in *Luther's Works* 25. *American Edition*, ed. Hilton C. Oswald (St Louis: Concordia Publishing House, 1972), 215.

23 *DBWE* 2, 137. There is a consequence here for homiletics. Clearly, the preaching of repentance is meaningful only within the community of the church, as a second manoeuvre, after the sinner has been met by Christ in the community.

24 Ibid., 151.

25 *DBWE* 4, 131.

26 Ibid., 131.

27 *DBWE* 1, 63.

28 *DBWE* 2, 137. See Jüngel: 'The Christian faith understands this ontic tendency towards self-grounding as *sin*. For faith, identity as self-identification is the mark of one who is losing him or herself. For according to faith's understanding of the matter, we never find ourselves in ourselves. In ourselves we cannot come to ourselves. We come to ourselves when we come to someone other than ourselves.' Eberhard Jüngel, *Theological Essays I* (Edinburgh: T&T Clark, 1989), 134.

29 *DBWE* 3, 115.

30 Ibid., 117–18.

31 Ibid., 118.

32 Ibid., 122.

33 Ibid., 124.

34 *DBWE* 1, 63.

35 *DBWE* 2, 139–41. For a further account of Bonhoeffer on conscience, see DeJonge, *Bonhoeffer's Theological Formation*, 118–27.

36 *DBWE* 2, 145–7.

37 My claim about dogmatic locatedness is the reverse of Nielsen, who states that
    Bonhoeffer's understanding of the church is influenced by his anthropology
    (including his hamartiology under this). My argument is that the distinctive
    flavour of his hamartiology stems from his ecclesial approach, which is
    the reason why there is a preoccupation with communal sin. The logical
    consequence of the influence of anthropology on the church does not
    necessitate either a relationality or a propensity to focus on the community;
    whereas the logical consequence of an ecclesial ultimate *res* (as I am arguing)
    would necessitate an anthropological account involving relationality and
    sociality, and an hamartiological account which focuses on the corporate as
    well as the individual. Nielsen herself, however, seems to reverse the doctrinal
    direction in her account of the movement from Bonhoeffer's ecclesiology to his
    anthropology, and then recapitulates it in the other direction once more. I wish
    to clarify the dogmatic topography in relation to these themes. See Nielsen,
    'Community Turned Inside Out', 92–5.
38 *DBWE* 1, 63.
39 Ibid., 34, emphasis in original.
40 Ibid., 63, emphasis added.
41 *DBWE* 2, 153
42 See Bruce McCormack on this point. McCormack, *Orthodox and Modern*
    (Grand Rapids: Baker Academic, 2008), 133.
43 *DBWE* 2, 115
44 For more on this concept, see Green, *Bonhoeffer*, esp. 29–45.
45 Being for others is contrasted to 'conceptual forms of the absolute, the
    metaphysical' (with the word metaphysical added later in the manuscript
    as a definitive addition). *DBWE* 8, 501. The metaphysical also comprises
    components of Bonhoeffer's critique of religion. Ibid., 372. Indeed, Bonhoeffer
    asks the question: 'How do we talk about God – without religion, that is,
    without the temporally conditioned presuppositions of metaphysics, the inner
    life, and so on?' Ibid., 364.
46 It is notable here that Bonhoeffer uses the idea of the likeness or analogy
    (*analogia*) and not directly the image of God. Classical theology has tended to
    suggest that humans lose the likeness but not the image of God; see for example,
    the *locus classicus* of Irenaeus, *Adversus haereses, Patrologia Graeca*, vol. 7, ed.
    J. P. Minge (Paris: 1857), 5.6.1 and 5.16.2 (though at other points Irenaeus is not
    quite so consistent).
47 *DBWE* 3, 65.
48 Ibid., 65–6.

49   Ibid., 115.

50   *DBWE* 2, 150.

51   See Athanasius, *De Incarnatione Verbi, Patrologia Graeca*, vol. 25, ed. J. P. Minge (Paris: 1884), para 54.

52   *DBWE* 4, 285.

53   Ibid., 285.

54   *DBWE* 6, 157.

55   Ibid., 95–6.

56   Ibid., 95.

57   *DBWE* 2, 114.

58   'Christ is the Kollektivperson of the new humanity, superseding Adam as the Kollektiveperson of the old humanity.' Green, *Bonhoeffer*, 53.

59   *DBWE* 5, 110.

60   Ibid., 110.

61   Ibid., 111.

62   *DBWE* 14, 593–4.

63   *DBWE* 6, 142.

64   *DBWE* 2, 112–13.

65   Ibid., 114.

66   *DBWE* 6, 136.

67   Ibid., 137.

68   Ibid., 135.

69   On Bonhoeffer's criticism of social gospel accounts of sinfulness, see *DBWE* 12, 241–2.

70   The notion of irreducible narratives is borrowed from David Kelsey, *Eccentric Existence: A Theological Anthropology* (Louisville: Westminster/John Knox, 2009).

71   Leahy puts it thus: 'Bonhoeffer brings together two important categories that flow from Christ who is present and are essential for members of the church – the soteriological motif of vicarious representative action (*Stellvertretung*) and the motif of the reciprocity of being *with* one another (*miteinander*) and *for* one another (*füreinander*). All communitarian life in the church is rooted in Christ's vicarious action on our behalf.' Brendan Leahy, '"Christ Existing as Community": Dietrich Bonhoeffer's Notion of Church', *Irish Theological Quarterly* 73 (2008): 32–59, 41.

72   This parallels Barth's account of the way in which students of Calvin should learn from Calvin; see Karl Barth, *The Theology of John Calvin* (Grand Rapids: Eerdmans, 1992), 1–10.

Chapter 6

'COMPLETELY WITHIN GOD'S DOING': SOTERIOLOGY AS META-ETHICS IN THE THEOLOGY OF DIETRICH BONHOEFFER

Philip G. Ziegler

Introduction

There is remarkably little ethics in Bonhoeffer's *Ethics*. That is, if one goes looking for discrete guidance on the content of Christian moral judgements about any number of perplexing questions of human conduct, one will come up almost entirely empty handed. Of course, that is precisely a good part of the point of what Bonhoeffer's intends with this work. For in a manner akin to what we find in Barth's later moral theology, Bonhoeffer's experiments in ethics drafted during the first years of the Second World War are preoccupied with something other than executing moral judgements or prescribing specific moral acts. Rather, these manuscripts represent so many efforts to describe the moral space or field within which human persons as ethical agents are located. And for Bonhoeffer, as for Barth, this business is relentlessly and properly theological work. It is the task that John Webster characterizes as 'moral ontology', which is to say, the effort to provide an ever more adequate dogmatic description of the reality of the world within which humans are given to act.[1] In a different idiom, we might speak of Bonhoeffer's theological ethics as thoroughly *metaethical* in character, being pre-eminently concerned with the fundamental presuppositions, commitments and dispositions of moral discourse, reflection and action, rather than with the content of particular moral judgements or the form of discrete moral acts.[2] In this venture of dense doctrinal description of the salient moral features of the reality of our world – a world lost in sin and now reconciled to God in Christ – Bonhoeffer's tone is assured; he deploys an array of doctrinal resources with open confidence in their meaning, intelligibility and explanatory power. His work in this regard seems largely unanxious about what Charles Taylor has called the 'great epistemological cloud' which hangs over all such exercises in moral ontology under the conditions of modernity.[3]

The epistemological trouble that concerns Bonhoeffer in his *Ethics* does not arise from uniquely modern challenges. Rather, what concerns him most basically is the way in which acts of moral knowing and the contents of moral reflection are fundamentally affected by the determinative and dynamic realities of sin and God. In fact, epistemology generally – and, in the context of ethics, the knowledge of good and evil in particular – is itself profoundly at issue in his description of the moral field in which the Christian life is set and enacted. Moral epistemology – i.e. the question of the nature and place of knowledge in the constitution of the human being as a moral agent – is a problem requiring a thoroughly theological contextualization.[4] For Bonhoeffer, this means grasping the consequences of the situation of human sinfulness, conceiving the nature of the gift of faith and the disposition of a life reconciled with God in Christ, and registering the abiding priority (indeed exclusivity) of God's gracious agency in delivering human beings and their own activity into truth, including moral truth. In short, mapping the moral field requires that we acknowledge and reflect upon the fact that, as Bonhoeffer writes, 'Holy Scripture puts human beings completely within God's doing, and subjects human doing completely to the doing of God'.[5]

In what follows I want briefly to pull this particular metaethical thread that runs – and is readily traceable – from the concluding section of *Act and Being* through to the *Ethics* in the essay 'The Love of God and the Disintegration of the World' where the earlier explorations are set explicitly and materially within a determinative account of divine election and salvation in Christ. In the course of this, I will attend in particular to the fate of the notion of *conscience* as an organ of moral knowledge. I suggest that Bonhoeffer's practice of appealing consistently to soteriological considerations as materially decisive in establishing moral reality, and so in orienting Christian moral reflection, is a key marker of its self-consciously Protestant character. His is a theological approach to ethics in which 'grace must be the story' as it is grace that finally 'determines the relationship between God, the creature, creation, and its destiny' since 'grace is what God is all about'.[6] Reflection on this approach challenges us to consider whether contemporary Protestant ethics can hold its nerve and register, at its base, the implications of the radical understanding of grace and faith that must animate and orient any moral theology whose centre of gravity rests firmly in the second-article of the creed, as does Bonhoeffer's own.

Soteriology as fundamental moral description

Act and Being: What the word makes of the world

For all the technicality of its execution, the programme of Bonhoeffer's early work *Act and Being* is clear enough: disputes about epistemology in modern philosophy are proxy battles fought over variant understandings of what it means to be a human being. Theology's stake in these epistemic debates is likewise funded by fundamental concerns in *theological* anthropology, in particular the need to do justice to the decisive import of the contingent revelation of God in Jesus Christ for human self-understanding. This divine revelation is not the mere disclosure of hitherto obscure knowledge, but comprises the saving advent of God himself for us. Doing justice to this first involves overreaching the categories of 'act' and 'being' by incorporating them into the more apposite and complex concepts of 'person' and 'community'. But beyond this, doing justice to divine revelation further requires that we acknowledge that the concrete determination of human beings by divine judgement in sin and in grace decisively overruns all our categories. As Bonhoeffer explains, all our concepts of human being 'insofar as they are acquired from revelation,' should always be 'determined by the concepts of sin and grace – by reference to 'Adam' and 'Christ' – such that theology can and must refuse any and all ways of conceiving of human beings 'that are primarily based in creation' as such.[7]

Bonhoeffer's book takes its title from the two concepts that frame the philosophical form of the epistemological problem going into the argument, namely 'act' and 'being'; but it could well have been titled for the two names that finally decide the theological form of the epistemological problem 'coming out' of the argument, namely *Adam and Christ*. For Bonhoeffer argues that the historic outworking of the drama of the human fall into sin and salvation by grace supervenes upon any and all thought of humanity as such, i.e. of human being in the world as pure or mere creature. Our conception of human being is fundamentally determined by the interrupting and transformative realities of sin and grace; human being is always being 'in Adam' or being 'in Christ'. In explicating this claim, Bonhoeffer has recourse in this work (as in no other) to concepts of *Dasein* and *Wiesein*, aiming thereby to signal that the fact *that* we are in the world is inseparable from just *how* we are in the world, which is to say, the way we exist before God as sinners and saved.[8] To think or speak of human beings as creatures as such is an impossible – and even dangerous – abstraction, and one that is simply disallowed by the formative realities of sin and grace.

Crucially, we must not be tempted to think that sin and grace are less fundamental anthropological categories because they are properly contingent, rather than essential determinations of our humanity. Sin and grace befall us *ab extra* to be sure: they are 'adventitious' realities which come upon humanity in the course of things, rather than arising of necessity 'from within' as it were; but they are no less constitutive of our actual reality for being so. All human being exists in the unfolding of the one economy of salvation – as Bonhoeffer says, in relation to the '*historical* church of Christ' – in the single transit from being 'in Adam' to being 'in Christ' and nowhere else, for there simply is nowhere else to be, no possibility of retreat to some 'deeper' and invariant 'being of their own'.[9] Tracking Paul's testimony in Romans 5, the names 'Adam' and 'Christ' exhaustively map the whole of human reality. 'There is no formal, metaphysical, psychological definition of the being of human beings', Bonhoeffer suggests, 'that is not comprehended in the statement that human beings are either "in Christ" or "in Adam"'.[10] His argument culminates in the following conclusion, one which Bonhoeffer claims to be definitive for any properly *Protestant* theology and ethics, and which I quote here at length:[11]

> Being-a-creature is in the agitation of being in faith. Ontologically this means that God is at once the creature's ground of being and Lord; transcendentally it means that *Dasein* is 'amidst' and 'in reference to' transcendence. There is no ontological specification of that which is created that is independent of God being reconciler and redeemer, and human beings being sinners and

forgiven. In the Christian doctrine of being, all metaphysical ideas of eternity and time, being and becoming, living and dying, essence and appearance must be measured against the concepts of the being of sin and being of grace, or else must be developed anew in light of them … . In the idea of the creature, however, the personal-being of God and revelation manifests itself as God being Creator and being the Lord over my human personal being. And the second of these is the more encompassing of the two latter determinations.[12]

For present purposes, two things are chiefly to be marked in this passage. The first is how recognition of God as Creator is subordinated to recognition of God as reconciler, redeemer and the Lord of life: we are given to know God as the origin of our being only after and as a reflex upon our being given to know God as the free and gracious agent of our salvation. We might say that it is the substance of the second and third articles of the creed that delivers us the truth of the first article as *evangelical* truth. To come to faith in the God *of the Gospel*, Bonhoeffer suggests, enjoins a specific material discipline upon the subsequent attention and movement of theological thought.

The second matter of note is how, following on from this, Bonhoeffer asserts that all the linguistic and conceptual tools theology has at its disposal must themselves be judged and renewed on the basis of the realities of sin and grace. Speaking grammatically, we might say that sin and grace are ever the proper *subjects* of our theology, of which everything else is a predicate. This is true of all our fundamental metaphysical categories but also, we must add, of all our fundamental moral concepts as well. This grammatical ordering is, Bonhoeffer suggests, irreversible: sin and grace are never functions or mere modifications of other realities; they are always the materially decisive realities in any theological description of human being. Thus, being disposed over by sin 'in Adam' and being disposed over by grace 'in Christ' represent two total determinations of human being and so also, for that same reason, of all thought and speech that would do justice to the truth of that being. They provide the comprehensive rubrics under which all humanity – and so also all human moral knowing and acting – must be ranged and understood if *theological* understanding is our aim.

The consequences of this last point for theological ethics can already be seen in *Act and Being* itself in Bonhoeffer's treatment of human *conscience*.[13] Abiding by his own stated theological discipline, conscience comes into view and is understood as a predicate first of our 'being in Adam' and then of our 'being in Christ', its meaning and importance being determined serially in this way. In the first case, Bonhoeffer argues that under the conditions of sin the conscience represents the last bastion of human efforts at self-control, the final moral spasm of the human self-turned-in-upon-itself, testimony to the desperate hope that we might yet be able to rectify our disintegrating moral situation ourselves; it is the device by means of which the sinner grasps one last time at the prospect of putting the house in order.[14] The moral knowledge delivered by the conscience under these conditions serves the isolationist policies of the self in revolt against God and neighbours, that is, a self ambitious to know and to do good and evil out its own perverse sense of *immediacy* and *aseity*, a self bound to itself in whom the *imago dei* has become the *sicut deus*.[15] Bonhoeffer here discerns the conscience 'in Adam' as a cunning, self-deceptive organ of sin, a faithful and ingenious servant of a moral subject who 'knows itself to be lord of its world'. This is conscience as the voice of 'a god', namely of the person I am in the contingency and continuity of my sin and as such a 'deflection from Christ'.[16]

Now, this old conscience is, like the sinner herself, brought to nought in the liberation of the self from itself by grace in Christ. Bonhoeffer emphasizes the radicality of this saving judgement by repeated reference to the cross, as well as by prominent recourse to the language of 'death' and 'resurrection' or 'new creation' as his primarily soteriological idiom.[17] The identity or continuity of human being across this saving transit from existence 'in Adam' to life 'in Christ' can only be received, acknowledged and wondered at *in faith*: it is not a function of any kind of 'general ontology' safely undisturbed by the outworking of the drama of salvation; it is rather a constituent part of the gift of that salvation: that *we* should be saved is part of the miracle that we should be *saved*.

As an exercise of the life of the liberated and reconciled self – the self placed and held 'in Christ' by grace – the *new* conscience is an organ of a moral agent turned out and away from itself, now disinterested and disregarding itself because its attention has been seized entirely by Christ. In making this point Bonhoeffer cites Luther's arresting claim that in the gift of salvation 'Christ and my conscience must become one body, so that nothing remains in my sight but Christ, crucified and risen'.[18] In winning the sinner from the immoral *and moral* solipsism of sin, grace seizes human being *in toto*, fundamentally establishing the self in Christ and directing the same self ever towards Christ. Grace, that is to say, elicits faith – 'faith, given and willed by God' as Bonhoeffer specifies – and within the life of faith the work of conscience is revolutionized. Conscience now names the self's newly retrospective confrontation with its own sin entirely 'within the forgiveness [won] through Christ' and 'in the context of Christ's forgiveness'.[19] The new conscience serves Christian freedom by relating that which is past and has no future – namely our 'being in Adam', our sin – to faith's exclusive 'intentionality toward Christ'. Holding the past in relation to the Christ who has come to dominate the total horizon of our future, the new conscience abets the mortification and repentance which are of a piece with the advent of faith, a faith Bonhoeffer characterizes as 'an act directed solely by and on Christ' and so 'the eschatological prelude under which life is placed' for the time being.[20] The work of the new conscience has become the opposite of its adamic twin: *then* it served to rivet human moral reflection to the self in a highly rarefied exercise of sinful ego; *now*, it serves the dispossession of the human self in witness to the 'new creation of those who no longer look back upon themselves, but only away from themselves to God's revelation, to Christ'.[21]

What are we to take away from these observations on the highly compressed moral theology that concludes Bonhoeffer's *Act and Being*? First, we note that the moral subject of Christian ethics has a history, namely the formative history of sin and grace. And what happens in this history – what becomes of human being in the thrall of sin and by virtue of the revelation of saving grace in the person and work of Christ – is, on Bonhoeffer's reading, much more ethically significant than attempts to access and describe any supposedly abiding architecture of human creatureliness as such. Bonhoeffer suggests that in as much as theological ethics aims to be realistic, it must always treat of human being 'in Adam' and 'in Christ' rather than aspiring after an abstract account of human being 'in Eden'. For any such 'general ontology', even if it were a possible object of theological knowledge, has been permanently and decisively overtaken by the ontological transformations of the world and humanity affected by sin and grace. The formative ontological weight – and so also the moral gravity – of the unfolding economy of salvation is simply greater than anything else at play on the moral field, as it were. We have seen the importance of this in the treatment of conscience just considered.

Second, all this is the case because, as Bonhoeffer contends, divine revelation decides the truth and falsity of human existence – indeed, the advent of divine grace kills and makes alive – by placing it 'in the truth' of God's own judgement.[22] This is crucial for our understanding of the tasks and aims of moral theology. Arising as it does from faith, theological ethics, no less than dogmatics, involves discursive acknowledgement of our 'being so placed' by God. It is thinking patient upon revelation, and so made responsible to discern and display the contours and consequences of such revelation for the living of this life. When Bonhoeffer claims that divine revelation will 'yield an epistemology [all] of its own', he has in view the kind of methodological entailments of the economy of salvation we have been outlining.[23] 'Just as the subject matter of doctrinal theology is the *truth* of God's reality revealed in Christ,' Bonhoeffer says in his *Ethics*, so the 'subject matter of a Christian ethic is God's reality revealed in Christ becoming real [*Wirklichwerden*] among God's creatures.'[24] In short, theological ethics concerns itself with the formative power, dynamics and effectiveness of the evangelical truth that Christian doctrine pursues.[25] This fact might be announced by talk of the *metaphysical* character of theological ethics, emphasizing thereby its concern with the *reality* made by the history of sin and grace. Better still, however, would be to say that theological ethics is primarily concerned with what we might call '*divine pragmatics*', which is to say, with the reality shaping power of the active divine address that is the Word of God in Jesus Christ together with its concrete practical entailments. Attending to what the Word makes of the world and we in it: *that* is the chief business of a Christian ethic.

'God's Love and the Disintegration of the World': Ethical action in a world of love

The *Ethics* manuscript entitled 'The Love of God and the Disintegration of the World'[26] resonates very closely with the approach and insights from *Act and Being* just considered. Indeed, it might well be envisaged to be an expansive theological gloss upon that earlier work. Here, once again, Bonhoeffer sketches an account of the moral field within which Christians act and ethical discernment takes place. As before, the antithetical realities of human existence 'in sin' and 'in Christ' decisively constitute and situate the human being, and therefore also the moral subject. As before, discussion of 'conscience' emerges as a bell-weather motif at a crucial juncture, and serves to signal just how radical the movement is between sin and grace.[27] And as before, Bonhoeffer's attention is riveted throughout to the reconciling and redeeming work of the Word of God incarnate as *the* fundamentally determinative factor giving shape to moral reality, a divine work summed up in the word 'love'. Bonhoeffer's preoccupations remain strictly meta-ethical and the tools he employs consistently dogmatic.

Bonhoeffer opens his discussion with the arresting claim that the fall into sin involves a fall into 'morality' understood simply as pursuit of the knowledge of good and evil. Ethics in this everyday sense is thereby cast as an originary mode of human rebellion against God, an exalted and sustained effort on the part of the human to repudiate life with God in favour of a life of self-legislation, i.e. of moral autonomy. The account of humanity 'in Adam' is entirely co-extensive with an account of *ethical* humanity. If the human being 'can know about good and evil only in opposition to God', then sinners are *per definitionem* moralists and *vice versa*, creatures asserting themselves as 'their own creator and judge'.[28] Bonhoeffer suggests that the fallen human self constitutes the encircling frontier of the moral world, within which and in terms of which everything else – including God – is located, adjudged and deployed. The *imago dei* has been unmade by the false promise and imperative of *sicut deus;* creaturely knowledge of God is thus displaced by the godlike knowledge of the creature. The moral project of fallen humanity is a project of self-making in which reference to God serves as but one possible means among many. Crucially, as Bonhoeffer stresses, morality no less than immorality serves and shapes this pernicious incurvature of the human self in sin. Liberation when it comes will, as Luther knew, be an exodus not from vice to virtue, but from vice and virtue to the grace of Christ.[29]

If human shame is an affective spectre of our primal disunity with God that haunts us still, then conscience, Bonhoeffer goes on to suggest, similarly reflects, enacts and buttresses this sinful breach. Akin to the discussion in *Act and Being*, conscience is fundamentally determined by its being 'in Adam', and as such is concerned solely with the integrity of the self; in this regard it amounts to the desperate 'voice of the fallen life that seeks to preserve unity at least within itself'.[30] Conscience does not and cannot break the closed circle in which all our moral knowing is founded upon and serves our self-knowledge; it can only compulsively reiterate this closure by its practice of judging good and evil for itself. Elsewhere in the *Ethics* – in the section 'History and the Good' – Bonhoeffer speaks of the exposure of this natural, fallen conscience 'as the most godless self-justification' precisely in the event of salvation in which it is 'overcome by the conscience that has been set free in Jesus Christ'.[31] Even more strongly than we have seen previously, the redemption of conscience now comprises its utter displacement and unmaking. The 'freed conscience' of which Bonhoeffer can speak no longer functions as a seat of moral judgement at all, but rather now simply names the total alignment of the human being with Christ. The argument culminates with the claim that 'Jesus Christ has become my conscience'.[32]

This explains why here in 'God's Love and the Disintegration of the World', Bonhoeffer offers no parallel account whatsoever of conscience on the other side of the advent of saving grace. We are met instead with a radicalization of the earlier argument: moral 'judging is itself the apostasy from God'; conscience is the highest organ of that act of ethical judging and, as such, is properly identified with the posture (being) and power (act) of sin. The salvation of conscience is therefore its ending, amounting to the complete displacement of human self-*knowing* by the gift of the knowledge of Christ and the complete displacement of *judging* good and evil by *hearing* and *doing* the will of God. The transition from existence 'in Adam' to existence 'in Christ' traverses a great antithesis in which the conscience is nullified as the sinful adamic struggle it serves 'vanishes out of sight' in the world reconciled to God in Christ once moral considerations have been set on a completely different plane.[33] Bonhoeffer's subsequent discussion of the running controversies between the figure of Jesus – who 'lives and acts not out of knowledge of good and evil' but with radical freedom and simplicity 'out of the will of God' – and the Pharisees – who embody conscience here – dramatically narrate these theological claims: to choose to know this Jesus, or better, to know as chosen by him, is to 'be filled with a new knowledge in which the knowledge of good and evil has been overcome', by an exclusive knowledge of Christ that fills the moral horizon and underwrites disinterest and even 'ignorance about one's own good and evil.'[34]

This treatment of conscience confirms for us the unparalleled importance of the outworking of the economy of salvation – i.e. the salutary transit from being 'in Adam' to being 'in Christ' – in the constitution of moral reality. And it leads us to consider more directly the substance and role of soteriology in Bonhoeffer's ethical thinking as displayed in this text. For Bonhoeffer, as has become clear, the space in moral theology that is commonly filled by philosophical or phenomenological analysis of the workings of human moral faculties in securing ethical knowledge is in fact fully occupied with discourse about the saving activity of God in Christ. He suggests that a theologically adequate moral description can sit very lightly upon investigation and analysis of human moral potential, moral psychology and moral formation – themes generally developed by appeal to fundamental anthropology within a doctrine of creation. This is because the contingent advent of sin upon creation, and its subsequent overcoming by the no less contingent advent of divine salvation in the coming of the God of grace in Christ are events of such total scope, comprehensive significance and ontological radicality that they effectively terraform the moral field and thus reconstitute the most morally salient features of our present reality anew.

It is on this basis that many motifs most closely associated with Bonhoeffer's work *Discipleship* reappear in this particular *Ethics* manuscript: the call that overcomes our intractable fixation with our own moral standing is precisely Jesus' 'liberating call to single-mindedness' in following him; the displacement of the question of good and evil by the discernment of the one will of God which is to be done 'in simplicity'; the immediacy of *doing* the divine command over against the discursive reception of that command as a mere possibility to be considered; the hiddenness of the Christian's own goodness from herself.[35] All this is possible Bonhoeffer contends because, by grace, 'Jesus Christ now occupies the very same space in them that had previously been occupied by their own knowledge of good and evil', a Christ alive and eloquent in them as their Saviour and Lord, the one to whom all self-examination and discernment may finally be surrendered.[36] It is the prevenient and salutary agency of God that is decisive here: Jesus' word 'without me you can do nothing' (Jn 15.5) is to be taken in its 'strictest sense', Bonhoeffer says; and precisely when taken in this way it comes upon us as promise and not threat. For while all our moral agency is utterly dependent upon and bound to Christ, Christ himself is the 'living one' who is well able to make us hear and so then also to do 'the law' as his living word 'which prevails of its own power without needing human assistance'.[37]

Expressed in another biblical idiom, as Bonhoeffer expounds in the final paragraphs, Christ is God's own act of sovereign love. This love is 'what God does to human beings to overcome the disunion in which they live', it is the power which human beings must 'suffer' in their liberation from sin, the power which draws them 'into the world in the only way in which the world is able to live before God and in God alone'. Love – what God does in Christ *for us* – is the election of women and men, their 'being placed into the truth' for the sake of life for one another; it is this 'utterly unique event of Jesus Christ giving up his life for us'.[38] This is what Bonhoeffer has foremost in mind when he makes the programmatic claim that Scripture 'puts human beings completely within God's doing, and subjects human doing completely to the doing of God'.[39] One of the first fruits of this divine love for us is to relieve us of the grinding sinful burden of judging good and evil ourselves, for the answer to the question 'What am I to do?' can and will only be provided by Jesus Christ himself.[40] The reconciling and redeeming love of God is, in this way, held forth as the necessary and sufficient condition for the establishment and animation of human moral agency in a world remade by the gospel.

One final observation to conclude this exposition: importantly, Bonhoeffer's intense and exclusive theological claims about the origins of human moral action and knowledge in Christ afford him an extraordinary freedom to acknowledge the manifold ways in which human beings may actually discern the will of God. The utter passivity of human beings at the hand of prevenient divine grace, Bonhoeffer stresses, is a '*theological* concept' and precisely not a psychological, sociological or physical description. As he explains, 'passivity with respect to God's love' does not exclude all 'thinking, speaking and acting', neither does affirmation of the simplicity and freedom of Christian obedience require that 'discerning the will of God must occur in the form of intuition, by abandoning all reflection, [and] naively grasping the first thought or feeling that insinuates itself': for it is precisely as 'thinking and acting human beings' that women and men are the objects and recipients of divine election, divine grace, divine love and the hearers of the divine claim and command in Christ.[41] As the ordained means by which divine revelation is publicly served by the Christian community in the world, Scripture, sacrament, prayer and preaching must always feature predominantly among these activities. But an evangelical moral theology cannot and need not further *prescribe* the creaturely channels and techniques of moral discernment precisely because it ascribes this discernment decisively to the gracious work of God, however variously we might penultimately understand, inhabit and enact our all-too human lives.

Conclusion: Theological ethics 'in Christ'

Karl Barth once remarked that in Christian theology human beings 'are not the subject of mere discussion or clarification but participants in a struggle … who have just emerged from the fray'.[42] In these brief remarks, I have argued that Bonhoeffer's practice as a moral theologian embodies this counsel, and does so precisely by the ferocity with which it holds the human being in the midst of the one struggle that is decisive, namely the struggle between sin and grace in the unfolding of the work of salvation. God's own prosecution of this struggle in Christ, and its ramifications for the situation and constitution of human existence, is Bonhoeffer's overarching concern in terms of which everything else comes to matter. It is solely with reference to this divine work that the depth of the problem of moral knowledge comes to light; and it is solely with reference to this same divine work that the revolution in the origins, shape and horizon of the *Christian* moral knowledge and the life it supports is acknowledged, owned and enjoined. The gospel tells of a world sorely oppressed by sin 'in Adam' being won by grace to freedom for God again 'in Christ'. Bonhoeffer takes this gospel to provide the most comprehensive theological context within which moral knowing and moral action must be understood Christianly. The eloquent presence of the living Saviour is the fundamental context within which the Christian moral life is set. It is the work of his Word of judgement and grace to announce and make effective the great antithesis between sin and faith that God has secured by way of incarnation, crucifixion and resurrection, and so to reconcile all things. All this tells of a theological intellect well furnished by a lively and creative reception of the genius of the theology that served the Protestant reformations of the sixteenth century.

As I hope to have shown, Bonhoeffer's interests and ambitions in moral theology are pre-eminently metaethical in character, committed first and foremost to calling to mind the revelation of the features of the divine economy of salvation as the chief and decisive landmarks on the field of human moral endeavour. What Nigel Biggar has recently written of the 'spiritual' character of Barth's ethics holds good for Bonhoeffer's too. He writes,

> The ethical task is not just – and not primarily – about our solving practical problems out there in the world. It is first and foremost about coming to terms with a true, theological, and soteriological description of our own creaturely nature and sinful condition, and of our standing before a benevolent forgiving, and saving God.[43]

In keeping with this, the work of theological ethics is not itself the work of discerning the will of God; it is not itself the enactment of a Christian moral life in which God's will is done. Faith in the living and sovereign God of the gospel precludes any such pre-emptive abstraction and foreclosure. Rather, Bonhoeffer's work suggests that the task of moral theology is to aid and abet the knowledge of God from which such actual discernment flows, namely 'the knowledge of being preserved, held and guided by the will of God' and of 'the gracious unity with the will of God that has already been granted' to faith. Ethics, in short, is a theological service to the life of faith as it 'seeks anew to solidify this knowledge in concrete living' as he says.[44]

In sum, a cardinal ambition of Bonhoeffer's moral theology is to secure soteriology as 'first moral philosophy' as it were, so that the generative impulse, form, substance and horizon of Christian ethics may be rightly discerned and inhabited by faith. This puts divine agency or divine pragmatics at the heart of the matter. For Bonhoeffer, a human life 'in Christ' is one subjected to the relentless gracious activity of the living God of our salvation. To be 'in Christ' is thus to be 'placed in the truth'; but because the truth at issue is the truth of the gospel – i.e. 'the truth of God's reality revealed in Christ' – the moral field is something dynamic, dramatic and historically shaped by the living realization of the work of salvation in which sin is overcome by the advent of the reign of God with all its profoundly humane implications.[45] 'In Christ' ethics is relieved of the impossible task of self-justification ascribed to it 'in Adam'. Instead, when properly ordered to and transformed by the absolute priority of grace, ethics 'in Christ' can, as Gerhard Forde suggests, 'take up its *rightful* task. Ethics is not the way of salvation. It is not, to use Luther's favourite image, the tree. It is the fruit of the tree.'[46]

Notes

1   See John Webster, *Barth's Ethics of Reconciliation* (Cambridge: Cambridge University Press, 1995), 1–2. See the discussion of this feature of Bonhoeffer's work in Barry Harvey, *Taking Hold of the Real* (Eugene, OR: Cascade, 2015), Chapter 1, 'A Sacramental This-Worldliness'.

2   See Geoff Sayre-McCord, 'Metaethics', *The Stanford Encyclopaedia of Philosophy*, ed. Edward N. Zalta, available at http://plato.stanford.edu/archives/sum2014/entries/metaethics/ (accessed summer 2014).

3   Charles Taylor, *The Sources of the Self* (Cambridge: Cambridge University Press, 1992), 5.

4   For the sense of 'contextualization' here see Walter Lowe, 'Why We Need Apocalyptic', *Scottish Journal of Theology* 63 (2010): 48–53.

5   *DBWE* 6, 327.

6   'Grace is what God is up to.' Gerhard Forde, 'Luther's "Ethics"', in *A More Radical Gospel: Essays on Eschatology, Authority, Atonement and Ecumenism* (Grand Rapids: Eerdmans, 2004), 140.

7   Bonhoeffer limns the argument as a whole at the outset of *Act and Being, DBWE* 2, 30–2.

8   See especially Ibid., 32, 138, 151–3.

9   Ibid., 136.

10   Ibid., 134.

11   Ibid., 138, 151.

12   Ibid., 151–2.

13   For a comprehensive discussion of the theme of conscience in Bonhoeffer's work see Reinhold Mokrosch, 'Das Gewissensverständnis Dietrich Bonhoeffers: Reformatorische Herkunft und politische Funktion', in *Bonhoeffer und Luther: Zur Sozialgestalt des Luthertums in der Moderne*, ed. C. Gremmels (Munich: Chr. Kaiser Verlag, 1983), 59–92. Also see Christiane Tietz, 'Dietrich Bonhoeffer: wer halt wir? Gewissen oder Verantwortung', in *Ringen um die Wahrheit: Gewissenkonflikte in der Christentumsgeschichte*, ed. M. Delgado, V. Leppin and D. Neuhold (Stuttgart: W. Kohlhammer, 2011), 325–37.

14   See *DBWE* 2, 139–44.

15   *DBWE* 3, 113.

16   *DBWE* 2, 141, 156.

17   See, for example, Ibid., 151.

18   Ibid., 150, fn.20. Bonhoeffer cites Luther's lectures on Galatians: 'Sed hic oportet Christum et conscientiam meam fieri unum corpus, ita ut in conspectua

meo nihil maneat nisis Christus crucifixus et resuscitatus.' Martin Luther, *Galatervorlesung*, Chaps. 1–4, 1535, *Weimar Ausgabe* 40.1. (Weimar, 1911), 282, lines 21–3.

19   Ibid., 154, 156.

20   Ibid., 156–7. Bonhoeffer goes on to stress in these closing paragraphs of his study the classical Protestant concept of faith as first and foremost *fides directa* and *actus directus*, i.e. an unreflective posture given to the self by the objective and eschatological force of the event of revelation in Christ. Ibid., 158–61.

21   Ibid., 161.

22   Ibid., 141.

23   Ibid., 31.

24   *DBWE* 6, 49.

25   On this theme see the programmatic essay by Paul L. Lehmann, 'The Formative Power of Particularity', *Union Seminary Quarterly Review* 18:3.1 (1963): 306–19.

26   *DBWE* 6, 299–338.

27   See a remark of Bonhoeffer's cited in a letter from K.-L. Schmidt from the 23 September 1936 on 'the dialectical connection between the unredeemed and redeemed state'. *DBWE* 14, 262.

28   *DBWE* 6, 300–1.

29   Martin Luther, *Lectures on Romans,* ed. and trans. W. Pauck (Philadelphia: Westminster Press, 1961), 5. For comment, see Forde, 'Luther's "Ethics"', 140.

30   *DBWE* 6, 307.

31   Ibid., 278. The exegetical basis for this radically negative assessment of conscience is found in *Creation and Fall*, when Bonhoeffer is glossing Gen. 3.8-13. *DBWE* 3, 127–30.

32   *DBWE* 6, 278–9.

33   Ibid., 309, 311.

34   Ibid., 313, 317, 323.

35   Ibid., 318, 318–24.

36   Ibid., 325.

37   Ibid., 328.

38   Ibid., 336, 335.

39   Ibid., 327.

40   Ibid., 325.

41   Ibid., 337, 321, 337–8.

42   Karl Barth, *Göttingen Dogmatics: Instruction in the Christian Religion*, ed. H. Reiffen, trans. G. W. Bromiley (Grand Rapids: Eerdmans, 1991), 77.

43 Nigel Biggar, 'Karl Barth's Ethics Revisited', *Commanding Grace: Studies in Karl Barth's Ethics*, ed. D. L. Migliore (Grand Rapids: Eerdmans, 2010), 28.

44 *DBWE* 6, 323.

45 *DBWE* 6, 49.

46 Forde, 'Luther's "Ethics"', 140.

Chapter 7

CREATURES BEFORE GOD: BONHOEFFER, DISABILITY AND THEOLOGICAL ANTHROPOLOGY

Michael Mawson

One striking feature of recent work in disability theology is the turn to the language of relational personhood as a means of developing a more expansive and inclusive theological anthropology. Thinkers such as Hans Reinders, John Swinton, Amos Yong and Michael Hryniuk have all sought to develop an anthropology along these lines. In addition, they have sought to show how such an anthropology can provide a basis for an ethic, that is, a basis for actively striving to care for those with profound disabilities. In this chapter, I review and endorse this basic development, but suggest that the theology of Dietrich Bonhoeffer may help with overcoming some problems with the turn to relational personhood as it stands.

In the first section I briefly indicate how personhood is typically defined and understood nowadays, that is, as involving the possession of certain capacities or attributes. In the second section I outline the theological alternative that has emerged in recent disability theology: an understanding of human beings as relational persons gifted to one another by God. In the third section, however, I express some concerns with one of the main ways that several theologians have sought to ground this relational personhood theologically, that is, by appealing to the divine persons and relations of the Trinity. I argue that this can potentially obfuscate or downplay the concrete and embodied nature of human personhood. Finally, I turn to Dietrich Bonhoeffer's account of the human being as a being-in-relation with a concrete other, suggesting that this creaturely anthropology provides a better theological basis for a relational anthropology.

Philosophical and cultural conceptions of personhood

In recent decades, questions such as 'Who is a person?', 'How do persons emerge?' or 'What does personhood entail?' have increasingly come to frame and organize how we negotiate basic issues of rights and responsibilities, as well as how we understand our individual and collective identities. How we respond to such questions can have profound implications at the level of public policy and practice.

One place where this is apparent is in dominant philosophical approaches to biomedical ethics. For example, in his influential *Practical Ethics*, the utilitarian philosopher Peter Singer has defined personhood in terms of 'self-awareness, self-control, a sense of the future, a sense of the past, the capacity to relate to others, concern for others, communication, and curiosity'.[1] Using such criteria, Singer has proposed including some non-animals as persons and – more controversially – excluding those human beings with profound intellectual disabilities, as well as fetuses, newborn infants, people with advanced dementia and various other groups with limited capacities due to ageing or terminal illness. For Singer, these groups are all essentially made up of non-persons; as such they have no recognizable human rights and we have strictly limited obligations to and responsibilities for them.[2]

In *Abortion and Infanticide*, Michael Tooley has proposed a definition of personhood with some similar ramifications: 'There are a number of necessary conditions that something must satisfy if it is to be a person', he writes, 'including the possession, either now or at some time in the past, of a sense of time, of a concept of a continuing subject of mental states, and of a capacity for thought episodes.'[3] According to Tooley, we are persons by virtue of a capacity to reflect upon and be aware of ourselves through time. Correlatively, he insists that 'an entity cannot be a person unless it possesses, or has previously possessed the capacity for thought'.[4] He draws out the implications of this with respect to newborns: It is 'unlikely that humans, in the first few weeks after birth, possess this capacity'.[5] This means, of course, that infanticide is not murder, and that we should reorder our ethical and legal systems accordingly.

If Singer and Tooley both closely identify personhood with the possession of certain attributes or capacities, this also resonates with many wider cultural assumptions about what it means to be human. Hans Reinders suggests that our 'culture is replete with images of self-determining bodies and minds, reflecting the deeply rooted cultural belief that the point of our lives is what we are capable of doing.'[6] Likewise, John Swinton notes that 'within a culture that is marked by … hypercognition … and hypermemory … the temptation to define the nature of personhood and humanness according to such criteria is alluring and perhaps inevitable.'[7] We implicitly understand what it means to be human on the basis of such cultural values and priorities. To be fully human involves being able to actively pursue and achieve the kind of existence or being that we collectively esteem.[8] It is these kinds of philosophical and cultural conceptions of personhood, then, that recent theologians working in the area of disability theology have sought to contest and overcome.

A theological approach to personhood

What insights does the Christian theological tradition have to offer for how we understand personhood? How can theology contribute to an alternative understanding of human life and its meaning? Traditionally, Christians have approached and negotiated questions surrounding anthropology with reference to Genesis 1: 'Then God said, "Let us make humankind in our image, according to our likeness …" So God created humankind, in his image, in the image of God he created them; male and female he created them' (Gen. 1.26–7). Genesis informs us that to be human fundamentally means to be created in the image of God.

On its own terms, however, the text provides few clues as to what this *imago Dei* specifically entails. This has led to diverging interpretations of the *imago Dei* within the Christian tradition. In a recent book James Mumford has identified a dominant strand of interpretation: the 'capacities-based or "immanentist" reading of the *imago* according to which human beings are thought to resemble God in so far as they possess specific attributes or properties.'[9] In line with recent philosophical conceptions of personhood, God created human beings in the *imago Dei* by endowing them with certain attributes. Drawing on Greek philosophy, the candidates for these have typically included reason, language, will or intellect. Thomas Aquinas, for example, insisted that 'since it is because of his intellectual nature that man is said to be made to the image of God, it follows that he is made to God's image to the highest degree to the extent that his intellectual nature is able to imitate God to the highest degree'.[10]

Yet if these kinds of interpretations of the *imago Dei* have a long and established pedigree, they have recently fallen from grace. In recent decades developments and insights from biology and phenomenology have undermined such immanentist or substantive interpretations. Wentzel Van Huyssteen summarizes these developments: 'Substantive interpretations of the *imago Dei*', he writes, 'have been replaced … precisely because substantive views were seen as too static, and too strongly expressive of mind/body dualism'.[11] As scientists and some philosophers have been attending to the bodily and embodied nature of human identity and intentionality, conceptions of human identity primarily in terms of a capacity for reason, language and intellect have become harder to sustain.[12]

The impact of all this is evident in recent disability theology. Over the last decade, theologians such as Hans Reinders, Thomas Reynolds, John Swinton and Amos Yong have sought to develop insights into theological anthropology by attending to the concrete realities and experiences of persons with physical and intellectual differences. Their interest has especially been in how the lives and experiences of those with profound physical and intellectual differences can help us to clarify the nature of personhood. Assuming that this group of human beings are persons in the full sense, what do their realities and experiences disclose about the nature of personhood?

On the one hand, these thinkers have drawn attention to the problems that immanentist or capacity-based interpretations of the *imago Dei* pose for many of those with disabilities. In *Theology and Down Syndrome*, Amos Yong writes: 'This view perpetuates a bias against persons with disabilities who are oftentimes less physically and intellectually capable than others'.[13] In *Receiving the Gift of Friendship*, Hans Reinders similarly insists 'the history of this doctrine shows' that 'the case for theological inclusiveness grounded in *imago Dei* is at best ambiguous', precisely because 'theological reflection has always been tempted to explain the divine image in terms of human capabilities'.[14] If to be created in the *imago Dei* means to be rational, self-determining or linguistic, then the status of those who lack or less clearly display such attributes becomes ambiguous at best.[15]

On the other hand, these theologians have also sought to recover and develop alternative ways of understanding the human being as *imago Dei*. They have interpreted the *imago Dei* not in terms of a capacity for reason or intellect, but in relational terms. Genesis 1.26–7 is read in light of Genesis 2.18: 'It is not good that the human being should be alone.' As Martin Buber influentially glosses this connection: 'In the beginning was the relation.'[16] At the most basic level what it means to be human or a human person is to be in relation to another.

Reflecting upon this point, Thomas Reynolds writes that 'interdependence is originary. It is the fulcrum from which we emerge as persons.'[17] We emerge as persons in and through our interactions with others. Yong draws out the significance of this for persons with disabilities in particular: 'An anthropology of interrelationality is able to account for the interpersonal encounters and intersubjectivity most palpably experienced in and between relationships involving people with disabilities.'[18] If immanentist or capacity-based interpretations of the human being place in question the full humanity or personhood of those with profound disabilities, a more thoroughly relational interpretation affirms that we are persons simply by being in relation.

In addition, some of these theologians have insisted that this relational being or personhood must be extrinsically grounded in and gifted by God.[19] They insist that an emphasis on relationality or relational personhood *per se* is insufficient. There could be a kind of relational personhood, for example, in which a human being *actively* realizes or achieves personhood in and through its interactions with another. This kind of relational personhood would still remain centred upon and directed by an active subject or agent, which would do little to secure the full humanity of those who less clearly display such agency.[20] Rather, they argue that relational personhood is not primarily something we can achieve or activate; it is more fundamentally a gift from God. As Reinders puts this point, relationality 'is not constituted by our subjectivity but by God's self-giving gift to humankind.'[21] God's free and gratuitous action grounds our relationality *ab extra*. In contrast to Singer and Tooley, such an extrinsic and transcendent grounding makes personhood unconditional and extends it to all human beings. We are related to one another prior to and apart from any capacity to recognize or realize this relationality ourselves.

This relational interpretation of the *imago Dei* not only allows for a more inclusive conception of personhood, it also provides a basis for an ethics that more actively strives to secure better lives for others, especially those with profound disabilities. Reinders aptly describes this as 'the other side of the unconditional gift' of our relational personhood: 'how we respond to it.'[22] As he succinctly puts it: 'the gift entails a mission.'[23] Reinders' point, then, is that even while relational personhood is itself unconditionally gifted by God, this gift brings with it an opportunity to embrace and serve all those who have been similarly gifted. Attending to the writing of Jean Vanier and the reflections of *L'Arche* communities, Reinders develops an account of this mission through the language of friendship and hospitality. We have been given an opportunity to embrace and serve our friends precisely because God has given them to us: 'God's gift is the gift that precedes Christian friendship and makes it possible.'[24] Crucially, his point is that God gives us our friends and that they are 'not chosen' by us.[25] This radically expands our social networks to include those who are different from us.[26] Christian friendship involves embracing all those who have been given to us, in particular those friends who we did not anticipate.

To be clear, however, any such active embrace or service to the other remains secondary and derivative. Neither our relational personhood nor these friendships *per se* require or depend upon a capacity to actively serve. Fundamentally, we have been given one another as friends; secondarily, this means we have an opportunity to actively serve one another insofar as we are able.

To summarize this section: these theologians rightly insist on a theological understanding of personhood as relational. Against Singer and Tooley, as well as 'immanentist' and 'substantivist' readings of the *imago Dei*, they recognize that we have all been created as persons in relation to one another. On this basis they affirm the personhood of all human beings, including those with profound intellectual and physical differences. And as Reinders shows, this relational anthropology also leads to an ethics. The recognition that we have been gifted to one another provides an opportunity to work to improve the lives of our friends.

Personhood and the Trinity

While I wish to endorse this account of relational personhood and its concomitant ethic, I have some concerns with one way in which it is often grounded theologically, that is, with reference to the divine persons and relations of the Trinity. Reinders in particular has sought to understand human relational personhood in terms of the relations and persons of the Triune God. God as Trinity provides the basic model for understanding what we are as relational persons at the human level.

This basic move of grounding human personhood in the Trinity appears in the work of a number of prominent modern systematic theologians more broadly, including Jürgen Moltmann,[27] Colin Gunton,[28] John Zizioulas and Miroslav Volf.[29] It appears in the work of feminist theologians such as Catherine LaCugna[30] and Patricia Wilson-Kastner,[31] philosophical theologians and political and liberation theologians,[32] and in the work of pastoral theologians like Peter Holmes and Stanley Grenz.[33] Indeed, Karen Kilby has aptly summarized this trend in modern theology: social trinitarianism 'has been gaining momentum especially since the publication of Jürgen Moltmann's *The Trinity and the Kingdom of God*, and by now has achieved in many quarters dominance – it has become the new orthodoxy'.[34]

This move of grounding a relational anthropology in the Trinity also appears in recent disability theology. John Swinton insists that 'properly understood, the relational nature of the Trinity is an important key to the relational nature of human beings. Something analogous to this divine dynamic is apparent within human personhood.'[35] Elsewhere Michael Hryniuk has suggested that 'just as God is a communion of persons who would not exist at all if not in relation toward one another and creation, so human beings are likewise persons, that is, existing only in and through relation to another, others, and God.'[36] For Hryniuk, the significance of this turn to the Trinity is that it disrupts our tendency and temptation to understand personhood in individualistic terms; it makes possible a 'recognition that personhood is not grounded essentially in one's power to think, reason or produce'.[37]

Hans Reinders, as already noted, likewise appeals to the Trinity to support his relational anthropology. In the core theological section of *Receiving the Gift of Friendship*, he turns to and draws upon the work of the Orthodox theologian John Zizioulas.[38] First, Reinders repeats and endorses Zizioulas' reading of the Greek Fathers who, according to Zizioulas, held that 'the *being of God himself* was identified with the three persons of the Trinity.'[39] For Zizioulas, Greek patristic theology revolutionized and overturned earlier Classical Greek conceptions of ontology and metaphysics, which had maintained a sharp opposition between *ousia* as general or universal being and *hypostasis* as the particular or concrete person. In Zizioulas' reading, the Greek Fathers disrupted this opposition by making being subordinate to the free relations of the divine persons. The effect of this move, he summarizes, is that 'to be and to be in relation becomes identical.'[40] For the Greek Fathers it was no longer possible to think of God prior to the persons and relations of the Trinity.

Moreover, Reinders takes over another move in Zizioulas' theology: the claim that human beings are relational by being ecstatically drawn towards and into God's intra-Trinitarian relations. 'We are truly human', he summarizes, 'because we are drawn into communion with God the Father, the Son and the Holy Spirit.'[41] Zizioulas himself describes this as opening ourselves up to the *perichoretic* fullness of the divine life: 'The life to which we open ourselves is expansive and unfathomable in its fullness, because it is the divine life: the life of the Trinity.'[42] Moreover, Zizioulas maintains that this ecstatic openness to God as Trinity is what grounds our relational personhood in the here and now. He understands the relational personhood of human beings on the basis of their *telos* or final end as union with God.[43]

My concern is that grounding relational personhood in the Trinity in this way obfuscates the more distinctly human or creaturely nature of human personhood. More specifically, my concern is that modelling a relational anthropology on Trinitarian relations and persons – human beings as relational through being drawn into the intra-Trinitarian relations – mitigates a more fundamental distinction between creator and creation. In a recent essay critiquing social Trinitarianism, Katheryn Tanner expresses this concern: 'No matter how close the similarities between human and divine persons, differences always remain – God is not us – and this sets up the major problem for theologies that want to base conclusions about human relations on the Trinity.'[44] Tanner locates the key difference in 'the essential finitude of human beings'.[45] For Tanner, by conflating the difference between divine and human persons, social trinitarianism marginalizes and downplays finitude or creaturely limitation in human personhood.[46]

One place where this is apparent in *Being as Communion* is in Zizioulas' central opposition between 'ecclesial being' and 'biological' or 'natural being'.[47] On the one side, he describes 'ecclesial being' as the new existence given in baptism, the free existence or personhood that is constituted in and by God as Trinity. On the other side, he further clarifies this ecclesial being by positioning it over against a prior 'biological' or 'natural existence.' He construes the latter in wholly negative terms: 'Man as a biological hypostasis is intrinsically a tragic figure.'[48] Or as he describes this opposition in a later essay: 'Man is called to preserve the image of God in him as much as possible, striving to free himself from the necessity of nature, to experience "sacramentally" the "new being" as a member of the community of those "born again."'[49] For Zizioulas, we should strive to embrace the freedom of our ecclesial being, moving beyond the necessities and vicissitudes of human nature or natural being.

Both Reinders and Hryniuk take up this opposition between ecclesial and biological being in their theological reflections on disability. Reinders, for example, insists that being drawn into God 'means that we no longer fear the limitations of our biological and historical being because we have been accepted as who and what we are.'[50] Similarly, Hryniuk (citing Catherine LaCugna) insists that when 'the Spirit deifies human beings' this 'makes them holy, sets them free from sin, free from the conditions of their biological hypostasis.'[51] In other words, both Reinders and Hryniuk posit an opposition between the ground of our relational personhood in God and our natural embodied limitations. Accordingly, when human beings are drawn into or constituted by the relations of the Trinity, they are simultaneously drawn out of or away from their natural situations and limits. Summarizing this aspect of Zizioulas' theology, Douglas Farrow writes that the human being on its own terms is 'bound by finitude, by his biological nature, by the necessities of his body, and by the self-centredness which all of this inevitably entails'. 'If he is to be free at all', Farrow continues, 'he must overcome his natural or biological hypostasis, and all that it stands for.'[52] For Zizioulas, and consequently for Reinders and Hryniuk, the limits of our biological embodied being are progressively overcome or displaced by our ecstatic transformation.

One problem, then, is that this suggests that biological and creaturely limits, including the physical and intellectual limits of persons with disabilities, will be overcome in and through this transformation. Bodily limits and experiences play no role in our new ecclesial being or identity. This in turn suggests that disability and its realities are not finally constitutive of identity; they do not fundamentally inform our identities as human beings and our standing in relation God and one another.[53]

To be clear, neither Reinders nor Hryniuk *directly* advocate dispensing with concrete embodiment or limits. Indeed, Reinders explicitly insists that the new 'ecclesial being does not abandon the concreteness of the body, nor does it ignore concrete differences between bodies. Both aspects, concreteness and difference, are included in the transformation through the Eucharist.'[54] The problem, however, is that he does not provide an account of how this is the case. Reinders' basic emphasis on theosis and deification undermines, or at least sits in tension with, these more explicit affirmations of concrete bodily life.[55]

This leads to a second problem. If our ecstatic transformation draws us away from our concrete and embodied limits, then this has implications for the kind of ethics that proceeds from this anthropology. It has implications for how we understand our friendships with and responsibilities to others, including those with profound disabilities. If we are in relation to such persons primarily because we are together being drawn into communion with God, then the mission or ethics that proceeds from this is similarly directed to and by this ecstatic transformation. We recognize and attend to others not in terms of their natural and biological limits *per se*, but by looking beyond or behind these to who they truly are. My own worry, then, is that this means that Christian friendship is not directly determined by embodiment and concrete limitation. If Christian relationality and friendship are directed (ultimately) to the inner communion of the divine persons, it is unclear that this is a *necessarily* embodied and creaturely relationality or friendship.

Finally, this raises the question of whether a Trinitarian grounding of relational personhood leaves too much room for an idealization or romanticization of both disability and being friends with those with disabilities. If it is not inherently necessary to attend to embodiment and limitation as part of our friendships, would it not be easier to neglect or downplay the ways in which we continually encounter and experience concrete limitation through them? Does a Trinitarian approach allow us to neglect the necessarily limited and limiting nature of all human relationships? Could this lead us to neglect or downplay how such friendships limit us in ways that are often costly and painful?

To reiterate: my concern in this section is that theologically basing a relational anthropology on Triune persons and relations, and our own ecstatic transformation towards the communion of the Trinity, threatens to undermine or obfuscate the necessarily bodily and concrete nature of human relationality. And if such an anthropology provides a basis for an ethics of friendship, then it is similarly left unclear how this is an ethic that is necessarily attentive to what is concretely entailed by in our friendships. Rather than viewing the other human being in terms of their transformation away from concrete limits, we need an anthropology and ethics that more clearly places embodiment and concrete limitation at its centre.

Bonhoeffer and creaturely personhood

In this final section, I shall suggest that Bonhoeffer's theology – in particular his *Creation and Fall* – provides just such an anthropology. In his 'theological exposition of Genesis 1–3' from 1933, Bonhoeffer presents a rich and detailed account of human beings as created by God in relation to one another. At the same time, however, he avoids grounding this relationality in Triune persons and relations, more directly insisting on the limited and necessarily creaturely nature of human relationality. Furthermore, in this section I shall suggest that Bonhoeffer's *Ethics*, and especially his concepts of 'vicarious representative action' and 'responsibility', significantly take up and expand such a creaturely anthropology.

At the outset it is important to note the overlaps and resonances between Bonhoeffer's anthropology and the recent work on personhood in disability theology. In *Creation and Fall*, Bonhoeffer similarly provides an account of human beings as fundamentally relational, as well as insisting that this relationality is grounded in God *ab extra*. Bonhoeffer insists that God has created human beings in the *imago Dei* by setting them in relation to one another:

'God created them man and woman.' This means, he continues, that 'the human being is not alone. Human beings exist in duality, and it is in this *dependence on the other that their creatureliness consists*'.[56] In other words, human beings have their existence and being only as those who God has set in relation.

Bonhoeffer develops his account of this relational existence with the language of freedom. That God has created human beings as *imago Dei* means we are free for God and one another. Moreover, Bonhoeffer connects this freedom to our relationality directly. For human beings, he writes, 'being free means "being-free-for-the-other", because I am bound to the other. Only by being in relation with the other am I free.'[57] Human beings are truly free only in relation and in service to one another.

Bonhoeffer is also clear that this relational freedom is not to be understood as a human possession or capacity. When God sets us in relation to one another, he writes, this 'is not a human potential or possibility or a structure of human existence; instead it is a given relation, a relation in which human beings are set, a *justitia passiva!*'[58] Like Reinders, Bonhoeffer holds that to be created in the *imago Dei* does not mean to have a capacity for relationship. God sets us in relation prior to and more directly than can any ability or capacity to understand or realize this relation.

Nonetheless, while Bonhoeffer is in these ways similar to Reinders and other recent advocates of relational personhood, it is significant that he avoids grounding this relationality and freedom in a doctrine of the Trinity. Instead he maintains that we are created as relational and free in a more distinctly human way. When discussing human freedom, he insists that this is a distinctly '*created* freedom'.[59] That we are free in relation to the concrete other does not mean that we are free in the same sense that God is free.

Bonhoeffer further develops this difference between divine and creaturely freedom in his discussion of the '*analogia relationis*'. Our freedom, he writes, is not an '*anaologia entis,*' or something in us that is 'like God's being.' Rather, we are free like God only through the creaturely and bounded 'relation that God has established'.[60] We are 'in the image of God in being for God and neighbor, in its original creatureliness and limitedness'.[61] Accordingly, Bonhoeffer is clear that being in the image of God does not mean being free as God is free. It means simply reflecting and participating in God's own purposes in creating the free human being.

Moreover, Bonhoeffer claims that we are in the *imago Dei* as bodily beings bound to the earth. Humankind 'is the image of God not in spite of but precisely in its bodily nature. For in their bodily nature human beings are related to the earth and other bodies; they are there for others and dependent upon others.'[62] This stands in contrast to Zizioulas' (and Reinders') claim that being drawn towards the Trinity involves being drawn away from our natural and biological limits. Bonhoeffer explicitly affirms that 'human beings have their existence as existence on earth. They do not come from above; they have not by some cruel fate been driven into the world and been enslaved by it.'[63] Our existence is inextricably tied to the world and even our salvation and redemption restores us to our status as creatures of the world.

In *Creation and Fall*, Bonhoeffer develops his account of relational and bodily freedom in a detailed exposition of the second Genesis narrative. He describes Eve, for example, as 'the limit given to Adam in bodily form'.[64] Adam's existence is *for* Eve as his concrete other, and vice versa. Moreover, Bonhoeffer maintains that it is in terms of Eve as concrete limit that Adam is the recipient of God's grace: 'This very revelation of the limit in bodily form, in the love he has for the other person, would have brought Adam into an even deeper knowledge of the grace of the creator.'[65] It is only in relation to the concrete other as bodily limit that we encounter God's grace and goodness. We are human beings precisely in and through such concrete relations.

Again, there is an ethics entailed in this theological anthropology. If we are human beings or persons only as set in relation to a concrete other – and also in relation to the concrete other as embodied limit – then this too entails an opportunity for attending to and serving the other. As Bonhoeffer writes in his later *Ethics*: 'To live as a human being before God … can only mean to be there not for oneself, but for God and for other human beings.'[66] To live before God means that we do not have to pursue or secure our own meaning: we are free for God and free for serving the other.

One way that Bonhoeffer develops this claim in his *Ethics* is through his concepts of 'vicarious representative action' (*Stellvertretung*) and 'responsibility' (*Verantwortlichkeit*). To live as a human being before God means to follow Christ by acting for the other and in the place of the other. Our action and responsibility flows from and reflects Christ's prior action upon the cross. In other words, we are free to respond to and serve others because Christ has freed us from ourselves and for this other. As Bonhoeffer writes: 'Vicarious representative action and therefore responsibility is only possible in completely devoting one's life to another person.'[67] Christ frees us to respond and be responsible without expectation of reward or reciprocation.

The point here, however, is that we are not responsible for the other *per se* or in the abstract, but only for *this particular* other in his or her given situation: 'The attention of responsibility is directed to concrete neighbors in their concrete reality.'[68] We respond to the concrete neighbour as and where we encounter them, and not in terms of their *telos* towards something higher. At the same time, this means that being responsible involves attending to actual human beings and not the idea of a human being. For Bonhoeffer, 'God loves the world. Not an ideal human, but human beings as they are.'[69] With Christ, we do not embrace and serve others on the basis of what we think they should be or become, but simply as we find them.

This means that our action and responsibility for the other remains limited or bounded. Bonhoeffer states that 'action in accord with reality [in Christ] is limited by our *creatureliness*. We do not create the conditions for our action but find ourselves already placed within them ... Our responsibility is not infinite but limited.'[70] Our responsibility and service are limited in that they are defined and guided by creaturely limits.[71] As creatures we respond to and are responsible for the ones who God sets before us. Bernd Wannenwetsch also makes this point: 'every individual is to respond in his life at the very place in which he finds himself placed'.[72] Accordingly, Bonhoeffer writes that responsible action is not 'unbounded or frivolous [*übermütig*]', but 'creaturely and humble [*demütig*]'.[73] 'The transcendent', as he puts it in his later 'Outline for a Book', 'is not the infinite unattainable tasks, but the neighbor within reach in any given situation'.[74] We encounter God in our everyday tasks and responsibilities, not in terms of any ecstatic transformation out of or away from these.

To be clear, in both *Creation and Fall* and *Ethics* Bonhoeffer carefully insists on the impossibility of directly recognizing or positively responding to the other as limit after the fall. After Adam and Eve's fall into sin, we still experience the other as a concrete limit, but no longer as the means of God's grace unambiguously. Rather, in the concrete other we now primarily experience and encounter God's judgement and wrath: 'Adam has transgressed the boundary, and now hates his limit.'[75] With Adam, we strive to dominate and control this other who presents a limit and limits us: 'One thing is quite certain, namely that at the point where love for the other is obliterated, a human being can only hate the limit. A person then desires only, in an unbounded way, to possess the other or to destroy the other.'[76] While God continues to encounter us through the concrete other, we are no longer open to the other as God's Word. Instead we desire to live without limits and thus experience the limit of this other negatively.

This means that for Bonhoeffer any positive recognition or embrace of the other as limit is now possible only in Christ, and thus fully possible only eschatologically. Indeed, Bonhoeffer holds that we cannot even have knowledge of or access to creation or creaturely relationality apart from Christ.[77] This also means that all genuine human relationships and community are only possible as they are mediated by Christ. In *Life Together*, he writes that 'without Christ we would not know other Christians around us; nor could we approach them … Christ opened up the way to God and one another.'[78] We can now properly recognize the other creature as God's gift and grace only through the intervention and mediation of Christ.

However even when we recognize the other in Christ it is significant that we still do so as creatures: Life in Christ 'means to assume the place assigned to us as creatures,'[79] as Wannenwetsch puts it. In Christ, we are to embrace and attend to the other as a concrete and creaturely limit. This indicates that when Christ overcame sin and the fall, he did so in a way that re-established, rather than displaced or abolished, the creaturely limit that is integral to human beings and all human relationality. Bonhoeffer explicitly rejects the kind of deification or theosis that is central for Zizioulas' Trinitarian notion of personhood. As he writes in his *Ethics*, 'God changes God's form into human form in order that human beings can become, not God, but human before God.'[80] God's work in Christ restores and redeems fallen human beings to their status as creatures, that is, creatures set in relation to one other as concrete limit. Even more pointedly, he insists that 'human beings are not transformed into an alien form, the form of God, but into the form that belongs to them, that is essentially their own.'[81]

So what are the advantages of Bonhoeffer's insistence on the specifically creaturely form of our relationality and redemption? How can a theological anthropology and ethics that more clearly insists on the other as an embodied and concrete limit help us to better understand and negotiate our friendships and relationships with those with profound disabilities? First, Bonhoeffer's theology more clearly requires that we attend to the concrete situations and particular needs of our friends. As we have seen, God has created us by setting us in relation to a concrete and embodied other, which means that we are to attend to this other in his or her givenness. We are to attend to this other in terms of his or her specific limitations, not in terms of an ecstatic transformation away from these. 'The human being is a bodily being and remains so in eternity as well. Bodiliness and being human [*Menschsein*] belong indivisibly together.'[82]

Second, Bonhoeffer's firmer emphasis on the other as concrete limit allows for a clearer recognition of how our relationships with others, especially those with profound disabilities, are themselves limiting. Bonhoeffer's theology recognizes the pain that is inherent in all human relationships after the fall, which we cannot ourselves mitigate or overcome: 'What we shrink back from with pain and hostility, namely, real human beings, the real world, this is for God the ground of unfathomable love.'[83] After the fall, we inevitably try to control others and shrink back from them because of how they challenge and limit us. Bonhoeffer recognizes the deeply painful aspects of human community, and yet he does so without making this the final word: 'While we exert ourselves to grow beyond our humanity, to leave the human being behind us, God becomes human; we recognize that God wills that we be human, real human beings.'[84]

Finally, I would suggest that Bonhoeffer's theology provokes an understanding of our relationships and friendships that is more realistic and ultimately more sustainable. As we have seen, he maintains that God has indeed set us in relation to one another as a grace and blessing, but we no longer directly recognize or experience other people in this way. This is why our friendships and responsibility must be grounded in Christ, and not a recognition or embrace of the other directly or apart from Christ. 'Our living as real human beings, and loving the real people next to us is ... grounded only in God's becoming human, in the unfathomable love of God for us human beings.'[85] On our own terms we remain unable to recognize and respond to others in the ways that we should. While we may catch occasional glimpses of God's grace in the concrete other, this is more often the exception than the rule. Following Bonhoeffer, we hold in faith that Christ is present in the limit of the other even when we cannot recognize this to be the case. It is this kind of Christian friendship – grounded upon the other as concrete limit rather than in an anticipation of community in the Trinity – that better enables us to attend to others and improve their lives and situations over the long haul.

Conclusion

In this chapter I have claimed that the approach to theological anthropology and ethics displayed by Reinders and several other disability theologians provides an important alternative to dominant secular and cultural conceptions of personhood. A theological account of human being as both relational and gifted by God properly challenges and expands our understanding of what it means to be human. Moreover, this anthropology provides a basis for an ethics of hospitality and friendship. All of the theologians I have in mind are themselves deeply attentive to and engaged with the concrete situations of their friends in precisely the right ways.[86]

Nonetheless, I have expressed concerns with a tendency to both model human relational personhood on the Trinity directly and ground human personhood in terms of a teleological metaphysics. My basic concern is that this subtly undermines and displaces an ethics of friendship that attends to others in their concrete givenness. By modelling relational personhood and Christian friendship on the Trinity, Reinders, for example, potentially obfuscates how our relational personhood is constituted by the other as bodily limit.

In Bonhoeffer's theology we find resources for an anthropology and ethics that avoids this potential idealization or abstracting of the other. While Bonhoeffer similarly develops an account of relational personhood as gifted by God, his theology more clearly insists upon the concrete and embodied particularity of the other human being, and to the ways we are limited through such relationships. Ultimately, it is this creaturely anthropology, I would suggest, that can provide a better basis for attending to and actively caring for others, that is, for taking action and responsibility in the world.

Notes

1   Peter Singer, *Practical Ethics*, 2nd edn (Cambridge: Cambridge University Press, 1993), 86.

2   See ibid., 192.

3   Michael Tooley, *Abortion and Infanticide* (Oxford: Clarendon, 1983), 419–20.

4   Ibid., 421.

5   Ibid.

6   Hans Reinders, *Receiving the Gift of Friendship: Profound Disability, Theological Anthropology and Ethics* (Grand Rapids: Eerdmans, 2008), 8.

7   John Swinton, *Dementia: Living in the Memories of God* (Grand Rapids: Eerdmans, 2012), 110.

8   Reflecting on this, Gilbert Meilaender notes that, 'it has become common to define personhood in terms of certain capacities. To be a person one must be conscious, self-aware, productive.' Meilaender, *Bioethics: A Primer for Christians* (Grand Rapids: Eerdmans, 2005), 6.

9   James Mumford, *Ethics at the Beginning of Life* (Oxford University Press, 2013), 186.

10 Thomas Aquinas, *Summa Theologica,* I. 93.4.

11 J. Wentzel van Huyssteen, *Alone in the World: Human Uniqueness in Science and Theology* (Grand Rapids: Eerdmans, 2006), 134.

12 See Maurice Merleau-Ponty, *Phenomenology of Perception*, trans. Colin Smith (New York: Routledge, 2002), 202–34.

13 Amos Yong, *Theology and Down Syndrome: Reimagining Disability in Late Modernity* (Waco: Baylor University Press, 2007), 173.

14 Reinders, *Receiving the Gift of Friendship*, 229.

15 See Yong, *Theology and Down Syndrome*, 169–74.

16 Martin Buber, *I and Thou*, trans. Walter Kaufmann (Edinburgh: T&T Clark, 1970), 69.

17 Thomas Reynolds, *Vulnerable Communion: A Theology of Disability and Hospitality* (Grand Rapids: Brazos Press, 2008), 117.

18 Yong, *Theology and Down Syndrome*, 184.

19 Molly Haslam is an exception here. In a recent book she directly argues for grounding relationality primarily in inter-human reciprocity and mutuality. Molly Haslam, *A Constructive Theology of Intellectual Disability: Human Being as Mutuality and Response* (New York: Fordham University Press, 2012).

20 This approach could, however, conceivably still secure the significance of recognizing and caring for those with disabilities, insofar as this activity

contributes to the cultivation of one's own subjectivity or rationality. This is essentially Alasdair MacIntyre's position in *Dependent Rational Animals: Why Human Beings Need the Virtues* (Chicago: Open Court, 1999), 99–118.

21 Reinders, *Receiving the Gift of Friendship*, 252.

22 Ibid., 287.

23 Ibid., 314.

24 Ibid., 15.

25 Ibid., 355.

26 Reinders contrasts this Christian vision of friendship with the Aristotlean one, wherein friendships are governed by rationality and have a certain level of reciprocity. Ibid., 358–63.

27 Jürgen Moltmann, *The Trinity and the Kingdom: The Doctrine of God*, trans. Margret Kohl (London: SCM, 2000).

28 Colin Gunton, *The One, The Three and the Many* (Cambridge: Cambridge University Press, 1993).

29 Miroslav Volf, *Exclusion and Embrace: Theological Exploration of Identity, Otherness and Reconciliation* (Nashville: Abingdon Press, 1994).

30 Catherine LaCugna, *God For Us: The Trinity and Christian Life* (Chicago: HarperOne, 2000).

31 Patricia Wilson-Kastner, *Faith, Feminism and the Christ* (Philadelphia: Fortress, 1983).

32 Leonardo Boff, *Trinity and Society* (Maryknoll, NY: Orbis, 1988).

33 Stanley Grenz, *The Social God and Relational Self: A Trinitarian Theology of the Imago Dei* (Louisville: Westminster/John Knox, 2002).

34 Karen Kilby, 'Perichoresis and Project: Problems with Social Doctrines of the Trinity', *New Blackfriars* 81 (2000): 432–3.

35 John Swinton, *Dementia: Living in the Memories of God* (Grand Rapids: Eerdmans, 2012), 159, fn.10. Swinton writes that 'the inherently relational nature of human beings emerges from the nature and relational shape of the God in whose image they are created.' Ibid., 158.

36 Michael Hryniuk, *Theology, Disability and Spiritual Transformation: Learning from the Community of L'Arche* (Amherst, NY: Cambria Press, 2010), 247.

37 Ibid., 249.

38 Hans Reinders writes, 'my being as imago Dei is not to be taken ontologically as subsistent being, but as a relationship that is ecstatically grounded in God's loving kindness towards me.' Reinders, *Receiving the Gift of Friendship*, 273.

39 Ibid., 258.

40   John Zizioulas, *Being as Communion: Studies in Personhood and the Church* (London: Darton, Longman and Todd, 1985), 88.

41   Reinders, *Receiving the Gift of Friendship*, 274.

42   Zizioulas, *Being as Communion*, 122.

43   Reinders, *Receiving the Gift of Friendship*, 267.

44   Kathryn Tanner, 'Trinity, Christology, and Community', in *Christology and Ethics*, ed. F. LeRon Shults and Brent Waters (Grand Rapids, MI: Eerdmans, 2010), 65.

45   Ibid., 66.

46   Ibid., 65–9.

47   Zizioulas, *Being as Communion*, 49–65.

48   Ibid., 52.

49   John Zizioulas, 'On Being a Person: Towards an Ontology of Personhood', in *Persons, Divine and Human*, ed. Christoph Schwöbel and Colin E. Gunton (Edinburgh: T&T Clark, 1992), 44.

50   Reinders, *Receiving the Gift of Friendship*, 368.

51   Hryniuk, *Theology, Disability and Spiritual Transformation*, 265.

52   Douglas Farrow, 'Person and Nature: The Necessity-Freedom Dialectic in John Zizioulas', in *The Theology of John Zizioulas: Personhood and the Church*, ed. Douglas Knight (Burlington, VT: Ashgate, 2007), 111.

53   One of the main claims of disability studies during recent decades is precisely that disability is constitutive of identity. See, for example, Simi Linton, *Claiming Disability: Knowledge and Identity* (New York: New York University Press, 1998).

54   Reinders, *Receiving the Gift of Friendship*, 263.

55   It is significant that this language is largely absent from Reinders' more recent book. Here Reinders draws more heavily upon Calvin, which leads to a clearer distinction between Creator and creature and avoids the kinds of problems that can result from a Trinitarian metaphysics. Hans Reinders, *Disability, Providence and Ethics* (Waco: Baylor University Press, 2014), 145–56.

56   *DBWE* 3, 64.

57   Ibid., 63.

58   Ibid., 65.

59   Ibid., 64. Bonhoeffer frames this as a question: 'In what way does the freedom of the Creator differ from the freedom of that which is created?' Ibid.

60   Ibid., 65.

61   Ibid., 113.

62   Ibid. As Bernd Wannenwetsch notes, 'it is precisely as bodily beings that humans experience their mutual dependency, both in the most pleasurable and

the most painful way.' Bernd Wannenwetsch, 'Angels with Clipped Wings: The Disabled as Key to the Recognition of Personhood,' in *Theology, Disability and the New Genetics: Why Science Needs the Church*, ed. John Swinton and Brian Brock (London: T&T Clark, 2007), 189.

63 *DBWE* 3, 77. Bonhoeffer writes that, 'humanity is derived from a piece of the earth … From it human beings have their *bodies*.' Ibid., 76.

64 Ibid., 122.

65 Ibid., 118.

66 *DBWE* 6, 400.

67 Ibid., 259.

68 Ibid.

69 Ibid., 84.

70 *DBWE* 6, 267.

71 As Paul makes this point in Ephesians, 'we are what he has made us, created in Christ Jesus for good works, which God prepared beforehand to be our way of life.' Eph. 2.10.

72 Bernd Wannenwetsch, 'Responsible Living' or 'Responsible Self'? Bonhoefferian Reflections on a Vexed Moral Notion,' *Studies in Christian Ethics* 18:3 (2005): 131.

73 *DBWE* 6, 269.

74 *DBWE* 8, 501.

75 *DBWE* 3, 127.

76 Ibid., 99.

77 'It is because we know of the resurrection that we know of God's creation in the beginning, of God's creating out of nothing.' *DBWE* 3, 35.

78 *DBWE* 5, 33.

79 Bernd Wannenwetsch, 'Christians and Pagans: Towards a Trans-Religious Second Naiveté or How to be a Christological Creature,' in *Who Am I? Bonhoeffer's Theology through his Poetry*, ed. Bernd Wannenwetsch (London: T&T Clark, 2009), 190.

80 *DBWE* 6, 96.

81 Ibid.

82 Ibid.

83 Ibid., 84.

84 Ibid.

85 Ibid., 87.

86 For Reinders, this is apparent through his rich descriptions of his own friendships and engagements with Kelly and Ronald. Reinders, *Receiving the*

Gift of Friendship, 19–23, 354–6. Also see his extraordinary rich and concrete discussions in the chapter 'Stories we Live By', *Disability, Providence, and Ethics* (Waco: Baylor University Press, 2012), 167–90.

Chapter 8

BONHOEFFER'S TWO-KINGDOMS THINKING IN 'THE CHURCH AND THE JEWISH QUESTION'

Michael P. DeJonge

'The Church and the Jewish Question', published in June 1933, is one of Bonhoeffer's most discussed and controversial writings. As Kenneth Barnes puts it, 'This short essay has been perhaps the most scrutinized, by both his hagiographers, who wish to find in this essay the basis of a strong defence of the Jews, and his detractors, who find the essay anti-Jewish. These varying assessments are possible because Bonhoeffer contradicts himself throughout the essay.'[1] One place where the essay contradicts itself, Barnes details, is on the issue of church action against the state. 'For each argument for church action,' he writes, Bonhoeffer 'presented a counter-argument which invalidated that action.'[2]

On the issue of church action, I argue, 'The Church and the Jewish Question' is in fact entirely consistent. Seeing this requires recognizing something about the essay that is too little discussed: the essay is driven by the logic of the two kingdoms, that Lutheran way of understanding God's action in two dimensions of life, the spiritual and temporal. 'The Church and the Jewish Question' is virtually incomprehensible without the logic of the two kingdoms in mind, and with this logic in mind it is consistent at least on the issue of church action towards the state. I demonstrate this by presenting the relevant aspects of Lutheran two-kingdoms thinking before interpreting Bonhoeffer's essay in light of them. After doing so, I suggest one implication of such an analysis, namely that more attention should be given to the Lutheran background for Bonhoeffer's resistance[3] to the state.

Luther's two kingdoms

I want to present Luther's thinking about the spiritual and temporal kingdoms by beginning with the centre of his thinking, justification by grace alone through faith alone. Before doing this, though, I need to clarify the terms 'law' and 'gospel', which are closely related to Luther's understanding of both justification and the two kingdoms, and which are so important in Bonhoeffer's 'The Church and the Jewish Question'.

Broadly speaking, the law for Luther is the demand God places on human beings.[4] In Luther's thinking, the law has two purposes or uses. The first use of the law is to restrain sin. Although the restraint of sin is part of the individual Christian's life as well,[5] this first use of the law is sometimes called the civic use because God tasks civic or temporal rulers with restraining sin in society. The second purpose of the law, often called the spiritual or theological use, is to lead sinners to despair at their inability to fulfil God's demands. Such despair is necessary for hearing the message of the gospel, namely that Christ has fulfilled the law's demands for us.

With this we arrive at the 'gospel', which also requires clarification. In short, the gospel is the message concerning Christ, especially his redemptive activity.[6] It is necessary, though, to recognize that there is in Lutheran thinking a narrow and broad sense of 'gospel'. Mary Jane Haemig summarizes this nicely: '"Gospel" can be used in two senses. When "gospel" is used to designate the entire Christian message, the term includes both the proclamation of repentance (law) and the forgiveness of sins. When "gospel" is opposed to law, the term is limited to the proclamation of the forgiveness of sins and reconciliation with God.'[7] As we will see, interpreting 'The Church and the Jewish Question' requires attention to both the narrow and broad sense of the gospel.

With this background in mind, an examination of the place of the two kingdoms in Luther's thinking can begin with the centre of this thought, justification by grace alone through faith alone.[8] The believer becomes righteous before God through God's grace rather than any human merit, and this grace is received in faith rather than earned through good works. This, said Luther, is 'the central article of our teaching', 'the sun, the day, the light of the church'.[9]

Justification is necessary since humans are in a sinful state. Luther speaks of sin in many ways, but one way he talks about it is in terms of self-justification.[10]

This is the attempt to be like God, the delusion that we can perform the work that only God performs. In other words, we think that we can earn our righteousness, that we can justify ourselves. Or if we are not quite so grandiose, we might think that we can at least get started along the way towards righteousness, with God providing grace when we falter. In this way, the sinful state from which God redeems sinners can be described as one of self-justification.

Given the character of sin as self-justification, Luther's doctrine of justification cannot be separated from his notion of law and gospel. The sinful presupposition that we can earn favour from God needs to be discredited. In Luther's terms, it needs to die. Here the theological use of the law goes to work. By presenting an unattainable standard of holiness, the law makes us despair of our own ability.[11] The law leads the sinner into despair, into the realization that nothing in her can earn favour from God. Only when the law (in its theological use) leads the sinner to despair at his own ability is he prepared to truly hear the promise of justification (the gospel in the narrow sense). In this way, justification is necessarily connected to law and gospel.

Law and gospel, then, belong together but must always be distinguished. Failing either to relate or distinguish them means the message of justification cannot be heard. On the one hand, law and gospel belong together. If the law is not preached, justification will not be heard for what it really is, a totally gracious, unmerited gift. On the other hand, law and gospel must not be confused. The law is not the gospel and the gospel is not the law. To treat the law as the path to righteousness confuses it with the gospel. Similarly, treating the gospel as a task confuses it with the law, undermining the very character of the gospel as something freely received rather than earned. While justification is the centre of Luther's thinking, distinguishing between the law and gospel is theology's central task. As Luther said, what makes a real theologian is the ability to distinguish between law and gospel.[12]

The believer who has heard the gospel is simultaneously justified and a sinner (*simul justus et peccator*), and in two senses. This is so, first, because the righteousness of the believer is 'alien righteousness'; it is Christ's own righteousness that, depending on the interpretation of Luther, is counted as or becomes one's own.[13] Paradoxically, because the believer's righteousness is Christ's, the believer remains sinner. This should not be interpreted to mean that, for Luther, the believer does not really becomes more righteous. As

Luther never tires of saying, 'It is impossible for [faith] not to be doing good works incessantly.'[14] The believer, on the basis of Christ's alien righteousness, increases in 'proper righteousness'.[15] But because this proper righteousness is not perfected in this life, the believer remains always sinful. Thus there emerges a second sense of *simul justus et peccator*, less paradoxical than temporal.[16] The believer increases in proper righteousness but does not reach perfection. In these two ways, the one who is justified is simultaneously sinner and saint.

Having begun with justification we now arrive at the issue of the two kingdoms. And, in fact, all of the foregoing can be translated into that language. The temporal kingdom is the place where non-believers are restrained from sin and impelled towards good works. Here the restraining use of the law is at work. In the preaching of the gospel, an activity of the spiritual kingdom, the law works theologically to convict persons of their sin. For those who despair of their own ability and throw themselves into the arms of Christ, there is justification. But because justification creates a *simul* situation, the believer is a citizen of both worlds, the spiritual and the temporal. The believer stands side by side with the unbeliever under the law, which believers fulfil by virtue of faith (insofar as they are righteous) and by compulsion (insofar as they are sinners). Thus the centre of Luther's theology, justification, is intimately connected with the two kingdoms.

Although the above has been presented from the perspective of the believer, it is crucial to note that Luther's thinking about the two kingdoms, like his theology as a whole, is focused on God's action. Luther's two-kingdoms thinking is theological rather than anthropological or ethical or political. The two kingdoms are ultimately about the twofold way that God preserves the sinful world from falling into unfettered chaos while ushering it towards redemption.[17] God preserves the world through the law and redeems the world through Christ's work preached in the gospel.

Church and state from a Lutheran confessional perspective

Because the two kingdoms are interwoven into Luther's theology as a whole, and because Luther was a theologian rather than a political theorist, his two-kingdoms thinking is not primarily about the relationship of church and state. Nonetheless, it clearly has implications for church-state issues, which were taken up and formalised in the Lutheran confessional documents. Similarly, while Bonhoeffer's two-kingdoms thinking always radiates outward from the centre of his thinking (Christ present in the church-community), his explicit use of two-kingdoms language often comes in the context of discussing church–state issues. For that reason, it is necessary to look at the impact of Luther's two-kingdoms thinking on confessional Lutheranism's conceptions of church and state.

According to the Lutheran confessional perspective,[18] the church is 'the assembly of all believers among whom the gospel is purely preached and the holy sacraments are administered according to the gospel'.[19] Following Luther's claim that God's word cannot be without God's people and God's people cannot be without God's word,[20] the church is defined here from a twofold perspective as: 1) the assembly of people among whom 2) God is active in preaching and administration of sacraments. In shorthand, the church is the assembly where the gospel is preached and heard.

The church is defined, then, in terms of the gospel. But here it is necessary to keep both senses of gospel in mind. Yes, the church preaches the gospel in the narrow sense – the message that the believer is justified by faith through God's gracious work in Christ. But preaching the gospel in the narrow sense also requires preaching the law in its theological use; only if sinners despair of their own ability to fulfil the law will they recognize and accept Christ's gracious work. To say that preaching the gospel in the narrow sense requires also preaching the law is another way of saying that the church preaches the gospel in the broad sense. Thus when the church is defined in terms of the gospel, both senses of the gospel are at work. The importance of defining the church in terms of the gospel's broad sense is that this further defines the church as the custodian of the distinction between law and gospel.[21] The church is the place where the relationship between law and gospel is understood.

One more thing about the church. Notice that saying the church is the assembly where the gospel is preached and heard means the church is defined functionally rather than institutionally. This is not an institutional definition of the church where, as in some Catholic ways of thinking, the church is the church because it can trace its lineage back to Peter, the first pope. Rather, the church is the church because something happens there, namely the preaching and hearing of the gospel. The functional definition of the church means the church stops being the church if it stops preaching and hearing the gospel.

Now onto the state. The Lutheran confessional perspective defines the state, too, in terms of its function. '[I]t is taught that all authority, orderly government, laws, and good order in the world are instituted by God.'[22] Temporal authority's divinely given task is to uphold the law (in its civic or first use) to combat the chaotic effects of sin. On the Lutheran confessional view, the state has a high but limited status. Its status is high because its task is divine. As God tasks the church with preaching the gospel, so God tasks the state with upholding the law. In this way, the state's temporal authority is of equal status to the church's spiritual authority. The state's status is limited, however, since it answers to God and God's law. Its status is also limited because, like the church, the state is defined functionally rather than institutionally. Thus just as the church stops being church when the gospel is no longer preached and heard, so the state stops being state when it fails to uphold the law.

The relationship of church and state on this view, then, is co-operative. They differ as to function and mode of rule; the church preaches the gospel by the word while the state maintains the law through the sword. But they each play a role in God's redemptive action. God preserves the world from chaos through the state while redeeming it through the gospel preached by the church. State and church co-operate by performing their distinct tasks.

As with the two kingdoms in general, the concepts of church and state relate directly to the central concern of the Lutheran tradition: justification and the closely related distinction between law and gospel. The church preaches the gospel (in the broad sense) and the state maintains the law (in its first use). In order for the gospel to be heard, these two tasks must be properly co-ordinated. What is ultimately at stake in the relationship of church and state, as with the relationship of the two kingdoms in general, is the relationship of law and gospel and with it the purity of the gospel message. As we will see, the preaching and hearing of the gospel is the driving concern of 'The Church and the Jewish Question' as well.

'The Church and the Jewish Question'

Bonhoeffer wrote 'The Church and the Jewish Question' in response to 'the Aryan paragraph', a law excluding Jews from various organizations and professions, and in reaction to the perceived threat that similar legislation preventing the participation of ethnic Jews in Christian churches was on its way. As Bonhoeffer puts it in the essay's introduction, such legislation raises two questions for the church. The first question has to do with the church's relationship to the state: 'How does the church judge this action by the state, and what is the church called upon to do about it?' The second question is more of an internal church issue, namely 'What are the consequences for the church's position towards the baptized Jews in its congregations?'[23] The two sections of the essay correspond to these two questions, so I will be discussing primarily the first half of the essay.

Immediately after raising these two questions, Bonhoeffer states, 'Both these questions can only be answered on the basis of the right concept of the church.'[24] Much of the essay, therefore, is about developing the right concept of the church, which in turn forms the basis for how the church should respond to the state's action against Jews.

Bonhoeffer's initial response to the first question, about how the church should respond to the state's action, is, 'There is no doubt that the church of the Reformation is not encouraged to get involved directly in specific political actions of the state. The church has neither to praise nor to censure the laws of the state.'[25] 'Even on the Jewish question today, the church cannot contradict the state *directly* and demand that it take any particular different course of action.'[26] Bonhoeffer argues that it is not the church's task to advocate for or against particular policy decisions.

The reason for this restraint is the concept of the church: the 'true church of Christ … lives by the gospel alone'.[27] Thus Bonhoeffer, following the Lutheran tradition, defines the church as the community whose power rests in the preaching of the gospel. In defining the church in terms of the 'gospel alone', Bonhoeffer draws distinctions between the church and two other institutions.

On the one side, the church is not the state. It is the state's mandate to maintain order, and it does so by 'creating law and order by force'.[28] So, consistent with the Lutheran tradition, the state preserves the world through law and order, and the church preaches the gospel. If the church were to focus on advocating this or that policy position, it would risk abandoning its own task for the state's. Put otherwise, if the church were to see its task as advocating policy positions, it would risk turning the gospel into law, thereby undermining the gospel. So that the church can preach the gospel, the church should recognize that its task differs from the state's.

On the other side, Bonhoeffer defines the church against ethical or humanitarian organizations. While Bonhoeffer discourages the church from speaking out on particular actions of the state, he encourages humanitarian organizations (and individual Christians) to do so, 'to accuse the state of offenses against morality'.[29] But this moral activism is not generally the task of the church. For Bonhoeffer as for Luther, the gospel message of justification cannot but generate moral actions, but the church stands or falls not with ethics but with the gospel. It is the preaching of the gospel that distinguishes the true from the false church, and it is the preaching of the gospel that distinguishes the church from a humanitarian organization.[30] If the church speaks on every unjust action of the state, it ceases to become the church and becomes a humanitarian organization.

Driving Bonhoeffer's claim that the church 'is not encouraged to get involved directly in specific political actions', then, is his concept of the church defined by the preaching of the gospel. The preaching of the gospel in its purity requires distinguishing it from the law. The particular policies advocated by the state, as well as the objections to it by individuals and humanitarian organizations, are matters of the law, from which the church should generally keep its distance for the sake of the purity of the gospel.

Now we arrive at the most important distinction for reading the essay, the hinge on which the argument turns. This distinction can be put in several ways. One way to put it is in terms of state and law, namely to distinguish between the *content* and the *purpose* of the law. The state's mandate is to uphold the law in its first, 'civic' use. The state has access to the content of the law, so defined, through reason and without the aid of the church.[31] The state knows without the church's help that, for instance, murder is unlawful. While the state knows the content of the law, it does not know the greater purpose of the law in God's plan, namely that the law (in its first use) restrains sin for the sake of redemption and (in its second use) convicts of sin. These purposes of the law are not accessible to reason and therefore are not known by the state without the aid of the church. The state knows the content of the law but not its purpose.

Another way of putting this same point is in terms of the church and the gospel, namely the distinction between the narrow and broad senses of the gospel. Bonhoeffer's definition of the church in terms of the 'gospel alone' means, given the narrow sense of gospel, that the church does not under normal circumstances directly concern itself with the state's enforcement of the law in its first use. But Bonhoeffer's definition of the church in terms of 'gospel alone' also means, given the broad sense of the gospel, that the church is the guardian of the distinction between law and gospel. This distinction between the narrow and broad sense of the gospel maps onto the previous distinction between the content and purpose of the law. The gospel in the narrow sense means that the church, under normal circumstances, leaves the state to deal with issues of the content of the law, but the gospel in the broad sense means the church vigilantly watches over issues related to the state and the purpose of the law. Given the broad and narrow sense of gospel in the Lutheran tradition, Bonhoeffer's concept of the church, which is the centre of this essay, must be read in these two senses.

A third way of putting this same distinction, and the one that is most explicit in the essay itself, is the distinction between the state's action and the state's character (*Staatlichkeit*). While this distinction is difficult to discern in practice, an issue to which I return, Bonhoeffer asserts the importance of recognizing that judging a particular action of the state is something different from judging the character of the state itself. This way of expressing the distinction maps onto the previous two. On the one side are particular state actions, which are about the content of the law in its first use, which fall out of the purview of the gospel in the narrow sense; this has to do with *how* the state fulfils its mandate. On the other side of the distinction is the character of the state itself, which has to do with the purpose of the law, which falls within the purview of the gospel in the broad sense; this has to do with *whether* the state fulfils its mandate.

This distinction, variously expressed, is the hinge of Bonhoeffer's argument, for on the issue of *how* the state fulfils its mandate the church should generally be silent, but on the issue of *whether* the state fulfils its mandate the church has the divine obligation to speak. Here is the passage where Bonhoeffer's argument turns on this hinge. Having discouraged the church from direct political action on particular state policies, Bonhoeffer goes on to say, this

> does not mean that the church stands aside, indifferent to what political action is taken. Instead, it can and must, precisely because it does not moralize about individual cases, keep asking the government whether its actions can be justified as *legitimate state* actions, that is, actions that create law and order, not lack of rights and disorder. It will be called upon to put this question as strongly as possible wherever the state seems endangered precisely in its *character as the state* [Staatlichkeit], that is, in its function of creating law and order by force. The church will have to put this question with the utmost clarity today in the matter of the Jewish question.[32]

The church speaks out against the state not in response to particular actions but on the question of the state's character as the institution entrusted by God with the mandate to maintain law and order. The church speaks in such cases because it alone knows the true distinction between law and gospel, the true purpose of the law as that which preserves the world towards Christ, and therefore the true nature of the state.

Bonhoeffer goes on to provide the criteria for adjudicating the character of the state. The church is compelled to speak, he says, when the state fails to fulfil its mandate by ceasing to maintain law and order. 'Either *too little* law and order or *too much* law and order compels the church to speak.' As an example of too little law and order, Bonhoeffer discusses the case where 'a group of people is deprived of it rights'.[33] As an example of too much law and order, Bonhoeffer imagines a situation where the state dictates to the church the exclusion of baptized ethnic Jews from its communion.[34] Such a case of too much law and order, he says, 'would mean the state developing its use of force to such a degree as to rob the Christian faith of its right to proclaim its message'.[35] Then the 'church must repudiate such an encroachment by the state authorities, precisely because it knows better about the state and the limits of its actions'.[36] Thus the church must speak against the state in cases where the state fails to maintain law and order, either through too little or too much. The church speaks when the state risks ceasing to be the state.

Therefore Bonhoeffer's entire argument about church action towards the state – from the prohibition of resistance on particular state actions to the incitement to resistance on the state's character – develops within the logic of his two-kingdoms thinking that works from the concept of the church outward. The church is defined by the gospel, in both the narrow and broad senses. For the sake of the purity of the gospel message as reconciliation with God apart from works of the law, the church refrains from criticizing the state's particular acts of law-making and law-enforcement. Here the law and gospel distinction generates the distinction between the two kingdoms and the distinction between church and state. But the law and gospel are also a unity, the co-ordinated, twofold mode of God's action in the world. The church's custodianship of the relation between law and gospel means it speaks against the state on issues of the state's character, 'precisely because it knows better about the state and the limits of its actions'.[37] The church speaks out in two kinds of cases: when the state abandons its mandate (too little order) and when the state oversteps its mandate and encroaches on the church's (too much). The entire argument, including the call for the church to resist the state, is governed by two-kingdoms thinking.[38]

When 'The Church and the Jewish Question' is read with the logic of the two kingdoms in mind, some of its apparent contradictions dissolve. As mentioned above, Kenneth Barnes argues that 'the force of Bonhoeffer's argument cancels itself out by his contradictory presentation. For each argument for church action he presented a counter-argument which invali-dated that action.' Barnes attributes these contradictions to his 'sheltered, upper-middle-class, Lutheran milieu', 'his penchant for language obscured by theological abstractions' and his youth.[39] There is no need, however, to point to Bonhoeffer's rearing, obscurantism or youth to explain his position. His position on church action in 'The Church and the Jewish Question' is a consistent construal of the Lutheran two kingdoms (which Barnes mentions but does not pursue), one the young Bonhoeffer maintained until his death.

Here is one instance where Barnes thinks Bonhoeffer's call for church action is invalidated by a counter argument: 'While on the one hand he called for the church to question Nazi policies aimed at Jews as to whether they fulfilled the state's role as an order of preservation, and even suggested the church might actively resist such state policies, elsewhere in his essay he had forbidden the church to speak or act in such a way.'[40] This is only an apparent contradiction; Bonhoeffer discourages one form of church action while encouraging another. Where Bonhoeffer 'had forbidden the church to speak', his concern was with the church taking issue with a particular state action.[41] Where he questioned the state on the basis of its treatment of the Jews, his concern was the character of the state.

This is not a contradiction so much as an expression of the admittedly difficult distinction between a state's actions and a state's character. When does the state's unjust treatment of Jews cease to be a particular action on which the church remains silent and become a sign of the state's character that compels church condemnation? As Bonhoeffer himself admits, 'in concrete cases it will always be extraordinarily difficult to distinguish actual deprivation of rights from a formally permitted minimum of rights'.[42] This is a difficulty inherent in the two-kingdoms position itself, which asserts, as a contemporary exponent puts it, that 'a line (admittedly not always easily discernible) exists between admonishing the government to do its job as laid out in the Lutheran understanding of government and advocating for specific policy prescriptions'.[43] What Barnes points to is less a contradiction than a tension or difficulty, and one that arises out of the two-kingdoms framework Bonhoeffer adopts.

This difficulty of determining when a question of state action becomes a question of state character is, from the perspective of the two-kingdoms tradition, necessary since the alternatives are worse. One alternative would be that the church never speaks against the state, either by being apolitical or entirely subservient to the state. In two-kingdoms language, this would either entirely separate the two kingdoms or subordinate the spiritual to the temporal. The other alternative would be to involve the church intimately in temporal affairs. This would confuse the kingdoms, as Bonhoeffer thinks is characteristic of medieval Catholicism, the social gospel and spiritualist theocracy. Bonhoeffer, with the Lutheran tradition, resists both these alternatives. This means he, like the tradition, must wrestle with the difficult distinction between state actions and state character.

Reading 'The Church and the Jewish Question' in this way with two-kingdoms thinking in mind shows that its apparent contradictions on church action towards the state are not contradictions at all. They are better described as difficulties that arise from a consistent and coherent interpretation of Lutheran two-kingdoms thinking, difficulties that the Lutheran tradition has been willing to accept as the logical consequence of protecting its central concern, the preaching and hearing of the gospel.

A theological rationale for resistance

As a way of transitioning to the implications this reading of 'The Church and the Jewish Question' has for thinking about Bonhoeffer's resistance, I briefly raise the issue of Bonhoeffer's discussion of Jews. Clearly, the topic of the Jews is central to this essay since it is the state's ill treatment of ethnic Jews that raises the essay's first question, about church action towards the state, and it is the increasingly tenuous status of baptized Jews in the church that raises its second question.

Appropriately, Bonhoeffer's discussions of Jews in this essay have drawn much attention from the scholarship. These passages have been central for trying to understand Bonhoeffer's attitudes and beliefs regarding Jews as well as the value of his theology after the Holocaust. As the quotation from Barnes at the opening of this chapter indicates, Bonhoeffer's 'hagiographers' have found here 'a strong defense of the Jews' while 'his detractors' have found 'the essay anti-Jewish'.

My concern here is not to weigh in on what these passages say directly about Bonhoeffer's attitudes towards Jews. Rather, I want to make the point that the discussions of Jews in this essay do not fundamentally alter the argument-analysis above. This is because Bonhoeffer's various discussions of Jews are governed by those same concerns that govern his discussion of the state, namely, the preaching of the gospel and the closely tied issues of the relationship between law and gospel and the relationship between the two kingdoms. Thus Bonhoeffer discusses the state's mistreatment of Jews as a case for discerning whether the state is maintaining too little order. Similarly, he discusses a situation in which the state would dictate the church membership status of Jews as an instance where the state maintains too much order by encroaching on the church's mandate.[44] And when Bonhoeffer discusses, in the second half of the essay, the intra-ecclesial issue of how the church should treat its ethnically Jewish members, his driving concern is the proper relationship of law and gospel, namely that the law of racial status not become a precondition for hearing the gospel.[45] Regardless of how one evaluates Bonhoeffer's discussions of Jews in this essay, those various discussions find their place within the structure of the argument as outlined above. That is, Bonhoeffer's discussions of Jews are governed by his primary concern of the gospel and the closely related issues of law and gospel and the two kingdoms.

I want to conclude by connecting what I have said so far to the broader issue of Bonhoeffer's resistance to the Nazi state. What does the above analysis of 'The Church and the Jewish Question' tell us about Bonhoeffer's theological rationale for resistance to the Nazi state?

Since the early 1980s, it has been common to locate the motivation or rationale for Bonhoeffer's resistance in his reaction to the ill treatment of Jews. Influential here is a lecture published in 1982 by Ebergard Bethge, Bonhoeffer's close friend, biographer, and leading interpreter, where it is argued that 'there is no doubt that Bonhoeffer's primary motivation for entering active political conspiracy was the treatment of Jews by the Third Reich'. This path into conspiracy, continues Bethge, 'started with the political laws of March 1933 which destroyed all civil liberties'.[46] Here Bethge traces Bonhoeffer's resistance back to, among other laws, the Aryan paragraph that was the immediate occasion for 'The Church and the Jewish Question'. Bethge's position that Bonhoeffer's primary motivation in resistance and conspiracy was the treatment of Jews has been adopted by the majority of scholars.[47]

This consensus is deteriorating, however. Stephen Haynes's *The Bonhoeffer Legacy* has challenged especially Bethge's claims that Bonhoeffer's theology provides a promising foundation for Jewish-Christian reconciliation after the Holocaust. In the process he casts serious doubt on the idea that Bonhoeffer's resistance was motivated by the plight of Jews. Haynes' work is invaluable, and it is especially good in its rhetorical analysis, showing the degree to which Bonhoeffer's writings in general and 'The Church and the Jewish Question' in particular trade in anti-Jewish and anti-Semitic rhetoric. What Haynes does not do is provide an alternative account of Bonhoeffer's theological rationale for resistance.[48]

On this count, the work of Victoria Barnett has been important.[49] Largely in agreement with Haynes, Barnett argues that neither Bonhoeffer's rationale for resistance nor his significance for post-Holocaust theology can be located definitively in his concern for Jews. She goes beyond Haynes, however, in arguing, as my own analysis above implies, that the issue of state legitimacy was for Bonhoeffer a driving concern. In her work, then, she has suggested an alternative to the consensus initiated by Bethge.

What Barnett misses, however, is how Bonhoeffer's thinking about state legitimacy was deeply informed by the Lutheran tradition. In her discussion of 'The Church and the Jewish Question', she notes that the essay begins with traditional Lutheran teachings about church and state. She continues by saying the essay 'at the same time offers a radical revision of Lutheran teachings about obedience to state authority by setting the criteria for establishing when Christians can oppose illegitimate state authority'.[50] Like many readers of the essay, she sees Bonhoeffer's call for church restraint with regard to the state as informed by the Lutheran tradition but his call for resistance as moving beyond that tradition. This is of course in direct contrast to the thesis I advance, that both Bonhoeffer's caution against *and* incitement towards church action against the state draw from the Lutheran tradition, specifically its two-kingdoms thinking.

Informing judgements like Barnett's, it seems, are two related scholarly commonplaces that cannot withstand scrutiny. The first is that the Lutheran tradition emphasizes subservience to political authorities and therefore lacks the resources for resistance. William Shirer's *The Rise and Fall of the Third Reich: A History of Nazi Germany*, initially published in 1960 and reprinted repeatedly, popularly perpetuated the stereotype of 'Luther as a preacher of quietism in the face of absolute authority and as a supporter of the ruler's right to wield the sword with brute force'.[51] In academic theological circles, particularly in the English-speaking world, the portrayal of Luther has often been only slightly more nuanced. Reinhold Niebuhr influentially disseminated to a generation of scholars and seminarians an image of Lutheran social ethics as 'defeatist',[52] 'quietest'[53] and excessively deferential to the state.[54]

But this idea that Luther was, and Lutheran social ethics necessarily are, deferential to the state simply cannot be maintained in light of textual and historical evidence. As the analysis above shows, two-kingdoms thinking includes within it at least an implicit logic of resistance since the state's authority is defined functionally and is limited by the authority of the church. The state should be disobeyed or resisted, then, when it either fails to fulfil its mandate (Bonhoeffer's *'too little* law and order') or encroaches on the mandate of the church (Bonhoeffer's *'too much* law and order'). Moreover, Lutherans have historically developed this implicit logic into explicit theories of resistance, most notably in the Magdeburg Confession of 1550.[55] As has been widely accepted for several decades among political historians of the early modern era, Western theories of resistance developed first on Lutheran soil before being exported to Calvinists.[56] The Lutheran tradition has ample resources for urging resistance to the state.

The second scholarly commonplace that hides Bonhoeffer's reliance on the resistance resources of the Lutheran tradition is the idea that Bonhoeffer rejects Lutheran two-kingdoms thinking. Clifford Green, for example, has made this argument both in his classic book *Bonhoeffer: A Theology of Sociality*[57] as well as in the introduction to the scholarly edition of Bonhoeffer's *Ethics*.[58] Stanley Hauerwas, too, has argued that Bonhoeffer's political ethics are 'expressed primarily by his critique and attempt to find an alternative to the traditional Lutheran doctrine of the two kingdoms'.[59] One even reads in the editor's introduction to Heinrich Bornkamm's helpful little book, *Luther's Doctrine of the Two Kingdoms in the Context of His Theology*, that Bonhoeffer 'condemned the doctrine as the source of a hopeless defeatism and dualism'.[60]

But this claim, too, cannot hold up under critical scrutiny. As I argue in a book-in-progress, two-kingdoms thinking is deeply embedded in Bonhoeffer's thinking through the end of his career. Realizing this is necessary for the proper interpretation of a number of Bonhoeffer's writings, including, as I hope to have shown here, 'The Church and the Jewish Question'.

The idea that the Lutheran tradition lacks resources for resistance and the idea that Bonhoeffer did not think in terms of the two kingdoms work together to hide the ways that he draws on the Lutheran tradition to justify resistance to the state. Returning to Barnett's judgement, the issue from 'The Church and the Jewish Question' that she singles out as a radical revision of the Lutheran tradition about obedience to the state is Bonhoeffer's articulation of 'criteria for establishing when Christians can oppose illegitimate state authority'.[61] But on this count Bonhoeffer is on solid Lutheran footing. In fact, in offering his criteria of 'too much' and 'too little', Bonhoeffer perhaps even alludes to the *locus classicus* of two-kingdoms thinking, Luther's own essay, 'Temporal Authority'. There Luther writes:

We must now learn how far [temporal authority's] arm extends and how widely its hand stretches, lest it extend too far and encroach upon God's kingdom and government. It is essential for us to know this, for where it is given too wide a scope, intolerable and terrible injury follows; on the other hand, injury is also inevitable where it is restricted too narrowly. In the former case, the temporal authority punishes *too much*; in the latter case, it punishes *too little*.[62]

Barnett is right to direct attention away from Bonhoeffer's attitudes towards Jews and towards his understanding of the state when investigating his rationale for resistance and conspiracy. In this she offers what may well become the new consensus. What I would like to add is that exploration of Bonhoeffer's resistance will need to take more seriously how his thinking draws from Lutheran resources, which speak to the issue of state character or legitimacy in a way that radiates outward from justification through law and gospel and into the two kingdoms.

Notes

1   Kenneth C. Barnes, 'Dietrich Bonhoeffer and Hitler's Persecution of the Jews', in *Betrayal: German Churches and the Holocaust*, ed. Robert P. Ericksen and Susannah Heschel (Minneapolis: Fortress, 1999), 114.

2   Ibid., 116.

3   I use the term 'resistance' broadly here to include any action against the state. This includes the church's proclamation against the state, which is at issue in 'The Church and the Jewish Question'.

4   Denis R. Janz, *The Westminster Handbook to Martin Luther* (Louisville: Westminster John Knox Press, 2010), 81.

5   See, for example, Martin Luther, 'Freedom of a Christian', *Career of the Reformer I. Luther's Works* 31, *American Edition,* ed. Harold J. Grimm, (Philadelphia: Fortress, 1957), 358.

6   Janz, *The Westminster Handbook to Martin Luther*, 67.

7   Mary Jane Haemig, 'The Confessional Basis of Lutheran Thinking on Church-State Issues', in *Church & State: Lutheran Perspectives*, ed. John R. Stumme and Robert W. Tuttle (Fortress Press, 2000), 172, fn.6. Haemig cites Robert Kolb and Timothy J. Wengert, eds., *The Book of Concord: The Confessions of the Evangelical Lutheran Church*, 2nd edn (Minneapolis: Fortress Press, 2000), Formula of Concord (Epitome) V, 500–1.

8   Bernhard Lohse, *Martin Luther's Theology: Its Historical and Systematic Development*, trans. Roy A. Harrisville (Minneapolis: Fortress Press, 1999), 258. For a classic expression of justification's centrality, see Luther, 'Freedom of a Christian', 345–7.

9   Quoted in Lohse, *Martin Luther's Theology*, 258.

10   Martin Luther, 'Heidelberg Disputation', *Career of the Reformer I. Luther's Works* 31, *American Edition,* ed. Harold J. Grimm, (Philadelphia: Fortress, 1957), 39–42.

11   Luther, 'Freedom of a Christian', 348.

12   Janz, *The Westminster Handbook to Martin Luther*, 83.

13   Martin Luther, 'Two Kinds of Righteousness', *Career of the Reformer I. Luther's Works* 31, *American Edition,* ed. Harold J. Grimm (Philadelphia: Fortress, 1957), 297. See also Luther, 'Freedom of a Christian', 347.

14   Martin Luther, 'Preface to the Epistle of St. Paul to the Romans', *Word and Sacrament I. Luther's Works* 35, *American Edition*, ed. E. Theodore Bachmann (Philadelphia: Fortress Press, 1960), 370.

15   Luther, 'Two Kinds of Righteousness', 299.

16   The existence and the nature of this second sense in Luther is controverted. My presentation here follows Lohse, *Martin Luther's Theology*, 260–4.

17   For this reason, some scholars prefer the language of God's twofold reign or twofold rule. See, e.g. Haemig, 'Confessional Basis', 9.

18   Throughout this section I rely heavily on Mary Jane Haemig's lucid, helpful account: 'Confessional Basis'. She defines 'Lutheran confessional perspective', following Wilhelm Maurer, to mean more than the confessional documents, including the ways of thinking in Wittenberg in the 1520s that are presupposed in those documents. See ibid., 172 fn.1.

19   Kolb and Wengert, *The Book of Concord*, Augsburg Confession VII, 42.

20   Martin Luther, 'On the Councils and the Church', in *Church and Ministry III. Luther's Works* 41, *American Edition,* ed. Eric W. Gritsch (St Louis: Concordia, 1966), 150. Cited in Haemig, 'Confessional Basis', 4.

21   Kolb and Wengert, *The Book of Concord*, Formula of Concord (Epitome) V, 500.

22   Ibid., Augsburg Confession XVI, 48.

23   'The Church and the Jewish Question', *DBWE* 12, 362.

24   Ibid.

25   Ibid.

26   Ibid., 363.

27   Ibid.

28   Ibid., 364.

29 Ibid., 363.

30 'The Confessing Church and the Ecumenical Movement.' *DBWE* 14, 393–412. There Bonhoeffer uses the criterion of the gospel to distinguish between the true and false churches in Germany, and to call the ecumenical movement to clarity regarding its position as either a church or a humanitarian organization.

31 'The Nature of the Church.' *DBWE* 11, 332.

32 'The Church and the Jewish Question', *DBWE* 12, 363–4.

33 Ibid., 364.

34 Ibid., 368–9.

35 Ibid., 365.

36 Ibid.

37 Ibid.

38 Marikje Smid, *Deutscher Protestantismus und Judentum, 1932/1933* (Munich: Chr. Kaiser Verlag, 1990), 462. She writes, 'Both in terms of the foundation as well as in view of the potential practical consequences the conclusion can be drawn that Bonhoeffer's position on the Jewish question rests on his own version of the Lutheran two-kingdoms teaching.'

39 Barnes, 'Dietrich Bonhoeffer and Hitler's Persecution of the Jews', 116–17.

40 Ibid., 116.

41 'The Church and the Jewish Question.' *DBWE* 12, 363.

42 Ibid., 364.

43 Haemig, 'Confessional Basis', 10.

44 'The Church and the Jewish Question.' *DBWE* 12, 364–6.

45 Ibid., 368–70.

46 Eberhard Bethge, 'Dietrich Bonhoeffer and the Jews', in *Ethical Responsibility: Bonhoeffer's Legacy to the Churches*, ed. John D. Godsey and Geffrey B. Kelly (New York: Mellen, 1982), 76–7.

47 Stephen R. Haynes, *The Bonhoeffer Legacy: Post-Holocaust Perspectives* (Minneapolis: Fortress Press, 2006), 33.

48 Haynes discusses Bonhoeffer as a 'rescuer', placing him in the context of Holocaust studies treatments of the phenomenon of Christian rescue. But Haynes does not provide (nor intend to provide) an analysis of Bonhoeffer's theological writings relevant to resistance. Ibid., 125–43.

49 See especially Victoria J. Barnett, 'Dietrich Bonhoeffer's Relevance for Post-Holocaust Christian Theology', in *Bonhoeffer and Interpretive Theory: Essays on Methods and Understanding*, ed. Peter Frick (Frankfurt: Peter Lang, 2013), 213–37. A version of this was first published as Victoria J. Barnett,

'Dietrich Bonhoeffer's Relevance for a Post-Holocaust Christian Theology', *Studies in Christian-Jewish Relations* 2(1) (2006): 53–67.

50 Barnett, 'Bonhoeffer's Relevance', 225.

51 Uwe Siemon-Netto, *The Fabricated Luther: Refuting Nazi Connections and Other Modern Myths*, 2nd edn (St. Louis: Concordia Publishing House, 2007), 43.

52 Reinhold Niebuhr, *The Nature and Destiny of Man*, vol. 2 (New York: Scribners, 1964), 191.

53 Ibid., 187.

54 Ibid., 194–5.

55 *The Magdeburg Confession*, trans. Matthew Colvin (North Charleston: CreateSpace, 2012).

56 Oliver K. Olson, 'Theology of Revolution: Magdeburg, 1550–1551', *Sixteenth Century Journal* 3(1) (1972): 56–79; Cynthia G. Shoenberger, 'Luther and the Justifiability of Resistance to Legitimate Authority', *Journal of the History of Ideas* 40(1) (1979): 3–20; Cynthia G. Shoenberger, 'Development of the Lutheran Theory of Resistance: 1523–1530', *Sixteenth Century Journal* 8:1 (1977): 61–76; Quentin Skinner, 'The Origins of the Calvinist Theory of Revolution', in *After the Reformation: Essays in Honor of J. H. Hexter*, ed. Barbara C. Malament (Philadelphia: University of Pennsylvania Press, 1980), 309–30; Quentin Skinner, *The Foundations of Modern Political Thought*, vol. 2 (Cambridge: Cambridge University Press, 1978), 206–7.

57 Clifford J. Green, *Bonhoeffer: A Theology of Sociality*, rev. edn (Grand Rapids: Eerdmans, 1999), 290.

58 Clifford J. Green, 'Editor's Introduction', *DBWE* 6, 21.

59 Stanley Hauerwas, *Performing the Faith: Bonhoeffer and the Practice of Nonviolence* (Grand Rapids: Brazos Press, 2004), 48.

60 Heinrich Bornkamm, *Luther's Doctrine of the Two Kingdoms in the Context of His Theology*, trans. Karl H. Hertz (Philadelphia: Fortress Press, 1966), iii. The Introduction's author is Franklin Sherman.

61 Barnett, 'Bonhoeffer's Relevance', 225.

62 Martin Luther, 'Temporal Authority: To What Extent It Should Be Obeyed', *The Christian in Society II. Luther's Works 45, American Edition,* ed. Walther I. Brandt (Minneapolis: Fortress, 1962), 104. My emphasis.

Chapter 9

DIETRICH BONHOEFFER AND THE JEWS IN CONTEXT
Andreas Pangritz

It has become commonplace among scholars to point out the exceptional attitude Dietrich Bonhoeffer adopted with respect to what was called the 'Jewish question' in the years of the Nazi regime in Germany. It is emphasized that Bonhoeffer was one of the few, perhaps the first, if not the only theologian who, as early as April 1933, urged the Protestant Church to declare its solidarity not only with Christians of Jewish descent but also with the Jewish minority outside of the Church.[1] Frequently Karl Barth's confession on the occasion of the publication of Eberhard Bethge's biography of Bonhoeffer is quoted in this context, in which he admits that he had long considered himself 'guilty' of not having expressed his solidarity with the Jews 'with equal emphasis during the Church struggle'. In the *Barmen Theological Declaration* of May 1934 composed by Barth, for example, the theme was omitted.[2]

More recent research, however, has demonstrated that the image of Bonhoeffer as the singular exception has to be revised. It is no longer possible to isolate him as the great hero from his context. His position regarding the so-called 'Jewish question' must be contextualized and related to similar commitments among his contemporaries. Only in so doing can the distinctive profile of Bonhoeffer's position be described in a comparative way. There were others (including Barth himself) who, more or less at the same time as or even earlier than Bonhoeffer, were concerned about the subject. In what follows I contextualize Bonhoeffer's attitude by drawing comparisons with Karl Barth, Elisabeth Schmitz and Wilhelm Vischer, three theologians who were in contact with Bonhoeffer and one another during those years, forming a kind of network in which Bonhoeffer participated.

While Barth and Bonhoeffer are well known, we should perhaps introduce Elisabeth Schmitz and Wilhelm Vischer since, in spite of their pioneering work, they have long been nearly forgotten. Elisabeth Schmitz (1893–1977) has been ignored by historical research until recently. Between 1923 and 1938 she worked as a teacher of German literature, history and religious education in Berlin. She had studied under Adolf von Harnack, the figurehead of liberal theology, and had written her dissertation under the renowned historian Friedrich Meinecke in Berlin. In the 1920s she participated in Harnack's private seminar and befriended his youngest daughter Elisabet. In 1934 she joined the Confessing Church and committed herself especially to the support of persecuted Jews. For decades she has been a forgotten hero. She has only been rediscovered in the last fifteen years by critical historians like Manfred Gailus, who published her biography in 2010.[3] In 2011 she was posthumously honoured as a 'righteous among the nations' by the Jerusalem Holocaust memorial 'Yad va-Shem'.

Wilhelm Vischer (1895–1988) was a Swiss Reformed theologian, a friend of Barth's, and from 1928 professor of Old Testament at the Bethel 'School of Theology' near Bielefeld. After attacks by Nazi students and the Nazi '*Gauleiter*', he was suspended in May 1933 for having expressed doubts concerning the racist ideology of the Nazi movement.[4] In 1934 he was expelled from Germany and had to return to Switzerland, where he served as a pastor, first in Lugano, then in Basel. After the war he became a professor of Old Testament at the Reformed School of Theology in Montpellier, France.

This essay comprises five sections: In the first, I consider reactions to the boycott of Jewish businesses and to the adoption of the 'Aryan clause' in April 1933; second, I discuss issues relating to the *Bethel Confession* in August 1933; third, I examine Elisabeth Schmitz's memorandum 'On the situation of German non-Aryans' of September 1935–May 1936, before, fourth, moving to consider reactions to the '*Kristallnacht*' of 9–10 November 1938; fifth and finally, I reflect upon Bonhoeffer's *Ethics* and Barth's 'doctrine of Israel' in the face of the deportation of the Jews (1941–2).

Reactions to the boycott of Jewish businesses and the adoption of the 'Aryan clause' in April 1933

The boycott of Jewish businesses on 1 April 1933 and the adoption of the 'Law for the Reconstitution of the Civil Service', which included a so-called 'Aryan clause', on 7 April 1933 provoked a number of reactions by leading figures in the Protestant Church. At the same time, the German Christians started a campaign in order to abolish the use of the Old Testament and to enforce an 'Aryan clause' within the Protestant Church as well.

Most typical is the reaction of Otto Dibelius, general superintendent of the Kurmark province of the Evangelical Church of the Old-Prussian Union, who later became a prominent representative of the Confessing Church and, after the war, of the Evangelical Church in Germany. In his weekly column '*Wochenschau*' of 9 April 1933, he wrote: 'Understandably, the Jewry feels threatened by a national movement with antisemitic impact.' He then justifies everything, because 'the government of the Reich has felt compelled to organize the boycott of Jewish businesses – in the correct perception that, because of the international relations of the Jewry, the foreign agitation will probably cease the soonest when it becomes dangerous in economic terms'.[5] Even later Dibelius did not retract his antisemitic statements of 1933.

In contrast to Dibelius, Elisabeth Schmitz wrote a letter to Karl Barth on 18 April 1933, because she felt that the Church had to declare its solidarity at least with the baptized Jews and to recognize 'its responsibility on the other hand for *those* members [of the Church] who are the source of the hatred'.[6] Barth answered that he, too, was 'in deep concern not only, however, with respect to the Jewish question, but with respect to all those complexes by which its treatment is caused today'. On the other hand he was not convinced that the moment for a public statement had arrived.[7] His attitude would change only eight weeks later, when he published his pamphlet *Theologische Existenz heute!* (see later).

On 30 April 1933 Wilhelm Vischer presented a paper in Lemgo on the significance of the Old Testament for the Christian Church. An extract of Vischer's paper was published together with some biblical explanations in the May–June 1933 issue of the renowned *Monatsschrift für Pastoraltheologie*.[8] In his paper Vischer maintained that the Old Testament 'directs faith towards recognizing Jesus as the Christ', because 'the Old Testament shows, *what* the Christ is', whereas 'the New Testament shows, *who* he is'. A faith rejecting the Old Testament was a 'pagan faith'.[9]

Vischer's essay is one of the earliest statements explicitly dealing with the attitude of the Church towards the persecution of Jews in the Nazi state. On the one hand Vischer emphasizes the theological significance of Israel, treating the so-called 'Jewish question' as a 'question of God'. On the other hand he does not hesitate to speak of 'God's politics' in this context, suggesting that the predestinatarian perspective on salvation history – that is on Israel as God's chosen people – has political implications as well, for instance in the criticism of the boycott of Jewish businesses and in the warning against the burning of Jewish books.

Bonhoeffer's own essay 'The Church and the Jewish Question' was finished on 15 April 1933 and published in the rather obscure journal *Der Vormarsch* in June 1933. It has become famous because of the often quoted sentence according to which in certain situations it might become necessary for the Church 'to fall within the spokes of the wheel', in order to rescue people in danger.[10] However, the essay contains a number of theological ambiguities. Some commentators even find traits of the traditional 'teaching of contempt' (Jules Isaac) in Bonhoeffer's treatment of the subject.[11]

In a recent analysis I have pointed to the handwritten headings to the two sections of the essay in Bonhoeffer's typescript, which were not reproduced in the published version in 1933: '*Ahasver peregrinus*' [Wandering Ahasuerus] and '*Modernes Judenchristentum*' [Modern Jewish Christianity]. While the first heading suggests that Bonhoeffer regarded the Jewish history of suffering as a divine punishment, because the Jews allegedly had crucified the Messiah, the second heading blames the German Christians for representing – in Bonhoeffer's perspective – a modern type of Jewish Christianity, because they have reintroduced a law – the racial law – into the Church of the gospel.[12] Both headings can be traced back to an anti-Judaic Lutheran tradition.[13]

Karl Barth's famous pamphlet *Theologische Existenz heute!* (25 June 1933), by which he publicly opened the Church struggle from his side, has become the source of a number of misunderstandings. In part of its reception it has been reduced to the statement according to which Barth wanted to speak objectively ('*zur Sache*'), that is, to continue 'doing theology and only theology', refusing to speak about the situation ('*zur Lage*'). However, it should not be overlooked that according to Barth this theological concentration was 'a statement as well, an ecclesial-political statement and indirectly even a political statement'.[14] And it should not be forgotten that Barth's pamphlet included a warning against the adoption of an 'Aryan clause' by the Church: 'The fellowship of those belonging to the Church is not determined by blood nor, therefore, by race, but by the Holy Spirit and baptism. If the German Evangelical Church excludes Jewish Christians or treats them as second-class Christians, it ceases to be a Christian Church.'[15] These two sentences were to become a central point of reference for the oppositional movement within the Protestant Church, including Bonhoeffer's activities. Elisabeth Schmitz immediately wrote to Barth that it was 'a salvation' to her that 'finally someone takes a position in such a clear and unambiguous way without the usual bows'.[16]

The chapter 'The Church and the Jews' in the Bethel Confession

In August 1933 Bonhoeffer participated in the attempt to formulate a Lutheran confession, the so-called *Bethel Confession*, which contained a chapter 'The Church and the Jews', initially drafted by the Reformed theologian Wilhelm Vischer.[17] In his original draft Vischer deals first with the position of the Church towards the Jews outside the Church, before discussing the status of Jewish Christians within the Church.[18] Writing about Israel as the 'chosen people', he resumes the predestinatarian approach of his essay '*Zur Judenfrage*'. Speaking about the crucifixion of Christ as having broken down the 'fence' between Jews and Christians, and using the provocative phrasing of the '*character indelebilis*', the indestructible character of the Jewish people, he resumes the soteriological perspective of his essay.

After his draft had provoked some controversy within the Bethel working circle, Vischer sent it to Barth, asking him for a comment:

> The people around Bodelschwingh asked me to write some sentences on the Church's position towards the Jews. I first referred them to the sixth point against the German Christians in your article *Theologische Existenz heute!* But

they wanted it in more detail, such as some points about the unbaptized Jews. So then I put together what I hear the Bible saying on this. I am not surprised that the people who made this request (with the exception of Bonhöffer [!]) do not agree with what I have written. But I am surprised that [Georg] Merz maintains that you, too, certainly would not agree with me. That I cannot believe. Therefore I permit myself to send you what I have written down and ask you to write me what is wrong about it ...[19]

Barth's 'sixth point' mentioned by Vischer is the statement against an 'Aryan clause' in the Church quoted above. Provoked by Vischer's report Barth immediately answered that he completely agreed with his text: 'Tell them there that I give my consent to every word and that I very well would wish that they would, too.'[20]

As has been noted by Bethge, the text of the *Bethel Confession* was considerably altered after August 1933, so much so that Bonhoeffer and Vischer ultimately refused to sign the published version.[21] However, a detailed comparison of Vischer's original draft with the 'August version' reproduced in *Dietrich Bonhoeffer Works*[22] proves that the version that had emerged from the discussions between Vischer, Bonhoeffer and Merz in August 1933, was already watered down in some respect. More precisely, it represented a compromise between Bonhoeffer's Lutheran and Vischer's Reformed approaches.[23]

For instance, Vischer's explanation of the ecclesial 'fellowship with the Jewish Christians' and his rejection of 'the formation of Jewish-Christian congregations' is preceded in the 'August version' by two sentences, which obviously have been contributed by Bonhoeffer: 'We object to the attempt to make the German Evangelical Church into a Reich Church for Christians of Aryan race, thus robbing it of its promise. This would set up a racial law at the entrance to the Church, making such a Church itself into a Jewish Christian, [i.e.] legalistic congregation.'[24]

Fifty years later in a letter to Eberhard Busch, Vischer recalled:

Concerning the Bethel Confession I was put in charge to draft the article 'Israel', because I always and especially since my employment in Bethel (1928) had dealt with the topic. Bonhoeffer worked on other articles. We talked a lot with each other and were in agreement about Israel, with the difference that Bonhoeffer was especially concerned about the full community with the Jews within the

Church, whereas I in addition was concerned about Israel in service of God's world politics.[25]

In other words, whereas Vischer's perspective was conceived along the line of the doctrine of predestination, according to which Israel is God's chosen people to which God remains faithful in his 'world politics' – that is, in salvation history – Bonhoeffer's main interest seems to have consisted in giving the text a more Lutheran shape.[26] He therefore insisted on inserting the distinction between 'law and gospel' into the chapter, a move that led to the problematic definition of Jewish Christians as 'legalistic'.

By opposing law and gospel, as is characteristic of Lutheran theology, this insertion clearly recalls Bonhoeffer's reasoning in the second part of his essay 'The Church and the Jewish Question', where 'Jewish Christianity' and Judaism are defined as a 'religious concept', which – 'from the perspective of the Church' – is 'legalistic' or a religion of the law.[27] One may doubt whether the polemical comparison of the 'Aryan clause' as a 'racial law' with the alleged 'legalism' of Jewish Christianity is serviceable. For the comparison does not really hit the point: after all the 'Aryan clause' was not a 'religious' but a political law, the purpose of which was not to prevent a 'legalistic' heresy, but to exclude Christians of Jewish descent from the Church.

On 9 September 1933, after the 'brown' synod of the Old Prussian Church had adopted an 'Aryan clause' (5–6 September 1933), Bonhoeffer wrote to Barth, referring to the warning against an ecclesial 'Aryan clause' in *Theologische Existenz heute!* and asking him for advice regarding the practical consequences of the *'status confessionis'*. In addition, he asked him for a critical review of the 'August version' of the *Bethel Confession*.[28] In his answer, Barth recommended assuming 'a highly active, polemical position of waiting', instead of leaving the Church and joining a 'Free Church', as Bonhoeffer had suggested.[29] In a letter to Bodelschwingh, Barth communicated his reservations regarding the 'August version' of the *Bethel Confession* not least with respect to the altered text of the chapter 'The Church and the Jews'. He regretted the lack of any declaration of solidarity with those persecuted outside the Church or any related criticism of the state policies against the Jews. In addition, he missed an explicit refutation of the ecclesial 'Aryan clause', after it had been adopted by the 'brown' synod.[30]

We may take Barth's comments on the 'August version' of the *Bethel Confession* as an explanation of what he had meant by 'a highly active, polemical position of waiting' in his answer to Bonhoeffer. Such waiting would imply an active fight against the discrimination and persecution of the Jews in the Nazi state and a polemical protest against the heresy within the Church.[31] Already in a discussion on the occasion of his speech 'What is Reformation?' on 31 October in Berlin, Barth had asked: 'What has the Church to say with respect to what is going on in the concentration camps? Or to the treatment of the Jews?'[32] Further, in a sermon in Bonn on the second Sunday of Advent that same year Barth – expositing Rom. 15.5–13 – addressed the Jewish-Christian relationship, suggesting that we always have to remember, when thinking about the Jews, that 'the gentiles praise God because of his mercy' (Rom. 15.9).[33]

Elisabeth Schmitz and her memorandum 'On the Situation of the German non-Aryans'

Against the background of the discussions around the antisemitic developments at the beginning of the Nazi era, we must ask the embarrassing question as to why the founding synod of the Confessing Church at Barmen did not deal with the 'Jewish question', and why the problem of an 'Aryan clause' did not become a topic in the *Theological Declaration* drafted by Barth and adopted by the synod on 31 May 1934.[34] We have evidence from Elisabeth Schmitz's correspondence with Barth that she fought for keeping the problem on the public agenda.

In a letter of 1 January 1934 Schmitz had asked Barth for expressions of solidarity not only with Jewish Christians, but also with Jews, outside of the Church.[35] Schmitz discerned that the Church struggle could be distorted to an 'end in itself':

> It comforts the conscience – one fights against the Aryan clause (but certainly only within the Church!) – and one blinds the people about the fact that other urgent tasks, or even the most urgent task is forgotten. Where have we heard a comforting word of the Church towards its persecuted members, not to mention a thought of compassion with respect to the persecuted – persecuted by *Christians* – in general?

According to Schmitz, the Church does not need 'a new confession'. It needs 'very simple, plain, self-evident Christian love'. There is no field, in which the Church 'has failed as completely as in this one'.[36] In his answer Barth completely agrees: 'The thought of your letter from New Year was with me those weeks. You should know that I have been moved by it to an extraordinary extent'.[37]

In a letter of 12 February 1934, Schmitz explains why she expects more commitment precisely from the Church. Reflecting on how readily the universities, the woman's liberation movement and everyone had capitulated to the state, she asks: 'Shouldn't it do honour to the Church that one demands more from her than from any of these institutions?' But full of shame she has to admit: 'Time and again I come to the point when everything threatens to collapse around myself, when it becomes totally *unbearable* to me that I nearly cannot find any understanding, not even in ecclesial circles, but only complete blindness with regard to the weight of guilt under which I place myself completely and *must* do so.'[38]

Again, we ask why was the topic of solidarity with the Jews missing in the *Barmen Declaration*?

In spite of her disappointment, Schmitz joined the Confessing Church on 18 September 1934. She felt a special responsibility to push the Confessing Church towards solidarity with the persecuted 'non-Aryans'. And so she wrote a memorandum 'On the Situation of German non-Aryans'.[39] In her memorandum, completed mid-September 1935, Schmitz urges uncompromising practical solidarity with the Jews:

> Where is Abel, your brother? In our case, too, in the case of the Confessing church, there can be no answer other than that given by Cain … And if the church, afraid for its own destruction, can do nothing in many instances, why is it not at least aware of its guilt? Why does it not pray for those who are afflicted by this undeserved suffering and persecution? Why are there no services of intercession as there were for the imprisoned pastors? The church makes it bitterly difficult for anyone to defend it.[40]

In addition to her call for practical solidarity with the persecuted, Schmitz pursues theological matters, challenging the traditional 'teaching of contempt' prevalent among most leading theologians of the Confessing Church as well:

The fact that there can be people in the Confessing church who dare assume that they are entitled, even called, to preach God's justice and mercy to the Jews in the present historical situation when their present sufferings are our crime, is a fact that must fill us with icy fear. Since when has the evil-doer had the right to pass off his evil deed as the will of God? Since when is the claim that our evil deed is God's will anything but blasphemy? Let us take care that we do not conceal the horror of our sins in the sanctuary of God's will. Otherwise it could well be that we too will receive the punishment of those who desecrated the temple, that we too must hear the curse of him who made the scourge and drove them out.[41]

To the disappointment of both Schmitz and Bonhoeffer, the treatment of the Jews was not discussed at the Old-Prussian confessing synod in Berlin-Steglitz on 23–26 September 1935. However, Schmitz did not give in and she circulated her memorandum among leading theologians of the Confessing Church. Bethge mentions that Bonhoeffer passed the memorandum to his friend Julius Rieger in London. Later, in May 1936, Schmitz added 'a postscript regarding the consequences of the Nuremberg Laws and the experiences of non-Aryan children'.[42] In July 1936 she visited Barth in Basel to deliver a copy to him personally. Afterwards she wrote him: 'What I wish is chiefly that *the Church* acknowledges that this is a field of its concern and that it accepts my work in some way as a service to the Church.' In addition, she cautiously distanced herself from what she had realized as a certain reluctance on Barth's side with respect to 'the Jewish':

I would have to ask and to say a lot regarding the Jewish question, for instance with respect to the sensation of strangeness that one allegedly has towards the Jewish, a sensation that one perceives even in a 'quarter-Jew' – if I have got well what you said … In any case there is sensation against sensation … . Therefore in any case: This cannot be the starting point … . Because this has been your opinion, too, and it is about a theological issue, I may repeat my request once more: You should attend to this theological issue, and you should do it in such a way that those circles in the Confessing Church, on whom it depends, learn about it.[43]

Reactions to *Kristallnacht*

The persecution of the Jews in Nazi Germany reached a new climax with the pogroms of *Kristallnacht* on 9–10 November 1938. It seems that on this occasion Bonhoeffer 'underlined the verse in Psalm 74, "they burned all the meeting places of God in the land"' in the Bible he 'used for prayer and meditation', 'and wrote beside it "9.11.38"'. In addition 'he urged the Finkenwaldians … to heed the words: "He who touches you touches the apple of his eye (Zach. 2.8)."'[44]

Already in October 1938 the 'Swiss Evangelical Relief Agency for the Confessing Church in Germany' had published a memorandum titled 'Salvation comes from the Jews'. The memorandum was co-signed by Karl Barth, but it was Wilhelm Vischer who had authored the text.[45] Vischer's memorandum was occasioned by measures taken by the Swiss government in August 1938 in order to close the border to Jewish refugees from Germany. In this context, the title 'Salvation comes from the Jews' (Jn 4.22) receives a clear theological-political meaning. Obviously the purpose of the quotation from the gospel of John was to emphasize that the admission of Jewish refugees was to be regarded as an expression of thanks owed by the world of nations to the Jews, because 'every Jew *eo ipso* is a witness to God's sanctity and faith-fulness'. In the Christian 'attitude towards the Jews', a decision is taken about the sincerity of 'faith, love and hope of Christianity'.[46] With the Jews, God 'has initiated the revelation of his grace in face of the world, with them he will complete it'. The eschatological expectation has implications in the present time:

> The Jews and the Christians stand in face of each other as the two servants of the one true God, separated in greatest depth and joined to each other through the one Lord, who is full of mercy according to his will and who hardens according to his will, each one as a witness to the other, so that salvation and condem-nation depend completely on his free grace.[47]

Talk of the 'two servants of the one Lord' and God's 'free grace' situates the Jewish-Christian relationship in the context of the doctrine of predestination, as had already been the case in Vischer's essay *'Zur Judenfrage'* of June 1933 and in Barth's sermon on Romans 15 of December 1933. Rightly, Eberhard Busch emphasizes that on this view, election and rejection, salvation and condemnation, cannot simply be mapped onto Christians and Jews respectively. Rather, no one can rely upon God's gracious salvation who does not 'recognize that it is first of all aimed at the Jews'.[48] Both these phrases – talking of the 'two servants of the one Lord' and about God's 'free grace' – would find their reception after the 'night of crystals' in the Confessing Church in Berlin (see below).

Immediately after *Kristallnacht*, Elisabeth Schmitz visited pastors of the Confessing Church to ask them to deal with the pogroms in their sermons on the coming 'Repentance Day'. In a letter of 15 November, probably addressed to pastor Eitel-Friedrich von Rabenau,[49] she emphasized that a public statement by the Confessing Church was necessary.[50] She argues that the Christian Church and the Jewish congregations are two branches of the one people of God, who must publically co-operate and support each other. 'After what has happened in Germany, a Protestant Church, one that calls itself a Confessing Church, should immediately organize repentance services in every congregation. And now there *is* Repentance Day, and the Church should keep silent? Is there any other possibility as to bring this awful guilt of our people *collectively* before God and to confess it *collectively*?'[51]

It was Helmut Gollwitzer (1908–93), friend of Karl Barth and unofficial replacement for the imprisoned pastor Martin Niemöller in the Confessing congregation in Berlin-Dahlem, who spoke publically to the matter in his Repentance Day sermon. He expressed shame for the guilt of Christianity, and asked:

> Who should still dare to preach today? Who should dare to preach repentance? Are we not silenced all together on this day? … What an impertinence, to come to God now, to sing and to read the bible, to pray, preach, confess our sins, as if it was to expect that God is still there and that it is not only an empty religious business! Our presumptuousness and impudence must be disgusting for God. Why don't we at least keep silent?[52]

Schmitz, together with her friend Martha Kassel, a Jewish physician, had attended Gollwitzer's service and on later wrote a letter of thanks to the preacher:

> Please, let me thank you out of a deeply felt need for the service on Repentance Day … . This is the only way in which a Christian congregation can and may

come together after what has happened. To my friend who expects to emigrate (although at the moment it seems to be impossible) your words have been helpful and encouraging in a situation of deep embitterment and desperation.[53]

Schmitz reminds Gollwitzer that she had visited him a few weeks ago in order to talk about the necessity,

> that the Church had to say a word to the congregations about the treatment of the Jews in Germany … . The word of the Church has not come. Instead we have experienced the atrocities, and now we have to live on knowing that we are guilty … . It seems that this time again, where in reality the stones are crying, the Church leaves it to the insight and courage of the single pastor, if he wants to say something and what he wants to say. But what has to come now is intercession, not only for the Christians, but also for the Jews.

She asks if anyone has had the idea to write a letter of solidarity to Rabbi Leo Baeck on behalf of the Church, or to the Jewish congregations who have lost all their synagogues in Germany because of the burnings.[54]

Schmitz closes her letter with a prophetic warning: 'According to the annunciations of the government a complete separation of Jews and non-Jews will come … . Rumors are circulating … that a sign on the clothing is planned … . We have seen the destruction of Jewish properties, to this end their businesses had been marked in summer. When one moves to mark human beings, a consequence suggests itself' – one that she does not want to specify. By this time she has already 'heard about horrible bloody excesses' and she is convinced that should this plan be executed, 'Christianity will disappear from Germany with the last Jew'.[55]

Three days later in another letter to Gollwitzer, Schmitz reflects further, asking why the Church cannot put her buildings at the disposal of Jewish congregations as a place in which to continue their worship. In any case, she insists that the Church must 'find a way to demonstrate to Jewish congregations that we stand together with them as the two servants of the one Lord' and thinks this should be expressed 'by a personal letter on the one hand and by intercession on the other hand'.[56]

Schmitz emphasizes that her talk of the 'two servants of the one Lord' refers to Barth's position set out in Vischer's '*Memorandum zur Judenfrage*', which had recently circulated. She had evidently seen a copy herself. By alluding to the 'two servants of the one Lord' she wants to remind Gollwitzer of the description of the Jewish-Christian relationship as it had been formulated by his own friends in Basel.[57]

On 5 December 1938, Barth reacted to *Kristallnacht* in his speech 'The Church and the Political Question of Today', presented at the first Wipkingen meeting of the 'Swiss Evangelical Relief Agency for the Confessing Church'. Here Barth explains that the 'decisive, biblical-theological reason' why National Socialism has to be regarded as a 'strictly anti-Christian counter-Church' does not consist 'in the various anti-Christian assertions and activities of National Socialism, but in the issue that has moved us exactly during the last weeks, that is its *antisemitism* in principle'. In the face of the 'physical extermination' of the Jews, which was clearly being undertaken in Germany, in the face of the 'burnings of synagogues and Torah scrolls', the 'decrying of the "Jewish God" and the "Jewish Bible"', it has to be said: 'Whoever rejects the Jews and persecutes them, rejects and persecutes Him, who … has died for our sins. Whoever is an enemy of the Jews in principle, reveals himself as an enemy of Christ in principle. Antisemitism is sin against the Holy Spirit.'[58] This sentence can be regarded as Barth's most explicit theological-political statement against National Socialism.

Bonhoeffer's 'Heritage and Decay' and Barth's 'Doctrine of Israel'

The relationship between Barth und Bonhoeffer had become difficult during the war years. However they co-operated in the attempt to rescue a number of people of Jewish descent in relation to 'Operation 7'.[59] And there is evidence of a close theological connection between Barth and Bonhoeffer on the issue of Jewish-Christian relations at this time. This can be seen in Bonhoeffer's manuscript '*Erbe und Verfall*' (Heritage and Decay), drafted in 1940 and revised in the autumn of 1941,[60] which demonstrates that in those years he shared Barth's predestinatarian perspective on the relationship between Church and Israel.

Originally, Bonhoeffer had written in 'Heritage and Decay' that 'the primal fact … of the appearance of Jesus Christ [2,000] years ago … evokes the question of our historical heritage'. More precisely, 'the line of our forebears reaches back' even 'before the appearance of Jesus Christ into the people Israel'. Therefore 'Western history is by God's will inextricably bound up with the people Israel'.[61] In the later revision, he specified the year as 1941 and also added in the margins the contention that this inextricable bond between the history of the West and the people Israel is to be understood 'not just genetically but in a genuine, unceasing encounter'. According to Bonhoeffer: 'The Jews keep open the question of Christ; they are the sign of God's free, gracious election and of God's rejecting wrath'. Here Bonhoeffer refers to Romans 11.22: 'See the kindness and the severity of God'. At the end, he draws out the present significance: 'Driving out the Jew(s) from the West must result in driving out Christ with them, for Jesus Christ was a Jew'.[62]

The passage is one of the most important in Bonhoeffer's *Ethics*, not least because it largely overcomes the theological ambiguities of the earlier essay 'The Church and the Jewish Question'.[63] Talk of a 'genuine, unceasing encounter' between the Christian West and the Jews seems to renounce the claim for a Christian mission to the Jews prevalent in the theology of the Confessing Church. To be sure, in face of the 'Aryan clause' and the racist exclusion of Jews from baptism, proselytism was well-meant at that time. Nonetheless, such proselytism contributed in its own way to the depreciation of the Jews, because in this perspective Judaism was regarded as deficient and at best tolerable only as the precurser of Christianity. The editors of the critical edition of Bonhoeffer's *Ethics* note that it was on the night of 16–17 October 1941 that 'the mass deportation of Jews from Berlin residences began'.[64] Against this background it is appropriate to interpret Bonhoeffer's marginal additions to the original text of 'Heritage and Decay' as an immediate response to the deportations.[65]

However, there is a philological difficulty: where the English translation of Bonhoeffer's *Ethics* reads 'driving out the Jew(s) from the West', the German original reads '*Verstoßung d. Juden aus dem Abendland*'. The German term '*Verstoßung*' is significant. While the English translation obviously alludes to the expulsion of the Jews, Bonhoeffer does not just speak of '*Vertreibung*', that is, of 'expulsion' or 'driving out'. In fact, after *Kristallnacht* expulsions had come to an end and deportation to extermination had begun. But Bonhoeffer does not speak of '*Verschleppung*' [deportation] either. Instead, he chooses the theological term '*Verstoßung*', clearly alluding to the doctrine of double predestination.[66] Luther had used the verb *'verstoßen'* in his translation of Rom. 11.1: *'Hat denn Gott sein Volk verstoßen? Das sei ferne!'* which the *New English Bible* translates: 'Has God *rejected* his people? I cannot believe it!' Bonhoeffer's term *'Verstoßung'* is best rendered in English as 'rejection'.

While admitting the historical contextualization of Bonhoeffer's text, an additional theological perspective seems necessary. The 1941 revisions of 'Heritage and Decay' relate Bonhoeffer's text to Barth's developing 'doctrine of Israel' within his *Church Dogmatics*.[67]

In his 'doctrine of Israel' Barth exposits Romans 11.17–22 – the very verses which Bonhoeffer refers to in his marginal insertions – so as to provide a Christological basis for solidarity with the Jews similar to that offered in Bonhoeffer's essay. Barth writes:

> Whoever has Jesus Christ in faith cannot wish not to have the Jews. He must have them along with Jesus Christ as His ancestors and kinsmen. Otherwise he cannot have even the Jew Jesus. Otherwise with the Jews he rejects Jesus Himself. This is what is at stake, and therefore, in fact, the very basis of the Church, when it has to be demanded of Gentile Christians that they should not approach any Israelite without the greatest attention and sympathy.[68]

Even Bonhoeffer's wording seems to refer to Barth's 'doctrine of God's gracious election'.[69] For instance, when he speaks about 'God's free, gracious election', he uses Barthian terminology, which does not seem to occur anywhere else in Bonhoeffer's writings. In Barth's treatment the term 'gracious election' – *'Gottes Gnadenwahl'* – was used to overcome the traditional misunderstanding of the doctrine of predestination. It was coined to emphasize the 'triumph' of God's grace over reprobation within the framework of 'double predestination'.[70] While God in his mercy chooses 'reprobation, perdition and death' for himself in Jesus Christ, no human being can be regarded as lost.[71] In short: it is not by chance that when Bonhoeffer speaks about the relationship of the Christian West towards the Jews he uses precisely this Barthian language of 'free, gracious election'.

There is a chronological difficulty, however. When Bonhoeffer revised his manuscript in autumn 1941 Barth's 'doctrine of Israel' had not yet appeared. It was only in May 1942, when Bonhoeffer visited Barth during a journey to Switzerland, that he asked Barth for the page proofs of the volume. Thus, he cannot have quoted *Church Dogmatics II/2* in his marginal insertions.

Moreover, we do not know if Bonhoeffer had received knowledge of Vischer's memorandum '*Das Heil kommt von den Juden*', where the conception of Israel in terms of the doctrine of election was already present. However, it is likely that the situation of the Jews in Germany was discussed by Barth and Bonhoeffer already during the previous journeys to Switzerland on behalf of the conspiracy in 1941.[72] In that context Vischer's memorandum may well have been discussed. Moreover, Bonhoeffer may have known of Barth's speech 'Our Church and Switzerland in Present Times' (November 1940), a speech which had prompted the Swiss authorities to ban Barth from public speaking.[73] In his speech, Barth had coined phrases that seem to presage Bonhoeffer's marginal additions to the manuscript of 'Heritage and Decay'. Barth had said that the 'most inward core of the world empire ascending today' consists of,

> hate against and rejection [*Verstoßung*] of the Jews … . However, the Son of Man, who was the Son of God, was a Jew … . The very fact that we cannot reject [*von uns stoßen*] God's salvation, that has come precisely to the Jews and from the Jews to us, makes it impossible for us to conform to the present world empire. On the same grounds we cannot participate in all the remaining inhumanities of this world empire.[74]

Obviously, the predestinatarian perspective does not exclude, but rather includes, ethical implications. It implies a recognition that since the 'teaching of contempt' against the Jews as a people allegedly rejected by God had produced fatal consequences – including the deportation and extermination of the Jews – a theological reversal was necessary.

It is important to realize that during the years when he worked on the 'doctrine of Israel', Barth participated in activities of solidarity with persecuted Jews organized by the 'Swiss Evangelical Relief Agency for the Confessing Church in Germany'.[75] During the Wipkingen meetings of the 'Relief Agency' a sharp controversy between Barth and Emil Brunner had developed about the understanding of the sentence 'Salvation comes from the Jews' (Jn 4.22).[76] The controversy reached its climax at the fourth Wipkingen meeting on 17 November 1941, one month after the beginning of the deportations in Berlin. According to Brunner, salvation once had come from the Jews, but meanwhile had been passed over to the Christians. Against this Barth insisted on the presentist meaning of the sentence, arguing that Brunner's interpretation failed to provide a theological basis for solidarity with the Jews in the present time.

The debate corresponds to Bonhoeffer's insistence that the history of the West is linked to Israel 'not just genetically but in a genuine, unceasing encounter'.

With his marginal additions to the manuscript 'Heritage and Decay' Bonhoeffer joined the theological debate concerning the Jewish-Christian relationship that had developed in the context of the 'Swiss Evangelical Relief Agency for the Confessing Church' at the beginning of the 1940s. With his choice of words he took a position at the side of Barth, emphasizing the enduring bond between Church and Israel.

Conclusion

Bonhoeffer was certainly not the only one to demand ecclesial solidarity with the Jews in the years of National Socialism in Germany. Rather, he participated in a network of theologians who were vitally concerned about the so-called 'Jewish Question' and who felt it necessary to revise the theological tradition in this respect. Neither was Bonhoeffer the first one to develop these new insights. Rather, the theological anti-Judaism inherent in Lutheran tradition made it difficult for him to overcome the 'teaching of contempt'. In his essay 'The Church and the Jewish question', the traditional conviction that the Jewish people had been rejected by God, together with the Lutheran distinction between law and gospel, produced theological ambiguities. These made it difficult to accept the theological concept of the continuing relevance of God's covenant with Israel as God's chosen people. It was only in the chapter 'Heritage and Decay' drafted for his *Ethics*, that Bonhoeffer accepted a perspective on Israel framed by the doctrine of election, taking up insights previously advanced by Vischer, Schmitz and Barth.

Notes

1   Eberhard Bethge, *Dietrich Bonhoeffer. A Biography*, rev. and ed. Victoria J.
Barnett (Minneapolis: Fortress Press, 1999), 272. Throughout, I make use of
existing English translations where possible, citing other German sources in my
own translation unless otherwise noted.

2   Karl Barth, Letter to Eberhard Bethge, 22 May 1967, in *Evangelische Theologie*
28 (1968): 555; English translation in Karl Barth, *Fragments Grave and Gay*, ed.
H. M. Rumscheidt, trans. Eric Mosbacher (London: Collins, 1971), 119.

3   Manfred Gailus, *Mir aber zerriss es das Herz. Der stille Widerstand der Elisabeth
Schmitz*, 2nd edn (Göttingen: Vandenhoeck & Ruprecht, 2011).

4   See Christine-Ruth Müller, *Bekenntnis und Bekennen. Dietrich Bonhoeffer in
Bethel (1933) – ein lutherischer Versuch* (Munich: Chr. Kaiser, 1989), 27. Vischer
was not really convinced of the 'outstanding significance of the Nordic race'.

5   Otto Dibelius, 'Wochenschau', *Berliner Sonntagsblatt* (9 April 1933), 1.

6   Elisabeth Schmitz, Letter to Karl Barth, 18 April 1933 (Karl Barth Archives,
Basel); quoted by Dietgard Meyer, 'Elisabeth Schmitz: Die Denkschrift "Zur
Lage der deutschen Nichtarier". Einleitung', in Hannelore Erhart, Ilse Meseberg-
Haubold and Dietgard Meyer, *Katharina Staritz 1903–1953: Dokumentation*, vol.
1: 1903–1942 (Neukirchen-Vluyn: Neukirchener Verlagsgesellschaft, 1999), 201–2.

7   Karl Barth, Letter to Elisabeth Schmitz, 2 May 1933, in Karl Barth, *Briefe des
Jahres 1933*, ed. E. Busch (Zürich: TVZ, 2004), 187–8.

8   See Wilhelm Vischer, 'Zur Judenfrage. Eine kurze biblische Erörterung der
Judenfrage im Anschluß an die Leitsätze eines Vortrages über die Bedeutung
des Alten Testamentes', *Monatsschrift für Pastoraltheologie* 29 (1933): 185–90.

9   Ibid., 185–6.

10 'The Church and the Jewish question', *DBWE* 12, 365. The German *'dem Rad in
die Speichen fallen'* has been translated here as 'to seize the wheel itself'.

11 See Eva Fleischner, *Judaism in German Christian Theology Since 1945:
Christianity and Israel Considered in Terms of Mission* (Metuchen, NJ: Rowman
and Littlefield, 1975), 24. See also Eberhard Bethge, 'Dietrich Bonhoeffer und
die Juden', in *Konsequenzen. Dietrich Bonhoeffers Kirchenverständnis heute*, ed.
E. Feil and I. Tödt (Munich: Chr. Kaiser, 1980), 174; and Franklin H. Littell, *The
Crucifixion of the Jews*, rev. edn (Macon/GA: Mercer University Press, 1996),
51: 'The sad truth is that Bonhoeffer was much better than his theology … .
The man whose humanity and decency led him to run risks for Jews and to
oppose practical Antisemitism was better than the bad theology which laid the
foundations for Christian Antisemitism.'

12 Bonhoeffer repeats his polemic against the German Christians as representing 'modern Jewish Christianity' several times in 1933. See for instance his memorandum 'The Jewish-Christian Question as Status Confessionis', *DBWE* 12, 371–3.

13 For more details of this analysis see Andreas Pangritz, 'To fall within the spokes of the wheel. New-old observations concerning "The Church and the Jewish Question"', in *Dem Rad in die Speichen fallen. Das Politische in der Theologie Dietrich Bonhoeffers / A Spoke in the Wheel. The Political in the Theology of Dietrich Bonhoeffer*, ed. Kirsten Busch Nielsen, Ralf K. Wüstenberg and Jens Zimmermann (Gütersloh: Gütersloher Verlagshaus, 2013), 94–108.

14 Karl Barth, *Theologische Existenz heute!* [1933], Supplement No. 2 of *Zwischen den Zeiten* 11 (1933) *Theologische Existenz heute*, ed. Karl Barth and Eduard Thurneysen, No. 1, (Munich: Chr. Kaiser, 1933), 3.

15 Ibid., 45: '6. Die Gemeinschaft der zur Kirche Gehörigen wird nicht durch das Blut und also auch nicht durch die Rasse, sondern durch den heiligen Geist und die Taufe bestimmt. Wenn die deutsche evangelische Kirche *die Judenchristen ausschließen* oder als Christen zweiter Klasse behandeln würde, würde sie aufgehört haben, christliche Kirche zu sein.'

16 Elisabeth Schmitz, Letter to Karl Barth, 6 July 1933, in Barth, *Briefe das Jahres 1933*, 188.

17 Guy C. Carter, *Confession at Bethel, August 1933 – Enduring Witness: The Formation, Revision and Significance of the First Full Theological Confession of the Evangelical Church Struggle in Nazi Germany* [Dissertation Marquette University, 1987] (Ann Arbor: UMI, 1988), 81: The section on 'The Church and the Jews' was Vischer's 'contribution to the Bethel confessional project'. See Ibid., 255: 'Vischer's section'. Since this thesis was written, Vischer's original draft text has been published from the Karl Barth Archives in Basel, see Eberhard Busch, '"Die Kirche und die Juden". Der Beitrag Wilhelm Vischers zum sog. Betheler Bekenntnis', in *Gott wahr nehmen. Festschrift für Christian Link zum 65. Geburtstag*, ed. M. L. Frettlöh and H. P. Lichtenberger (Neukirchen-Vluyn: Neukirchener Verlagsgesellschaft, 2003), 47–50. See also Barth, *Briefe des Jahres 1933*, 59889.

18 See Carter, *Confession at Bethel*, 255: 'Here there is a reflection not only on the church's relationship to its members of Jewish ethnic descent. Here the Old Testament exegete, Vischer, attempts a statement of the Christian church's relationship to the Jewish community as such.'

19 Wilhelm Vischer, Letter to Karl Barth, 21 August 1933; see Brigitte Schroven, *Theologie des Alten Testaments zwischen Anpassung und Widerstand. Christologische Auslegungen zwischen den Weltkriegen* (Neukirchen-Vluyn:

Neukirchener Verlagsgesellschaft, 1995), 220, fn.279. See Eberhard Busch, *Unter dem Bogen des einen Bundes. Karl Barth und die Juden 1933–1945* (Neukirchen-Vluyn: Neukirchener Verlagsgesellschaft, 1996), 58. See also Busch, 'Die Kirche und die Juden', 50.

20 Karl Barth, Letter to Wilhelm Vischer, 24 August 1933, in Barth, *Briefe des Jahres 1933*, 347.

21 According to Bethge it was chiefly the fact that 'particularly … Vischer's chapter on the Jewish question' was 'watered down', that prevented Bonhoeffer from agreeing with the final version, Bethge, *Dietrich Bonhoeffer*, 303.

22 See 'The Bethel Confession', *DBWE* 12, 416–24.

23 For more details see Andreas Pangritz, 'Die "Politik Gottes" mit Israel. Über Wilhelm Vischers Beitrag zum "Betheler Bekenntnis"', *Evangelische Theologie* 72 (2012): 194–213.

24 'The Bethel Confession', *DBWE* 12, 420 (translation slightly altered). According to Vischer's later memory it was exactly at this place, that Bonhoeffer influenced style and phrasing of the *Bethel Confession*. See Vischer, 'Témoignage d'un contemporain', *Révue d'histoire et philosophie religieuses* 64 (1984): 118–19.

25 Wilhelm Vischer, Letter to Eberhard Busch, 15 April 1983; see Busch, 'Die Kirche und die Juden', 45.

26 This would correspond with the fact that the Bonhoeffer circle who had originally initiated the work on the *Bethel Confession* by its letter to Bodelschwingh of 1 August 1933, 'apparently thought it self-evident that the document ought to be a *Lutheran* confession of faith' (Carter, *Confession at Bethel*, 65). Accordingly Georg Merz, writing to Eberhard Bethge in 1956, recollected that during the work on the *Bethel Confession* Bonhoeffer was 'completely in favor of "the Lutheran way"'. Ibid., 152.

27 Bonhoeffer, 'The Church and the Jewish Question', *DBWE* 12, 368–70. Translation altered.

28 Dietrich Bonhoeffer, Letter to Karl Barth, 9 September 1933, *DBWE* 12, 164–6. Bonhoeffer writes that he had been 'expressly requested' in Bethel 'to ask you sincerely for your evaluation of and corrections to this text'. The reasons, why Bonhoeffer asked Barth for his review only with a delay of ten days are not clear.

29 Barth, Letter to Dietrich Bonhoeffer, Bergli, Oberrieden (Kt. Zürich), 11 September 1933, *DBWE* 12, 168.

30 Barth, Letter to Friedrich von Bodelschwingh (appendix), 12 October 1933, in Barth, *Briefe des Jahres 1933*, 606. Barth writes: 'Is the *civil* treatment of the Jews which is systematically permitted in present-day Germany something that '"we"

do not have to address? Something that "we" accept and support as willed by God because it is ordered by the "authorities" [*Obrigkeit*]? … Here the "Aryan clause", which has become legally binding for the Church of the Old Prussian Union, must be expressly mentioned and this Church expressly accused of heresy.' See Müller, *Bekenntnis und Bekennen*, 50. See also Vischer, Zeugnis eines Zeitgenossen, in *Bethel 30. Beiträge aus der Arbeit der v. Bodelschwinghschen Anstalten* (Bielefeld, 1985), 85, as well as Schroven, *Theologie des Alten Testaments*, 221.

31   Contrary to divergent rumours, Bonhoeffer himself did not feel abandoned by Barth, as can be seen from his letter to Barth from London, 24 October 1933. According to this letter he feels he has been 'personally disloyal' to Barth in his move to London. Bonhoeffer, Letter to Karl Barth, London, 24 October 1933, *DBWE* 13, 24.

32   Erica Küppers, Circular letter to friends, 11 November 1933, in Hans Prolingheuer, *Der Fall Karl Barth. Chronographie einer Vertreibung 1934–1935*, 2nd edn (Neukirchen-Vluyn: Neukirchener Verlagsgesellschaft, 1984), 239.

33   Karl Barth, *Die Kirche Jesu Christi*, Theologische Existenz heute 5 (Munich: Chr. Kaiser, 1933), 16. Regarding this sermon see Friedrich-Wilhelm Marquardt, *Die Entdeckung des Judentums für die christliche Theologie. Israel im Denken Karl Barths* (Munich: Chr. Kaiser, 1967), 86–97.

34   The silence of Barmen regarding the Jews is all the more surprising, when we take into account the fact that in January 1934 the declaration of the Reformed synod in Barmen had included a paragraph rejecting the introduction of an 'Aryan clause' in the Church. The declaration was authored by Karl Barth as well.

35   See Elisabeth Schmitz, Letter to Karl Barth, 1 January 1934 [Karl Barth Archives, Basel]; quoted by Meyer, 'Elisabeth Schmitz', in Erhart/Meseberg-Haubold/Meyer, *Katharina Staritz*, 201–2. Schmitz mentions that her friend Martha Kassel, who because of the 'Aryan clause' had lost her permission to practise as a physician, had left the Church. She emphasizes that she had 'not abandoned' her 'Christian faith'. According to Dietgard Meyer Martha Kassel was disappointed about the 'anti-Jewish attitude' of the Church and 'its servile behaviour towards the Nazi regime.'

36   Ibid., 202–3.

37   Barth, Letter to Elisabeth Schmitz, 18 January 1934 [Karl Barth Archives, Basel]; quoted by Werner Koch, 'Karl Barths erste Auseinandersetzungen mit dem Dritten Reich', in *Richte unsere Füße auf den Weg des Friedens. Helmut Gollwitzer zum 70. Geburtstag*, ed. A. Baudis et al. (Munich: Chr. Kaiser, 1979),

511: Barth agrees that 'the attempt to resolve the Jewish question in Germany is impossible from the perspective of humanity, politics, and the Church. The Protestant Church is obliged to say no! to everything currently happening in the "Aryan question" and "a word of comfort and hope for its members affected by this problem". Barth agrees that 'even a serious intercession for the members of the synagogue' is necessary.

38   Elisabeth Schmitz, Letter to Karl Barth, 12 February 1934 [Karl Barth Archives, Basel]; quoted by Meyer, 'Elisabeth Schmitz', in Erhart/Meseberg-Haubold/ Meyer, *Katharina Staritz*, 200, 202.

39   Elisabeth Schmitz, 'Zur Lage der deutschen Nichtarier', in Erhart/Meseberg-Haubold/Meyer, *Katharina Staritz*, 218–61. See Manfred Gailus (ed.), *Elisabeth Schmitz und ihre Denkschrift gegen die Judenverfolgung* (Berlin: Wichern, 2008), 191–223. See also Gailus, *Mir aber zerriss es das Herz*, 223–52. Bethge mentions the memorandum (Bethge, *Dietrich Bonhoeffer*, 488–90), however with the wrong ascription to Marga Meusel, which can be traced back to Wilhelm Niemöller. More recent research by Dietgard Meyer ('Elisabeth Schmitz', in Erhart/Meseberg-Haubold/Meyer, *Katharina Staritz*, 185–214) has clarified that the author was, in fact, Elisabeth Schmitz.

40   Schmitz, 'Zur Lage der deutschen Nichtarier', in Erhart/Meseberg-Haubold/ Meyer, *Katharina Staritz*, 240, 245. For the translation see Bethge, *Dietrich Bonhoeffer*, 488.

41   Schmitz, 'Zur Lage der deutschen Nichtarier', in Erhart/Meseberg-Haubold/ Meyer, *Katharina Staritz*, 246. For the translation see Bethge, *Dietrich Bonhoeffer*, 489–90 (one sentence added). Elsewhere Bethge interprets this passage as 'a kind of rejection of the Christian mission to the Jews' (Bethge, 'Dietrich Bonhoeffer und die Juden', 213, fn.18).

42   Bethge, *Dietrich Bonhoeffer*, 489.

43   Elisabeth Schmitz, Letter to Karl Barth, Basel, 16 July 1936 [copy in the literary estate of Elisabeth Schmitz, owned by Dietgard Meyer]; quoted by Meyer, 'Elisabeth Schmitz', in Erhart/Meseberg-Haubold/Meyer, *Katharina Staritz*, 190.

44   Bethge, *Dietrich Bonhoeffer*, 607.

45   See Wilhelm Vischer, 'Das Heil kommt von den Juden (Memorandum)', in *Juden – Christen – Judenchristen. Ein Ruf an die Christenheit*, ed. Schweizerisches Evangelisches Hilfswerk für die Bekennende Kirche in Deutschland (Zollikon: Verlag der Evangelischen Buchhandlung, 1939), 39–47.

46   Ibid., 45.

47   Ibid., 43: 'Die Juden und die Christen stehen einander gegenüber als die zweierlei Knechte des einen wahren Gottes, im Tiefsten geschieden und

verbunden durch den einen Herrn, der sich erbarmt, welches er will, und
verstockt, welchen er will, die einen den andern zum Zeugnis, daß Heil und
Verdammnis ganz von seiner freien Gnade abhängen.'

48   Busch, *Unter dem Bogen*, 324.

49   Elisabeth Schmitz, Letter to pastor [Eitel-Friedrich von Rabenau?], 11 November
     1938 [unpublished; copy in the literary estate of Elisabeth Schmitz, Hanau].

50   Ibid. Schmitz writes that '1) It is simply impossible that a people or rather
     the church of a people, where these things have happened, celebrates a
     national Repentance Day one week later, without mentioning all those things.
     2) Some representative person, not necessarily a member of the board of the
     Confessing Church, has to write a personal letter to [Leo] Baeck or to the Jewish
     congregations. 3) We have to help with money, too. First the affected members
     of our communities, *then the others, too*.'

51   Ibid. Schmitz continues: 'It is about an issue of the Church, about her
     obedience, her task, about the honour of God and of Christianity (and Jewry),
     but not before the world.'

52   Helmut Gollwitzer, Sermon on Lk. 3. 3–14, Repentance Day, 16 November
     1938, in Helmut Gollwitzer, *Dennoch bleibe ich stets an dir ... Predigten aus
     dem Kirchenkampf 1937–1940*, ed. J. Hoppe (Munich: Chr. Kaiser, 1988),
     52–3.

53   Schmitz, Letter to Helmut Gollwitzer, 24 November 1938, in Gerhard Schäberle-
     Koenigs, *Und sie waren täglich einmütig beieinander. Der Weg der Bekennenden
     Gemeinde Berlin/Dahlem 1937–1943 mit Helmut Gollwitzer* (Gütersloh:
     Gütersloher Verlagshaus, 1998), 203. See also Gailus, ed., *Elisabeth Schmitz und
     ihre Denkschrift*, 223–6, and Gailus, *Mir aber zerriss es das Herz*, 253–5.

54   Ibid.

55   Ibid. This resembles Bonhoeffer's later warning in his manuscript 'Heritage and
     Decay', where he writes that 'driving out the Jew(s) from the West must result in
     driving out Christ with them, for Jesus Christ was a Jew.' *DBWE* 6, 105.

56   Elisabeth Schmitz, Letter to Helmut Gollwitzer, 27 November 1938
     [unpublished; copy in the literary estate of Elisabeth Schmitz, Hanau].

57   In those years Gollwitzer, together with Gertrud Staewen, was regarded as the
     authentic voice of Barth in Berlin.

58   Karl Barth, 'Die Kirche und die politische Frage von heute', in Karl Barth, *Eine
     Schweizer Stimme 1938–1945*, 2nd edn (Zollikon-Zürich: Theologischer Verlag,
     1948), 89–90.

59   See Winfried Meyer, *Unternehmen Sieben. Eine Rettungsaktion für vom
     Holocaust Bedrohte aus dem Amt Ausland/Abwehr im Oberkommando der
     Wehrmacht* (Frankfurt am Main: Anton Hain, 1993), 70–82.

60   See *DBWE* 6, 103–33. Ilse Tödt dates the revisions and additions as having
     taken place between April and the end of 1941. See Ilse Tödt, 'Preparing the
     German Edition of *Ethics*', *DBWE* 6, 471.

61   *DBWE* 6, 105. Translation slightly altered.

62   Ibid. Translation altered.

63   For more details of the following analysis see Andreas Pangritz, 'Marginalie
     zu Bonhoeffers Ethik', in *Momente der Begegnung. Impulse für das christlich-
     jüdische Gespräch. Bertold Klappert zum 65. Geburtstag*, ed. M. Haarmann, J.
     Von Lüpke and A. Menn (Neukirchen-Vluyn: Neukirchener Verlagsgesellschaft/
     Wuppertal: Foedus, 2004), 206–12; also in *Dietrich Bonhoeffer Yearbook 2,
     2005/2006*, ed. Victoria Barnett et al. (Gütersloh: Gütersloher Verlagshaus,
     2005), 210–17.

64   *DBWE* 6, 105, fn. 9.

65   Dietrich Bonhoeffer and Friedrich Justus Perels, 'Report on the Mass
     Deportation of Jewish Citizens' [18 October 1941], *DBWE* 16, 225–7.
     Bonhoeffer and Perels, 'Report on the Evacuation of "Non-Aryans"' [20 October
     1941], Ibid., 227–9.

66   See Bertold Klappert, 'Weg und Wende Dietrich Bonhoeffers in der
     Israelfrage', in *Ethik im Ernstfall. Dietrich Bonhoeffers Stellung zu den Juden
     und ihre Aktualität*, ed. W. Huber and I. Tödt (Munich: Chr. Kaiser, 1982), 97.
     Klappert interprets Bonhoeffer's reflection as 'Umkehrung der traditionellen
     Verwerfungstheorie', i.e. a 'reversal of the traditional theory of rejection'.

67   See Karl Barth, *Church Dogmatics* II/2, ed. and trans. by G. W. Bromiley and
     T. F. Torrance (London: T&T Clark, 2009).

68   Ibid., 94.

69   The English translation of the title, 'the Election of God', is not precise,
     because it does not reflect the *gracious* character of this election in 'Gottes
     Gnadenwahl.'

70   Ibid., 203: 'This history is a triumph only for God's grace and therefore for God's
     sovereignty.'

71   Barth writes: 'Where man stands only to gain, God stands only to lose … .
     There is a sure and certain salvation for man, and a sure and certain risk for
     God … . In the election of Jesus Christ … God has ascribed to man … election,
     salvation and life; and to Himself He has ascribed … reprobation, perdition and
     death.'

72   Bonhoeffer, Letter to Charlotte von Kirschbaum, Zurich, 20 September 1941,
     DBWE 16, 219. Bonhoeffer writes: 'Please let Karl Barth know once again how
     happy I am about the conversations with him.'

73   In mid-June 1941, the published version of the speech was confiscated
     and censured by the police on grounds of an intervention of the German
     government. See Frank Jehle, *Lieber unangenehm laut als angenehm
     leise. Der Theologe Karl Barth und die Politik 1906–1968* (Zürich: TVZ, 1999),
     92.

74   Barth, 'Unsere Kirche und die Schweiz in der heutigen Zeit', in *Eine Schweizer
     Stimme*, 175.

75   See Marquardt, *Die Entdeckung des Judentums für die christliche Theologie*, 85.

76   See Busch, *Unter dem Bogen*, 373.

Bibliography

Anatolios, Khaled. *Retrieving Nicaea: The Development and Meaning of Trinitarian Doctrine* (Grand Rapids: Baker Academic, 2011).

Aquinas, Thomas. *Summa Theologica*, translated by Fathers of the English Dominican Province (Westminster, MD: Christian Classics, 1981).

Athanasius. *De Incarnatione Verbi. Patrologia Graeca*, volume 25, edited by J. P. Minge (Paris: 1884).

Augustine. *De Civitate Dei. Patrologia Latina*, volume 41, edited by J. P. Minge (Paris: 1864).

Augustine. *De Libero Arbitrio. Patrologia Latina,* volume 32, edited by J. P. Minge (Paris: 1841).

Augustine. *De Peccatorum Meritis et Remissione et de Baptismo Parvulorum. Patrologia Latina,* volume 44, edited by J. P. Minge (Paris: 1865).

Ayres, Lewis. *Nicaea and its Legacy: An Approach to Fourth-Century Trinitarian Theology,* (Oxford: Oxford University Press, 2004).

Barnes, Kenneth C. 'Dietrich Bonhoeffer and Hitler's Persecution of the Jews'. In *Betrayal: German Churches and the Holocaust*, edited by Robert P. Ericksen and Susannah Heschel (Minneapolis: Fortress, 1999), 110–28.

Barnett, Victoria J. 'Dietrich Bonhoeffer's Relevance for Post-Holocaust Christian Theology', in *Bonhoeffer and Interpretive Theory: Essays on Methods and Understanding*, edited by Peter Frick (Frankfurt: Peter Lang, 2013), 213–38.

Barnett, Victoria J. 'Dietrich Bonhoeffer's Relevance for a Post-Holocaust Christian Theology'. *Studies in Christian-Jewish Relations* 2 (2006): 53–67.

Barnett, Victoria J. *For the Soul of the People: Protestant Protest Against Hitler* (Oxford: Oxford University Press, 1992).

Barnett, Victoria, Sabine Bobert and Ernst Feil (eds). *Dietrich Bonhoeffer Yearbook 2, 2005/2006* (Gütersloh: Gütersloher Verlagshaus, 2005).

Barth, Karl. *Briefe des Jahres 1933*, edited by Eberhard Busch (Zürich: Theologischer Verlag, 2004).

Barth, Karl. *Church Dogmatics* I/1, translated by G. T. Thomson (London: T&T Clark, 2004).

Barth, Karl. *Church Dogmatics* II/2, edited by T. F. Torrance and G. W. Bromiley, translated by G. W. Bromiley et al. (London: T&T Clark, 2009).

Barth, Karl. *Church Dogmatics* IV/2, edited by T. F. Torrance and G. W. Bromiley, translated by G. W. Bromiley (London: T&T Clark, 2004).

Barth, Karl. *Eine Schweizer Stimme 1938–1945,* 2nd edn (Zollikon-Zürich: Theologischer Verlag, 1948).

Barth, Karl. *Die Kirche Jesu Christi. Theologische Existenz heute* 5 (Munich: Chr. Kaiser, 1933).

Barth, Karl. *Die Kirchliche Dogmatik,* vol. II: *Die Lehre von Gott: Gottes Gnadenwahl,* 2nd semi-vol. (Zürich: Theologischer Verlag, 1942).

Barth, Karl. *Fragments Grave and Gay,* edited by H. Martin Rumscheidt, translated by Eric Mosbacher (London: Collins, 1971).

Barth, Karl. *Göttingen Dogmatics: Instruction in the Christian Religion,* edited by H. Reiffen, translated by G. W. Bromiley (Grand Rapids: Eerdmans, 1991).

Barth, Karl. Letter to Eberhard Bethge, 22 May 1967. *Evangelische Theologie* 28 (1968): 555.

Barth, Karl. *Theologische Existenz heute!.* Supplement No. 2 of *Zwischen den Zeiten* 11 (1933).

Barth, Karl. *Theologische Existenz heute* 1, edited by Karl Barth and Eduard Thurneysen (Munich: Chr. Kaiser, 1933).

Barth, Karl. *The Theology of John Calvin,* translated by Geoffrey W. Bromiley (Grand Rapids: Eerdmans, 1992).

Bethge, Eberhard. *Bonhoeffer: A Biography,* revised edn, edited and revised by Victoria Barnett, translated by Eric Mosbacher, Peter and Betty Ross, Frank Clarke and William Glen-Doepel (Minneapolis: Fortress Press, 2000).

Bethge, Eberhard. 'Dietrich Bonhoeffer and the Jews', in *Ethical Responsibility: Bonhoeffer's Legacy to the Churches,* edited by John D. Godsey and Geffrey B. Kelly (New York: Mellen, 1982), 43–96.

Bethge, Eberhard. 'Dietrich Bonhoeffer und die Juden', in *Konsequenzen. Dietrich Bonhoeffers Kirchenverständnis heute,* edited by Ernst Feil and Ilse Tödt (Munich: Chr. Kaiser, 1980), 171–214.

Biggar, Nigel. 'Karl Barth's Ethics Revisited', in *Commanding Grace: Studies in Karl Barth's Ethics,* edited by D. L. Migliore (Grand Rapids: Eerdmans, 2010), 26–49.

Boff, Leonardo. *Trinity and Society,* translated by Paul Burns (Maryknoll, NY: Orbis, 1988).

Bonhoeffer, Dietrich. *Act und Sein: Transzendentalphilosophie und Ontologie in der Systematischen Theologie. Dietrich Bonhoeffer Werke* 2, edited by Hans-Richard Reuter (München: Chr. Kaiser Verlag, 1988).

Bonhoeffer, Dietrich. *Berlin 1932–1933. Dietrich Bonhoeffer Werke* 12, edited by Carsten Nicolaisen and Ernst-Albert Scharffenorth (München: Chr. Kaiser Verlag, 1997).

Bonhoeffer, Dietrich. *Ethik. Dietrich Bonhoeffer Werke* 6, edited by Ilse Tödt,
Heinz Eduard Tödt, Ernst Feil and Clifford Green (München: Chr. Kaiser Verlag,
1992).

Bonhoeffer, Dietrich. *Illegale Theologen-Ausbildung: Finkenwalde 1935–1937. Dietrich
Bonhoeffer Werke* 14, edited by Otto Dudzus and Jürgen Henkys (München: Chr.
Kaiser Verlag, 1996).

Bonhoeffer, Dietrich. *Oeuvres de Dietrich Bonhoeffer*, edited by H. Mottu (Geneve:
Labor et Fides, 1996–).

Bornkamm, Heinrich. *Luther's Doctrine of the Two Kingdoms in the Context of His
Theology*, translated by Karl H. Hertz (Philadelphia: Fortress Press, 1966).

Buber, Martin. *I and Thou*, translated by Walter Kaufmann (Edinburgh: T&T Clark,
1970).

Busch, Eberhard. "'Die Kirche und die Juden'. Der Beitrag Wilhelm Vischers zum
sog. Betheler Bekenntnis', in *Gott wahr nehmen. Festschrift für Christian Link
zum 65. Geburtstag*, edited by Magdalene L. Frettlöh and Hans P. Lichtenberger
(Neukirchen-Vluyn: Neukirchener Verlagsgesellschaft, 2003), 47–50.

Busch, Eberhard. *Unter dem Bogen des einen Bundes. Karl Barth und die Juden
1933–1945* (Neukirchen-Vluyn: Neukirchener Verlagsgesellschaft, 1996).

Calvin, John. *Institutes of the Christian Religion*, translated by Henry Beveridge
(Peabody, MS: Hendrickson, 2008).

Carter, Guy C. 'Confession at Bethel, August 1933 – Enduring Witness: The
Formation, Revision and Significance of the First Full Theological Confession of
the Evangelical Church Struggle in Nazi Germany'. PhD dissertation, Marquette
University, 1987.

Danz, Christian. *Grundprobleme der Christologie* (Tübingen: Mohr Siebeck 2013).

DeJonge, Michael P. *Bonhoeffer's Theological Formation: Berlin, Barth, and Protestant
Theology* (Oxford: Oxford University Press, 2012).

Dibelius, Otto. 'Wochenschau'. *Berliner Sonntagsblatt*, 9 April 1933.

Duchrow, Ulrich and Wolfgang Huber (eds). *Die Ambivalenz der Zweireichelehre in
lutherischen Kirchen des 20. Jahrhunderts* (Gütersloh: Gütersloher Verlagshaus
1976).

Dumas, André. *Dietrich Bonhoeffer: Theologian of Reality*, translated by Robert
McAfee Brown (London: SCM, 1971).

Fainlight, Ruth. 'The Other'. *Haphazard by Starlight*, edited by Janey Morley
(London: SPCK, 2013).

Farrow, Douglas. 'Person and Nature: The Necessity-Freedom Dialectic in John
Zizioulas', in *The Theology of John Zizioulas: Personhood and the Church*, edited by
Douglas Knight (Burlington, VT: Ashgate, 2007).

Feil, Ernst. *Die Theologie Dietrich Bonhoeffers. Hermeneutik – Christologie – Weltverständnis* (Münster: LIT, 2014).

Fleischner, Eva. *Judaism in German Christian Theology Since 1945: Christianity and Israel Considered in Terms of Mission* (Metuchen, NJ: Rowman and Littlefield, 1975).

Forde, Gerhard. *A More Radical Gospel: Essays on Eschatology, Authority, Atonement and Ecumenism* (Grand Rapids: Eerdmans, 2004).

Gailus, Manfred (ed.). *Elisabeth Schmitz und ihre Denkschrift gegen die Judenverfolgung* (Berlin: Wichern, 2008).

Gailus, Manfred. *Mir aber zerriss es das Herz. Der stille Widerstand der Elisabeth Schmitz,* 2nd edn (Göttingen: Vandenhoeck & Ruprecht, 2011).

Gerlach, Wolfgang. *And The Witnesses Were Silent: The Confessing Church and the Persecution of the Jews,* translated and edited by Victoria Barnett (Lincoln: University of Nebraska Press, 2000).

Gollwitzer, Helmut. Sermon on Luke 3.3–14, Repentance Day, 16 November 1938, in *Dennoch bleibe ich stets an dir … Predigten aus dem Kirchenkampf 1937–1940,* edited by J. Hoppe (Munich: Chr. Kaiser, 1988).

Green, Clifford J. *Bonhoeffer: A Theology of Sociality,* rev. edn (Grand Rapids: Eerdmans, 1999).

Grenz, Stanley. *The Social God and Relational Self: A Trinitarian Theology of the Imago Dei* (Louisville: Westminster/John Knox, 2002).

Gunton, Colin. *The One, The Three and the Many* (Cambridge: Cambridge University Press, 1993).

Haemig, Mary Jane. 'The Confessional Basis of Lutheran Thinking on Church-State Issues', in *Church & State: Lutheran Perspectives,* edited by John R. Stumme and Robert W. Tuttle (Minneapolis: Fortress Press, 2000), 3–19.

Harvey, Barry. *Taking Hold of the Real* (Eugene, OR: Cascade, 2015).

Haslam, Molly. *A Constructive Theology of Intellectual Disability: Human Being as Mutuality and Response* (New York: Fordham University Press, 2012).

Hauerwas, Stanley. *Performing the Faith: Bonhoeffer and the Practice of Nonviolence* (Grand Rapids: Brazos Press, 2004).

Haynes, Stephen R. *The Bonhoeffer Legacy: Post-Holocaust Perspectives* (Minneapolis: Fortress Press, 2006).

Hockenos, Matthew D. *A Church Divided: German Protestants Confront the Nazi Past* (Bloomington: Indiana University Press, 2004).

Hoye, William J. *The Emergence of Eternal Life* (Cambridge: Cambridge University Press, 2013).

Hryniuk, Michael. *Theology, Disability and Spiritual Transformation: Learning from the Communities of L'Arche* (Amherst, NY: Cambria Press, 2010).

Huyssteen, J. Wentzel van. *Alone in the World: Human Uniqueness in Science and Theology* (Grand Rapids: Eerdmans, 2006).

Irenaeus. *Adversus haereses. Patrologia Graeca,* volume 7, edited by J. P. Minge (Paris: 1857).

Janz, Denis R. *The Westminster Handbook to Martin Luther* (Louisville: Westminster/ John Knox Press, 2010).

Jehle, Frank. *Lieber unangenehm laut als angenehm leise. Der Theologe Karl Barth und die Politik 1906-1968* (Zürich: Theologischer Verlag, 1999).

Jenson, Matt. *The Gravity of Sin: Augustine, Luther, and Barth on 'homo incurvatus in se'* (London: T&T Clark, 2006).

Jüngel, Eberhard. *Theological Essays I*, edited and translated by J. B. Webster (Edinburgh: T&T Clark, 1989).

Kelsey, David. *Eccentric Existence: A Theological Anthropology*, 2 volumes (Louisville: Westminster/John Knox, 2009).

Kilby, Karen. 'Perichoresis and Project: Problems with Social Doctrines of the Trinity'. *New Blackfriars* 81 (2000): 432-3.

Klappert, Bertold. 'Weg und Wende Dietrich Bonhoeffers in der Israelfrage', in *Ethik im Ernstfall. Dietrich Bonhoeffers Stellung zu den Juden und ihre Aktualität*, edited by Wolfgang Huber and Ilse Tödt (Munich: Chr. Kaiser, 1982), 77-135.

Kolb, Robert and Timothy J. Wengert (eds). *The Book of Concord: The Confessions of the Evangelical Lutheran Church*, 2nd edn, translated by Charles Arand, Eric Gritsch, William Russell, James Schaaf and Jane Strohl (Minneapolis: Fortress Press, 2000).

LaCugna, Catherine. *God For Us: The Trinity and Christian Life* (New York: HarperOne, 2000).

Laube, Martin. 'Die Kirche als "Institution der Freiheit"', in *Kirche*, edited by Christian Albrecht (Tübingen: Mohr Siebeck, 2011), 131-70.

Leahy, Brendan. '"Christ Existing as Community": Dietrich Bonhoeffer's Notion of Church'. *Irish Theological Quarterly* 73 (2008): 32-59.

Lehmann, Paul L. 'The Formative Power of Particularity'. *Union Seminary Quarterly Review* 18: 3.1 (1963): 306-19.

Linton, Simi. *Claiming Disability: Knowledge and Identity* (New York: New York University Press, 1998).

Littell, Franklin H. *The Crucifixion of the Jews: The Failure of Christians to Understand the Jewish Experience*, new edn (Macon, GA: Mercer University Press, 1996).

Lohse, Bernhard. *Martin Luther's Theology: Its Historical and Systematic Development*, translated by Roy A. Harrisville (Minneapolis: Fortress Press, 1999).

Lowe, Walter. 'Why We Need Apocalyptic'. *Scottish Journal of Theology* 63:1 (2010): 48–53.

Luther, Martin. 'The Freedom of a Christian', in *Career of the Reformer I. Luther's Works* 31. *American Edition,* edited by Harold J. Grimm (Philadelphia: Fortress, 1957), 343–77.

Luther, Martin. *Galatervorlesung,* 1535, *Weimar Ausgabe* 40.1 (Weimar, 1911).

Luther, Martin. 'Heidelberg Disputation', in *Career of the Reformer I. Luther's Works* 31. *American Edition,* edited by Harold J. Grimm (Philadelphia: Fortress, 1957), 39–58.

Luther, Martin. 'Lectures on Romans', in *Luther's Works* 25. *American Edition*, edited by Hilton C. Oswald (St Louis: Concordia Publishing House, 1972).

Luther, Martin. 'On the Councils and the Church', in *Church and Ministry III. Luther's Works* 41. *American Edition,* edited by Eric W. Gritsch (St Louis: Concordia, 1966), 3–178.

Luther, Martin. 'Preface to the Epistle of St. Paul to the Romans', in *Word and Sacrament I. Luther's Works* 35. *American Edition*, edited by E. Theodore Bachmann (Philadelphia: Fortress Press, 1960), 365–80.

Luther, Martin. 'Temporal Authority: To What Extent Should it be Obeyed', in *The Christian in Society II. Luther's Works* 45. *American Edition,* edited by Walther I. Brandt (Minneapolis: Fortress, 1962), 77–129.

Luther, Martin. 'Two Kinds of Righteousness', in *Career of the Reformer I. Luther's Works* 31. *American Edition,* edited by Harold J. Grimm (Philadelphia: Fortress, 1957), 293–306.

MacIntyre, Alasdair. *Dependent Rational Animals: Why Human Beings Need the Virtues* (Peru, IL: Open Court, 1999).

The Magdeburg Confession, translated by Matthew Colvin (North Charleston: CreateSpace, 2012).

Marquardt, Friedrich-Wilhelm. *Die Entdeckung des Judentums für die christliche Theologie. Israel im Denken Karl Barths* (Munich: Chr. Kaiser, 1967).

Marsh, Charles. *Strange Glory: A Life of Dietrich Bonhoeffer* (London: SPCK, 2014).

McCormack, Bruce L. *Orthodox and Modern: Studies in the Theology of Karl Barth* (Grand Rapids: Baker Academic, 2008).

Meilaender, Gilbert. *Bioethics: A Primer for Christians* (Grand Rapids: Eerdmans, 2005).

Merleau-Ponty, Maurice. *Phenomenology of Perception*, translated by Colin Smith (New York: Routledge, 2002).

Metaxas, Eric. *Bonhoeffer: Pastor, Martyr, Prophet, Spy* (Nashville: Thomas Nelson Publishers, 2010).

Meyer, Dietgard. 'Elisabeth Schmitz: Die Denkschrift "Zur Lage der deutschen Nichtarier". Einleitung', in *Katharina Staritz 1903–1953: Dokumentation*, vol. 1: *1903–1942*, edited by Hannelore Erhart, Ilse Meseberg-Haubold and Dietgard Meyer (Neukirchen-Vluyn: Neukirchener Verlagsgesellschaft, 1999).

Meyer, Winfried. *Unternehmen Sieben. Eine Rettungsaktion für vom Holocaust Bedrohte aus dem Amt Ausland/Abwehr im Oberkommando der Wehrmacht* (Frankfurt am Main: Anton Hain, 1993).

Mokrosch, Reinhold. 'Das Gewissensverständnis Dietrich Bonhoeffers: Reformatorische Herkunft und politische Funktion', in *Bonhoeffer und Luther: Zur Sozialgestalt des Luthertums in der Moderne*, edited by C. Gremmels (Munich: Chr. Kaiser Verlag, 1983), 59–92.

Moltmann, Jürgen. *The Trinity and the Kingdom: The Doctrine of God*, translated by Margaret Kohl (London: SCM, 2000).

Müller, Christine-Ruth. *Bekenntnis und Bekennen. Dietrich Bonhoeffer in Bethel (1933) – ein lutherischer Versuch* (Munich: Chr. Kaiser, 1989).

Mumford, James. *Ethics at the Beginning of Life* (Oxford: Oxford University Press, 2013).

Nickson, Ann L. *Bonhoeffer on Freedom: Courageously Grasping Reality* (Aldershot: Ashgate, 2002).

Niebuhr, Reinhold. *The Nature and Destiny of Man*, vol. 2 (New York: Scribners, 1964).

Nielsen, Kirsten Busch. 'Community Turned Inside Out: Dietrich Bonhoeffer's Concept of the Church and of Humanity Reconsidered', in *Being Human, Becoming Human: Dietrich Bonhoeffer and Social Thought*, edited by Jens Zimmerman and Brian Gregor (Eugene: Wipf and Stock, 2010), 91–101.

Olson, Oliver K. 'Theology of Revolution: Magdeburg, 1550–1551'. *Sixteenth Century Journal* 3 (1972): 56–79.

Ott, Heinrich. *Reality and Faith: The Theological Legacy of Dietrich Bonhoeffer*, translated by Alex A. Morrison (London: Lutterworth, 1971).

Pangritz, Andreas. 'Die "Politik Gottes" mit Israel. Über Wilhelm Vischers Beitrag zum "Betheler Bekenntnis"'. *Evangelische Theologie* 72 (2012): 194–213.

Pangritz, Andreas. 'Marginalie zu Bonhoeffers Ethik', in *Momente der Begegnung. Impulse für das christlich-jüdische Gespräch. Bertold Klappert zum 65. Geburtstag*, edited by Michael Haarmann, Johannes von Lüpke u. Antje Menn (Neukirchen-Vluyn: Neukirchener Verlagsgesellschaft/Wuppertal, 2004), 206–12.

Pangritz, Andreas. '"To Fall Within the Spokes of the Wheel." New-old observations Concerning "The Church and the Jewish Question"', in *Dem Rad in die Speichen fallen. Das Politische in der Theologie Dietrich Bonhoeffers / A Spoke in the Wheel.*

The Political in the Theology of Dietrich Bonhoeffer, edited by Kirsten Busch
Nielsen, Ralf K. Wüstenberg and Jens Zimmermann (Gütersloh: Gütersloher
Verlagshaus, 2013), 94–108.

Pangritz, Andreas. 'Who is Jesus Christ, For Us, Today?', in *The Cambridge
Companion to Dietrich Bonhoeffer*, edited by John W. de Gruchy (Cambridge:
Cambridge University Press, 1999), 134–53.

Prolingheuer, Hans. *Der Fall Karl Barth. Chronographie einer Vertreibung 1934–1935*,
2nd edn (Neukirchen-Vluyn: Neukirchener Verlagsgesellschaft, 1984).

Reinders, Hans S. *Disability, Providence, and Ethics* (Waco, TX: Baylor University
Press, 2014).

Reinders, Hans S. *Receiving the Gift of Friendship: Profound Disability, Theological
Anthropology and Ethics* (Grand Rapids: Eerdmans, 2008).

Reynolds, Thomas E. *Vulnerable Communion: A Theology of Disability and
Hospitality* (Grand Rapids: Brazos Press, 2008).

Rumscheidt, Martin. 'The Significance of Adolf von Harnack and
Reinhold Seeberg for Dietrich Bonhoeffer', in *Bonhoeffer's Intellectual Formation*,
edited by Peter Frick (Tübingen: J. C. B. Mohr, 2008), 210–24.

Sayre-McCord, Geoff. 'Metaethics'. *The Stanford Encyclopaedia of Philosophy*, edited
by Edward N. Zalta, available at http://plato.stanford.edu/archives/sum2014/
entries/metaethics/ (accessed summer 2014).

Schleiermacher, Friedrich. *The Christian Faith*, 2 volumes, 2nd edn, edited by H. R.
MacKintosh and J. S. Stewart (Edinburgh: T&T Clark, 1963).

Schmitz, Elisabeth. Letter to Helmut Gollwitzer, 24 November 1938, in *Und sie
waren täglich einmütig beieinander. Der Weg der Bekennenden Gemeinde Berlin/
Dahlem 1937–1943 mit Helmut Gollwitzer*, by Gerhard Schäberle-Koenigs
(Gütersloh: Gütersloher Verlagshaus, 1998).

Schmitz, Elisabeth. Letter to Helmut Gollwitzer, 27 November 1938. Unpublished.
Literary estate of Elisabeth Schmitz, Hanau.

Schmitz, Elisabeth. Letter to Karl Barth, 18 April 1933. Karl Barth Archives, Basel.

Schmitz, Elisabeth. Letter to pastor (Eitel-Friedrich von Rabenau?), 11 November
1938. Unpublished. Literary estate of Elisabeth Schmitz, Hanau.

Schroven, Brigitte. *Theologie des Alten Testaments zwischen Anpassung und
Widerstand. Christologische Auslegungen zwischen den Weltkriegen* (Neukirchen-
Vluyn: Neukirchener Verlagsgesellschaft, 1995).

Seeberg, Reinhold. *Zum dogmatischen Verständnis der Trinitätslehre* (Leipzig:
Deichert, 1908).

Shoenberger, Cynthia G. 'Development of the Lutheran Theory of Resistance:
1523–1530'. *Sixteenth Century Journal* 8 (1977): 61–76.

Shoenberger, Cynthia G. 'Luther and the Justifiability of Resistance to Legitimate Authority'. *Journal of the History of Ideas* 40 (1979): 3–20.

Siemon-Netto, Uwe. *The Fabricated Luther: Refuting Nazi Connections and Other Modern Myths*, 2nd edn (St Louis: Concordia Publishing House, 2007).

Singer, Peter. *Practical Ethics*, 2nd edn (Cambridge: Cambridge University Press, 1993).

Skinner, Quentin. *The Foundations of Modern Political Thought*, vol. 2 (Cambridge: Cambridge University Press, 1978).

Skinner, Quentin. 'The Origins of the Calvinist Theory of Revolution', in *After the Reformation: Essays in Honor of J. H. Hexter*, edited by Barbara C. Malament (Philadelphia: University of Pennsylvania Press, 1980), 309–30.

Smid, Marikje. *Deutscher Protestantismus und Judentum, 1932/1933* (Munich: Chr. Kaiser Verlag, 1990).

Slenczka, Notger. 'Die Christologie als Reflex des frommen Selbstbewusstseins', in *Jesus Christus*, edited by Jens Schröter (Tübingen: Mohr Siebeck, 2014), 181–241.

Slenczka, Notger. 'Problemgeschichte der Christologie', in *Marburger Jahrbuch Theologie XIII: Christologie*, edited by Elisabeth Gräb-Schmidt and Reiner Preul (Leipzig: Evangelische Verlagsanstalt, 2011), 59–111.

Sonderegger, Kathryn. *Systematic Theology: Volume 1: The Doctrine of God* (Minneapolis: Fortress Press, 2015).

Swinton, John. *Dementia: Living in the Memories of God* (Grand Rapids: Eerdmans, 2012).

Tanner, Kathryn. 'Trinity, Christology, and Community', in *Christology and Ethics*, edited by F. LeRon Shults and Brent Waters (Grand Rapids: Eerdmans, 2010), 56–74.

Taylor, Charles. *The Sources of the Self* (Cambridge: Cambridge University Press, 1992).

Tietz, Christiane. *Bonhoeffers Kritik der verkrümmten Vernunft. Eine erkenntnistheoretische Untersuchung* (Tübingen: Mohr Siebeck 1999).

Tietz, Christiane. 'Dietrich Bonhoeffer: wer halt wir? Gewissen oder Verantwortung', in *Ringen um die Wahrheit: Gewissenkonflikte in der Christentumsgeschichte*, edited by M. Delgado, V. Leppin and D. Neuhold (Stuttgart: W. Kohlhammer, 2011), 325–37.

Tietz, Christiane. 'Friedrich Schleiermacher and Dietrich Bonhoeffer', in *Bonhoeffer's Intellectual Formation. Theology and Philosophy in His Thought*, edited by Peter Frick (Tübingen: Mohr Siebeck, 2008), 121–43.

Tietz, Christiane. 'Jesus von Nazareth in der christlichen Theologie heute'. *Zeitschrift für Dialektische Theologie* 31, Heft 62 (2015), 90–108.

Tooley, Michael. *Abortion and Infanticide* (Oxford: Oxford University Press, 1985).

Troeltsch, Ernst. *Die Soziallehren der christlichen Kirchen und Gruppen* (Tübingen: Mohr, 1912).

Vischer, Wilhelm. 'Das Heil kommt von den Juden (Memorandum)', in *Juden – Christen – Judenchristen. Ein Ruf an die Christenheit*, edited by Schweizerisches Evangelisches Hilfswerk für die Bekennende Kirche in Deutschland (Zollikon: Verlag der Evangelischen Buchhandlung, 1939), 39–47.

Vischer, Wilhelm. 'Témoignage d'un contemporain', in *Révue d'histoire et philosophie religieuses* 64:2 (1984): 177–22.

Vischer, Wilhelm. 'Zeugnis eines Zeitgenossen'. *Bethel 30. Beiträge aus der Arbeit der v. Bodelschwinghschen Anstalten bei Bielefeld* (1985): 79–85.

Vischer, Wilhelm. 'Zur Judenfrage. Eine kurze biblische Erörterung der Judenfrage im Anschluß an die Leitsätze eines Vortrages über die Bedeutung des Alten Testamentes'. *Monatsschrift für Pastoraltheologie* 29 (1933): 185–90.

Volf, Miroslav. *Exclusion and Embrace: Theological Exploration of Identity, Otherness and Reconciliation* (Nashville: Abingdon Press, 1994).

Wannenwetsch, Bernd. 'Angels with Clipped Wings: The Disabled as Key to the Recognition of Personhood', in *Theology, Disability and the New Genetics: Why Science Needs the Church*, edited by John Swinton and Brian Brock (London: T&T Clark, 2007), 182–200.

Wannenwetsch, Bernd 'Christians and Pagans: Towards a Trans-Religious Second Naiveté or How to be a Christological Creature', in *Who Am I? Bonhoeffer's Theology through his Poetry*, edited by Bernd Wannenwetsch (London: T&T Clark, 2009), 175–96.

Wannenwetsch, Bernd. '"Responsible Living or Responsible Self?" Bonhoefferian Reflections on a Vexed Moral Notion'. *Studies in Christian Ethics* 18:3 (2005): 125–40.

Webster, John. *Barth's Ethics of Reconciliation* (Cambridge: Cambridge University Press, 1995).

Webster, John. *The Domain of the Word: Scripture and Theological Reason* (London: T&T Clark, 2012).

Weinandy, Thomas. *Athanasius: A Theological Introduction* (Aldershot: Ashgate Press, 2007).

Wengert, Timothy J. 'Philip Melanchthon on Time and History in the Reformation'. *Consensus* 30(2) (2005): 9–33.

Williams, A. N. *The Architecture of Theology: Structure, System, and Ratio* (Oxford: Oxford University Press, 2011).

Williams, Rowan. *Arius*, 2nd edn (London: SCM Press, 2001).

Wilson-Kastner, Patricia. *Faith, Feminism and the Christ* (Philadelphia: Fortress, 1983).

Wüstenberg, Ralf K. *A Theology of Life: Dietrich Bonhoeffer's Religionless Christianity*, translated by Doug Stott (Grand Rapids: Eerdmans, 1998).

Yong, Amos. *Theology and Down Syndrome: Reimagining Disability in Late Modernity* (Waco, TX: Baylor University Press, 2007).

Zizioulas, John D. *Being as Communion: Studies in Personhood and the Church* (London: Darton, Longman and Todd, 1985).

Zizioulas, John D. 'On Being a Person: Towards an Ontology of Personhood', in *Persons, Divine and Human*, edited by Christoph Schwöbel and Colin E. Gunton (Edinburgh: T&T Clark, 1992), 33–46.

Index

9 780567 683793